Being and Truth

Studies in Continental Thought

Martin Heidegger

Being and Truth

Translated by
Gregory Fried and Richard Polt

Indiana University Press
Bloomington and Indianapolis

This book is a publication of

Indiana University Press
Office of Scholarly Publishing
Herman B Wells Library 350
1320 East 10th Street
Bloomington, Indiana 47405 USA
iupress.indiana.edu

Published in German as Martin Heidegger, *Sein und Wahrheit*
© 2001 German edition by Vittorio Klostermann, Frankfurt am Main
© 2010 English edition by Indiana University Press
First paperback edition © 2016 by Indiana University Press

Heidegger, Martin, 1889–1976
[Sein und Wahrheit. English]
Being and truth / Martin Heidegger ; translated by Gregory Fried and Richard Polt.
p. cm. — (Studies in continental thought)
ISBN 978-0-253-35511-9 (cloth : alk. paper) — ISBN 978-0-253-00465-9 (eb)
1. Ontology 2. Truth. I. Title.
B3279.H48 S3713 2010
193—dc22

2010005841

ISBN 978-0-253-02082-6 (pbk.)

1 2 3 4 5 21 20 19 18 17 16

BEING AND TRUTH

CONTENTS

ON THE ESSENCE OF TRUTH
Winter Semester 1933–1934

PART ONE

Truth and Freedom: An Interpretation of the
Allegory of the Cave in Plato's *Republic*

Chapter One

Translators' Foreword

Translators owe a double debt. To their sources, they owe fidelity. To their readers, they owe an explanation. Translators are intermediaries, and their work succeeds only if it can be trusted not to misdirect what they have been entrusted to convey. That responsibility is particularly pressing with a text such as Martin Heidegger's *Being and Truth*.

While Heidegger's language in *Being and Truth* is not as idiosyncratic as in his works of just a few years later (in particular, in the 1936–1938 *Contributions to Philosophy*), this text is challenging because of the diversity of its sources. Heidegger originally delivered the texts in this volume as a pair of lecture courses in 1933–1934, and as Hartmut Tietjen explains in his afterword, we have a variety of sources for what Heidegger actually presented: his own partial manuscript, his notes, and student transcripts. What this means is that the resulting text displays a wide range of styles: carefully prepared lectures that read like a book manuscript; transcriptions of what appears to be Heidegger's more relaxed and sometimes loose delivery during the lectures themselves; and aphoristic, even cryptic passages that often only sketch out a train of thought. The reader should be prepared for sudden alterations in style.

In discharging our debt to the author, we have attempted to be as faithful as possible to the German by following a few simple principles. As far as we can, we have endeavored to provide consistent renderings into English of Heidegger's terminology so that the reader may follow his usages as closely as possible. Because there is not always a one-to-one mapping of words and idioms from one language to another, truly literal translation is impossible, so the reader who wishes to pursue some of the complexities and connotations of Heidegger's vocabulary should consult the German–English glossary at the back of the volume. Heidegger's style is often very precise and carefully constructed; we have tried to reproduce this quality, even when a looser rendering in English might seem more elegant. But where Heidegger's style is more informal, we have tried to capture the mood of the text with corresponding English idioms, so long as we could maintain fidelity to his

meaning. In a number of cases where the text takes the form of gram-
matically or conceptually incomplete notes, we have formed complete
sentences and attempted to spell out the sense. Whenever we have had
to make decisions about missing words, our additions are enclosed in
square brackets, as are all our notes and our translations of Greek and
Latin terms. Readers should consult the editor's afterword for an explanation of other typographical devices.

Some of Heidegger's terminology is so specific to his thought, or to
the intellectual and historical context of these lecture courses, that we
owe the reader a more detailed explanation than we can offer in the
glossary.

Sein and *Seiendes*. Heidegger insisted that his lifelong theme was the
question of Being. We render *Sein* as capitalized "Being" in order to
distinguish it from our rendering of *Seiendes* (and its permutations) as
an individual "being" or "beings" in general. *Seiendes* literally means
"that which is" or "what is"; we have used these phrases when they
are not overly awkward. Some translations render *Seiendes* as "entities," but the rather scholastic flavor of this word would diminish the
freshness of many of Heidegger's formulations in these lectures. As for
"Being," many translators resist this usage out of a concern that the
capitalization will mislead some readers into believing that Being is a
metaphysical principle, a sort of transcendent super-being that constitutes or underlies the reality of all other beings. But rendering both
Sein and *Seiendes* as "being" can lead to serious confusions. In German,
Sein is the infinitive "to be" turned into a noun. For Heidegger, *Sein*
retains its verbal sense: Being is not a being, not a thing. As a first cut,
the reader might find it useful to understand Heidegger's question of
Being as a question about the field of meaning within which individual beings become accessible to us, a field that unfolds in time and as
time. As one can see in the following passage on Baumgarten, context
would not always be sufficient to save the reader from bewilderment
if *Sein* were rendered as "being" with the lowercase: "Is there anything
that stands even *above* Being, that accordingly is *non*-'Being'? What
could that *be*? Can such a thing still even *be* at all? Obviously not, for
if it still *is*, then it is a *being*, and *as* a being it *stands beneath* Being" (p.
54).[1] It should be noted that we do not capitalize our translation of
Sein in compound constructions where there is no possibility of mis-
taking it for *Seiendes*, such as "being seen" or "being-with."

---

1. All page numbers here refer to the pagination of the German edition of this
text, *Sein und Wahrheit, Gesamtausgabe* vols. 36/37, ed. Hartmut Tietjen (Frankfurt
am Main: Vittorio Klostermann, 2001). Further references to the Heidegger *Gesamtausgabe* will take the form "GA."

Dasein. In ordinary German, *Dasein* (literally, "being-there" or "being-here") means existence, usually in the sense of the existence rather than non-existence of some particular thing. Heidegger, however, uses this word in an idiosyncratic way to designate one being in particular: the human being, the being for whom its own existence can become a question. In designating human beings as *Dasein,* Heidegger is rejecting philosophical conceptions that treat the essence of the human as something independent of historical place and time. Instead, he wants to emphasize that human existence is rooted in a "here"; our distinct way of Being is enmeshed in a particular history and connected to a unique but transient place with all the filiations of language, cultural practices, and traditions that are our own. *As human beings, for Heidegger, we are here.* We follow the established tradition in leaving the term *Dasein* untranslated.

Volk. We translate this politically charged term consistently as "people," in the singular (not as the plural of "person"). It could also be translated as "community" or "nation," and in some contexts as "the masses." One could attempt to define a *Volk* by means of its shared language, history, or political system. For orthodox National Socialists, the *Volk* was primarily defined in racial terms, but Heidegger attacks this biological interpretation (see pp. 209–213). Despite the fact that Dasein is always engaged in a particular heritage and situation, our inheritance never locks us into a predefined essence. According to Heidegger, it is crucial that the identity of a people, as well as the identity of an individual, remain open to questioning. Dasein is a way of Being in which one's own Being is an issue for one (pp. 214, 218). Thus, "We are, insofar as we . . . ask who we are" (p. 4).

Kampf. In German, *Kampf* means fighting in the sense of actual battle as well as in the more abstract or metaphorical sense of struggle, as in the phrase *Kampf ums Dasein,* the "struggle for existence." We have chosen to render *Kampf* as "struggle" because this broader meaning is usually better suited to the contexts in which Heidegger uses the word. But the reader should realize that in German, even *Kampf* as struggle carries a strong sense of a willingness to fight in genuine combat. Furthermore, in the historical context of these lectures—delivered when Heidegger was serving as rector of the University of Freiburg as a dedicated supporter of the new National Socialist regime—the word *Kampf* had a very special resonance. Hitler's autobiography, *Mein Kampf,* was so famous a book that even English translations have kept its German title, which might be rendered as *My Struggle.* A fundamental component of Nazi rhetoric and ideology was the emphasis on *Kampf* as the spirit of the resurgent German nation. The reader should not assume that Heidegger simply echoed the term as it was being used in Nazi propaganda, but no one listening to Heidegger's lectures in 1933–1934 would have missed that he was attempting to appropriate this powerfully charged word in a distinctive way. This is most evident in his connection of *Kampf* to his interpretation of Heraclitus' πόλεμος (war).[2]

Geist, geistig. We translate these terms as "spirit" and "spiritual." They should not be taken as referring to religion in particular; in German, they indicate the entire realm of distinctively human culture and experience, including thought, history, and art. In some contexts *geistig* would be translated more naturally as "intellectual," but we have maintained consistency so that readers can follow Heidegger's ongoing exploration of the meaning of *Geist*. According to him, "there is no living spirit anymore" (p. 7); the *Volk* and the earth are in need of spiritual renewal (pp. 3–4, 7, 86, 120, 148). But those who wish to "spiritualize" the National Socialist revolution have failed to understand what spirit is (pp. 7, 14, 211, 213). Spirit is neither rootless intellect nor the "empty eternity" of the Hegelian absolute spirit (p. 77), but "breath, gust, astonishment, impulse, engagement" (p. 7).

For advice on the political connotations of several terms as well as on the translation of many difficult passages in this text, we are grateful to Dieter Thomä. We thank Michael Sweeney for his assistance with passages from Thomas Aquinas in Appendix II. Thanks also go to the students in Richard Polt's Heidegger seminar (fall 2008) and Gregory Fried's Heidegger seminar (spring 2009) for reviewing the manuscript, and to Ashley C. Taylor and Brian Smith for their assistance in preparing the manuscript for press. David L. Dusenbury provided numerous apt suggestions in the copyediting phase. And finally, we gratefully acknowledge Andrew Mitchell's careful comments on the translation, and his many helpful suggestions for improvement.

2. The lecture courses in the present volume are essential evidence for those who wish to judge the meaning and intent of Heidegger's support for National Socialism. While many texts are pertinent to this issue, other primary sources of particular relevance to this volume are the lectures and speeches Heidegger delivered during and immediately following his period as rector. Many such texts are collected in GA 16, *Reden und andere Zeugnisse eines Lebensweges (1910–1976)*, ed. Hermann Heidegger (Frankfurt am Main: Vittorio Klostermann, 2000). Translations of some of these speeches can be found in *The Heidegger Controversy: A Critical Reader*, ed. Richard Wolin (Cambridge, Mass.: MIT Press, 1993); in Heidegger's *Philosophical and Political Writings*, ed. Manfred Stassen (London and New York: Continuum, 2003); and in *The Heidegger Reader*, ed. Günter Figal, trans. Jerome Veith (Bloomington: Indiana University Press, 2009). Heidegger's lecture course of Summer Semester 1934, delivered immediately after his rectorate, has been published as *Logik als die Frage nach dem Wesen der Sprache* (GA 38), ed. Günter Seubold (Frankfurt am Main: Vittorio Klostermann, 1998), and translated as *Logic as the Question Concerning the Essence of Language*, trans. Wanda Torres Gregory and Yvonne Unna (Albany: State University of New York Press, 2009).

THE FUNDAMENTAL
QUESTION OF PHILOSOPHY

Summer Semester 1933

Introduction
The Fundamental Question of Philosophy and the Fundamental Happening of Our History

§1. The spiritual-political mission as a decision for the fundamental question

The German people is now passing through a moment of historical greatness; the youth of the academy knows this greatness. What is happening, then? The German people as a whole is coming to itself, that is, it is finding its leadership. In this leadership, the people that has come to itself is creating its state. The people that is forming itself into its state, founding endurance and constancy, is growing into a nation. The nation is taking over the fate of its people. Such a people is gaining its own spiritual mission among peoples, and creating its own history. This happening reaches far out into the difficult becoming of a dark future. And in this becoming, the youth of the academy is already there at the outset, and stands ready for its calling. And that means that the youth lives by the will to find the training and education that will make it ripe and strong for the spiritual-political leadership that is to be assigned to it in the future as its mission from the people, for the state, within the world of peoples.

All essential leadership lives by the power of a great vocation that is fundamentally concealed. And this vocation is first and last the *spiritual-popular mission* that the fate of a nation has reserved for it. We must awaken the *knowledge of this mission* and root it in the heart and will of the people and its individual members.

Yet such knowledge is not given to us simply when we get to know some contemporary matters of fact and circumstances —say, when we become aware of the political situation of the German people today. That is indispensable, of course, but it is not what is decisive. The knowledge of the spiritual-political mission of the German people is a knowledge of its future. And this knowledge, in turn, is not an awareness of what will be actual someday, and will someday be fixed upon as contemporary by the generation to come. Such prophetic knowledge is forbidden to us—and fortunately forbidden, for it would wear down and suffocate all action.

The knowledge of the mission is the demanding knowledge of that which must be *before* all else and *for* all else, if the nation is to grow into its greatness. This knowing demands what is not yet, and quarrels with what still is, and honors the greatness that has been. Such demanding, quarreling, and honoring are together that great restlessness in which we actually and as a whole are our fate. Our *Being* is this restless conjunction of the joining-in that honors amid the enjoining that demands. We are, insofar as we seek ourselves in demanding, quarreling, and honoring. We seek ourselves insofar as we ask who we are. Who is this people with this history and this destiny, in the ground of its Being?

Such questioning is no idle and curious brooding—instead, this questioning is the highest spiritual engagement, the most essential action. In such questioning, we hold on in the face of our fate, we endure it; we hold ourselves out into the darkness of necessity. *This questioning*, within which our people holds on to its historical Dasein, holds it through the danger, holds it out into the greatness of its mission—this questioning *is its philosophizing, its philosophy.*

Philosophy—that is the question of the law and structure of our Being. We want to make philosophy actual by asking this question, and to open this questioning by posing the *fundamental question of philosophy.* We want to open this questioning here and now, that is, not to talk *about* questions but to act questioningly, and to dare the engagement by asking the fundamental question of philosophy.

The fundamental question of philosophy! What question is that? How are we supposed to make it out? It seems that a simple reflection will suffice. The fundamental question of philosophy emerges when its task is known, and the task emerges when its essence has been defined.—But the essence is determined only in and through the fundamental question that it poses. So we are moving in a circle: the fundamental question is determined by the essence of philosophy, and the essence is determined by the fundamental question. It is so. To ask the fundamental question is in itself to unveil the essence of philosophy. Certainly. But what is the fundamental question, then? Who decides which question deserves this distinction?

Can the fundamental question be determined by the pronouncement of some authority somewhere, or by some notion that once struck somebody? Or is it the product of the accidental needs of some age? Or can it be settled by an agreement? Or is it a matter of preference, depending

on the so-called standpoint of each philosopher? Or does the fundamental question, the ground-question, have its own ground and basis,
and thus its own necessity? Has it already been decided somehow what
this fundamental question is? Yes, it has; and that is why the question
has already been called the fundamental question, the ground-question—as a grounded question and at the same time a grounding one.
What the fundamental question of philosophy is, is decided *with its inception.*

But it remains questionable whether we still understand this decision and are equal to it. Might it even be the case that we today have
grown unfamiliar with this decision, that even those before us were
no longer familiar with this decision, that is, no longer grasped it, that
is, were no longer equal to it? If so, then what must happen? And so it
is. And that means that there is no need for our most urgent effort to
aim at somehow thinking up and calculating what the fundamental
question is to be, but our sole task is to bring ourselves again to the
point where we can once more become equal to the decision about the
fundamental question of philosophy, the decision that has already
taken place—and remain equal to it. We have become unequal to it,
and this is why *an actual urgency* and a *highest necessity* must first assail
us and drive us to the renewed asking of the fundamental question.
Otherwise philosophy remains an empty idleness, through which we
might at most become somewhat more "cultured" and cultivated—a
remote concern with some arbitrary problems, completely free of dangers and of duties. And that is little enough—in fact, nothing at all, in
view of the rigors and darkness of our German fate and the German
calling. But when this fate has seized us, then we experience the *in-
eluctability* of philosophizing and the *urgency* of taking up the fundamental question of philosophy once again—of deciding again in a new
and unique way for the decision that has taken place.

---

§2. The Greek questioning in poetry and thought and the inception of philosophy. Philosophy as the incessant, historical, questioning struggle over the essence and Being of beings

But where and when did the first and only decision for the fundamental question of philosophy, and thus for philosophy itself, take place?
At the point when the *Greek people,* whose ethnicity and language have
the same provenance as ours, set about creating through its great poets
and thinkers a unique way of Dasein for a human people. What had
its inception there has remained unfulfilled to this day. But this inception still *is,* and it did not disappear nor is it disappearing just because
subsequent history has been less and less able to master it. *The inception*

still is, and it persists as a *distant enjoining* that reaches far out beyond our Western fate and links the German destiny to it.

The question concerns us and only us:

1. Whether we will the greatness of our people, whether we have the long will to realize a signal and singular mission among peoples.
2. Whether we experience and grasp in all its force the fact that the *current turn* of the German destiny brings with it the *sharpest affliction* for our Dasein, in that it places us before the decision: the decision whether we will to create the spiritual world that is still latent in the happening that is now coming to be, and whether we shall create this world—or not.

It is now a common opinion that "one's" task is to spiritualize and ennoble the conclusion of the National Socialist revolution. I ask: to spiritualize it with what spirit? For there is no living spirit anymore, one no longer knows anything about what spirit is (breath, gust, astonishment, impulse, engagement). Today, spirit drifts around as empty "cleverness," as the noncommittal play of wit, as the boundless pursuit of ratiocinative dissection and subversion, as the unbridled sway of a so-called world reason.

The spirit is already here, but it is constrained and lacks its world, a world formed for it. Not to spiritualize what is happening, on some basis or other, but to bring the world that is latent in this happening to light and form, and to bring it to power: if this should not succeed, then we are lost, and some barbarism, from some place or other, will sweep over us and past us. The role of a great, history-building people has then been played out.

But if this should succeed—and it must succeed—then we must learn to grasp and seize the current turn of German history *on the basis of an innermost ground,* that is, as the historical moment that is great enough and potent enough in forces, the moment from which we must dare to begin the authentic inception of our historical Dasein once again, solely in order to create our people's great future for it and to make the nation worthy of its mission—worthy, that is, equal to its fate and master of it—and thereby to raise this fate into its greatness. Only when we are what we are coming to be, from the greatness of the inception of the Dasein of our spirit and people, only then do we remain fit for the power of the goal toward which our history is striving.

This inception is the inception of philosophy among the Greeks. It was they who first threw themselves into that questioning in poetry and thought that is to determine our Dasein. The Greeks enabled this questioning to attain full spiritual actuality, precisely because they created it—that is, they gave it both a word and a name: philosophy, φιλοσοφία, the primal declaration in language of the essence of this questioning. A σοφός is one who can taste, who has the right taste for what is worthy in things, who can select in advance, set limits and keep within them; who, in short, can catch the right scent and reach out to the essence of things. φίλος, φιλία means inclination, the passion of pressing toward something, staying with it, staying true to it, and protecting it. Philosophy—the passion of pressing forward and catching the scent that reaches the essence of things: *the ceaseless questioning struggle over the essence and Being of beings.*

The outcome of this struggle created a new Dasein for humanity, brought about a completely new attunement in whose resonance we still stand. This struggle set humanity free into its world, in the face of the possibilities of its greatness and the powers of its obligation.

---

§3. What philosophy is not.
Rejection of inadequate attempts to define it

This characterization of the essence of philosophy is enough for now to say *what philosophy is not:* (1) not science, (2) not a worldview, (3) not laying a foundation for knowledge, (4) not absolute knowledge, (5) not concern with the existence of the individual. We will investigate what philosophy is not. We will defend against attempts that have arisen, that are disseminated again and again, and that are mutually dependent. Note well: in this way philosophy only moves away from inadequate attempts at definition and is forced more and more to itself—philosophy's own essence only *on the basis of* philosophy itself.

1. *Philosophy is not science.* Philosophy—as a widespread notion has it—is cognition, knowledge [*Wissen*], thus "science" [*Wissenschaft*]. Yet philosophy is not science; to the contrary, science is a subordinate mode of philosophy, if by science one understands, as is usual, the theoretical observation of and research into a particular region of beings. Philosophy has no particular region, but is concerned with all beings. And it does not observe and carry out research with a view to justifying a set of end results. It remains a questioning over which every result has already leapt. But if philosophy is concerned with all beings, and if it does not aim at theoretical, scientific results, then surely it must be the construction of a worldview.

2. *Philosophy is not a worldview* in the sense of the presentation of a picture of the world that is constructed from the current results of the sciences today, the dominant tendencies of the various directions of practical activity, and the currently valid demands of life, with the added intention of raising the individual out of his individual isolation in his occupation within his own domain, into the domain of a "universal cul-

tivation" and a universal consciousness. Making such pictures of the world is not only artificial, derivative, and ineffectual, but is a *fundamental delusion* about how humanity comes to know of beings as a whole, as well as about the character of this very knowing. Not to paint pictures of the world, but to attain world history in the struggle over our own history.

3. *Philosophy is not laying a foundation for knowledge.* Given the results of the sciences, the opinion that philosophy means laying a foundation for knowledge is certainly neither accidental nor difficult to conceive. To go back into the presuppositions of scientific knowledge—this would be a legitimate goal. And yet it is perverted if it aims solely at the logical structure and "logic" of the *fundamental concepts* of science. The goal remains derivative and gets stuck in its own rootlessness if it does not draw creatively on the essence of truth. (Cf. the theory of science in the sciences, Kant, 19th century.) Another legitimate goal is the delimitation of the *regions of research*, but only if that delimitation measures itself by the way these regions are revealed prior to scientific knowledge, in their own primordial connection within beings as a whole. Yet this connection is made inaccessible by the artificial system of the sciences that currently reigns.

4. *Philosophy is not absolute knowledge.* In what respect was such knowledge attributed to philosophy?

a) If it is supposed to be knowing about beings as a whole, then it is not supposed to know them in an isolated and necessarily narrowed perspective, but beyond all separation and finitude, it should be infinite, nonrelative knowing, released from all restriction.
b) If philosophical knowing reaches out beyond all special science, then it is also free of all uncertainty and questionability: it is insight pure and simple, ultimate, indubitable justification and irresistible convincing force.

But philosophy arises from the *ownmost urgency and strength of humanity,* and *not* of *God.* It is not absolute knowledge either in its content or in its form. Proper to it is the *highest essentiality,* and thus *necessity,* but not therefore infinity.

5. *Philosophy is not concern with the isolated existence of the individual human being as such.* To what extent is it this? To the extent that it is a resistance to absolute knowledge, to the forgetting of man in German idealism (*Kierkegaard*), the resistance to the dispersal of man into the rootless plurality of his machinations, to his dissolution and release into free-floating regions, "culture," sciences. Man reduced to a hireling—without ever having been independent. In the second half of the nineteenth century *Nietzsche* attempted to bring man as a historically spiritual entity back to himself again, and as far as possible beyond the

contemporary man: the over-man! And yet the two greatest voices of
warning did not find their way back into the true task. We must hear
them, but not become their adherents. They were broken under their
burden. In order to bring ourselves into the clear, an actual personal
engagement with our own destiny is required.

If we now think over everything at once that philosophy is not, and
remember at the same time its whole history from its inception with the
Greeks to Nietzsche, then we reach the unsettling and provocative conclusion that in its history, philosophy has been precisely everything that
we said is not its essence. It was and willed to be: science, worldview,
foundation for knowledge, absolute knowledge, concern with existence.
The history of Western philosophy thus turns out to be an ever steeper
decline from its own essence. More than that—insofar as in its history
philosophy appeals again and again to its start and inception among the
Greeks, philosophy makes this inception ever harder to recognize and
misinterprets it in terms of the later, degraded essence.

Decline from the inception, perversion of the inception—that does
not rule out the fact that in the course of the declining history, philosophers and philosophies of great rank and scope have always come to
light. This proves only that the greatness of the inception does not consist exclusively and primarily in the quality, so to speak, of the relevant
philosophy, but in the total character and style of its historical moment
and historical mission. *The essence of the inception itself turns itself around,*
the inception is no longer the *great, forward-reaching origin,* but is now
only the inadequate, groping beginning of the development to come.

You will immediately reply: why, then, should philosophy not be
defined by its history? Does it not go against all reason and objectivity
to assert that what philosophy actually was in its history is not its essence? Must we not say the very opposite: what philosophy *has been*
[gewesen] shows its *essence* [Wesen]? Where do we get the security of
our denial when we say: philosophy is not . . . ? From some sort of
suprahistorical standpoint? No—but precisely from history, from the
inception and from its end, yet in such a way that we do not stop at
their surface, but gain questioning access to what happened there. We
do not look down on history, but seek to grasp it in its innermost happening, which is stretched between inception and end.

To summarize:

1. Philosophy is the unceasing, questioning struggle over the essence and Being of beings.
2. This questioning is in itself historical, that is, it is the demanding, challenging, and honoring of a people for the sake of the
   hardness and clarity of its fate.

3. Philosophy is not: science, the formation of a worldview, laying a foundation for knowledge, absolute knowledge, concern for individual existence.

With this do we now know the *fundamental question of philosophy?* No—but we know the *direction and way* by which we are to *come into the asking of this question.* We do not entertain the misconception that this question can arbitrarily be thought up for the immediate future, in isolation from history. But we do not fall prey to the opposite error either, to the view that the question can be found somewhere by looking through the generally familiar history of philosophy.

Furthermore, we know:

1. that history must speak, because this question is itself the fundamental happening of our history;
2. that history is not the past, but happening, both as a heritage and as a future;
3. that history speaks only when we force it into confrontation;
4. that confrontation must arise among us from an actual urgency and necessity of Dasein;
5. that this confrontation may not set its sights on just any weak point of just any opponent, but instead, the attack must strike that *highest position of the entire history,* with whose conquest everything is decided.

---

§4. The fundamental question of philosophy and the confrontation with the history of the Western spirit in its highest position: Hegel

What is this highest position in which all essential forces of Western spiritual history gathered themselves as in a great block? That is the philosophy of *Hegel.* On the one hand and looking backward, it is the completion of the history of Western philosophy; on the other hand and looking forward, it is at the same time the direct and indirect point of departure for the opposition of the great voices of warning and pathbreakers in the nineteenth century: *Kierkegaard and Nietzsche.*

In the *confrontation with Hegel,* the entire history of the Western spirit before him and after him up to the present is speaking to us. In such truly historical confrontation we find our way back to the fundamental happening of our ownmost history. Only in this way can we make our way to the concealed trajectory of future spiritual action. The asking of the fundamental question of philosophy then stands before us as the highest effort of this very action. Philosophy must then set aside the illusion that it is the most innocuous occupation there can be, busying itself with the most remote thoughts there can be, thoughts that it artificially complicates to boot.

All the same—even if the necessity of asking the fundamental question of philosophy comes quite near to us, in the total historical urgency of our Western, German Dasein (the question never becomes coercion)—even then, it is always up to the decision we reach regarding our Dasein, that is, our historical being-with others in the membership of the people. It always remains up to us whether we will not, in the end, give way to spiritual torpor and willing cowardice; whether we will not hide the torpor and cowardice from ourselves behind apparently pressing tasks of the daily and current business at hand; whether we will not draw back into the placidity and apparent security of simply letting things run their course. No one will prevent you from doing so and standing aside from history.

But no one, either, is going to ask you whether you will it or not when the West cracks at its joints, and the derivative mock culture finally collapses into itself, and brings all forces into confusion and lets them suffocate in madness. Whether that will happen or not depends solely on whether we as a people still will ourselves, or whether we no longer will ourselves. Each one participates in this decision, even and precisely when he shrinks from this decision and believes he must act superior to today's awakening and play the part of the supposedly "spiritual" elite.

We want to find our way into the fundamental question of philosophy and thus into the fundamental happening of our history, in order to find our way to, build up, and secure the trajectories of our spiritual fate as a people. This is to happen through a *historical confrontation with Hegel.*

But perhaps, or even certainly, most of you will confess that you know nothing of Hegel and his philosophy. Yet the fact that you do not know his works does not mean that the world in which these works worked themselves out is not still actually here, and even so penetratingly and closely here that, on account of its very proximity, we no longer expressly feel it as such. And thus it is also questionable whether you will for the moment see today's actuality more sharply if you undertake, say, a hasty, supplementary study of Hegel's works. There are many experts on Hegelian philosophy—and they are just as clueless about what has happened in this philosophy, and consequently is still happening, as the non-experts are.

In this lecture course we do not want to, nor can we, present the entire work of Hegel, and we certainly do not want to promote the opinion that the confrontation could take place without the most thorough and long familiarity with this work. It is one thing *to conduct* this confrontation—it is another *to transpose* oneself into the asking of the fundamental question *on the basis of* this confrontation and *through* it. You are to follow only the fundamental features and major steps of this confrontation, with the sole intent of surveying for the first time the extent and scope of the fundamental question of philosophy and taking it up into an actual understanding.

Looking backward, Hegel means completion; looking forward, he means the starting point for Kierkegaard and Nietzsche.

MAIN PART

The Fundamental Question and Metaphysics:
Preparation for a Confrontation with Hegel

Chapter One
The Development, Transformation, and Christianization of Traditional Metaphysics

§5. Considerations for the confrontation with Hegel

The *historical path into the essence of philosophy*—there is no other, for the very reason that *philosophy itself is the fundamental happening of the history of our Dasein*. To be sure, the historical path is complex, but always because of an essential necessity in its outset, development, and goal. The goal is to overcome the accidental character of a particular preference and valuation; to overcome particular standpoints, whether genuine or ungenuine, in accordance with their provenance and the course of their development—to expose oneself to the driving need as a whole and detect the course of the history of spirit.

Hegel—in confrontation with him, we are to attain the overarching mood and fundamental attitude of our historical moment in the whole history of our Western Dasein and of the mission of our people in this history.

Who is Hegel? Hegel is one of the main figures who formed the "German movement" through which, between 1770 and 1820, a new German spiritual world was formed in great, creative thought and poetry.

Hegel was born in Stuttgart in 1770 and attended the University of Tübingen, where he studied philosophy and theology from 1788 to 1793. There he developed a friendship with his fellow students and countrymen, Schelling and Hölderlin. Upon finishing his studies he went to Berne until 1796 as a private tutor, and occupied himself there with theological questions (the introduction of Kant's moral philosophy into positive Christianity and nationality). After this rather unexciting period he went to Frankfurt as a private tutor. There he met Hölderlin again, who at the time was experiencing the years of his most intimate

15

fate. We know that the Hölderlin of that time had an essential influence on Hegel's further spiritual formation. It was the first real orientation to the *ancient world*, free of theological influence. At this time Hegel first confronts Aristotle and Plato, and this marks a decisive turn in the development of his thought into a great philosophy. With this preparation, Hegel is armed for his teaching position at Jena in 1801, where he delivers lectures on logic and metaphysics. At that time Schelling was already a celebrated teacher there (*System of Transcendental Idealism*).[1] On the evening of the battle of Jena and Auerstädt, he completes the *Phenomenology of Spirit*.[2] (Consciousness, self-consciousness, reason, ethical life, art, religion, absolute knowledge.) Hegel then moves to Bamberg, where he works as an editor. From 1808 to 1816 he directs a *Gymnasium* in Nuremberg; at this time he writes his *Science of Logic*.[3] In 1816, at age forty-six, he becomes professor of philosophy at Heidelberg, where he composes the *Encyclopedia*.[4] In 1818 Hegel goes to Berlin, where he develops a rich and influential career as lecturer up to his death in 1831.

When Hegel left Heidelberg, he noted in a text on the occasion of his departure[5] that he was not going to Berlin for philosophical purposes, but for political ones; his political philosophy was already complete. He said that he hoped to have a political effect, that he had no taste for mere instruction. His philosophy attained a most remarkable influence on the attitude of the state.

Hegel displays the specific nature and hereditary character of the Swabians. He pursues his whole path in a headstrong way from his youth onwards; his Swabian brooding gets to the bottom of things; he

1. {Friedrich Wilhelm Joseph Schelling, *System des transscendentalen Idealismus* (Tübingen, 1800).} [English translation: *System of Transcendental Idealism*, trans. Peter Heath (Charlottesville: University Press of Virginia, 1978).]

2. {*System der Wissenschaft von Ge. Wilh. Fr. Hegel, Erster Theil, die Phänomenologie des Geistes* (Bamberg and Würzburg: Joseph Anton Goebhardt, 1807).} [English translation: *Phenomenology of Spirit*, trans. A. V. Miller (Oxford: Oxford University Press, 1977).]

3. {*Wissenschaft der Logik. Von D. Ge. Wilh. Friedr. Hegel*, 2 vols. (Nuremberg: Johann Leonhard Schrag, 1812-1813, 1816).} [English translation: *Hegel's Science of Logic*, trans. A. V. Miller (London: Allen & Unwin, 1969).]

4. {*Encyclopädie der philosophischen Wissenschaften im Grundrisse. Zum Gebrauch seiner Vorlesungen von Dr. Georg Friedrich Wilhelm Hegel* (Heidelberg: August Oßwald, 1817).} [English translation: *Encyclopedia of the Philosophical Sciences in Outline*, trans. Steven A. Taubeneck, in *Encyclopedia of the Philosophical Sciences in Outline and Critical Writings*, ed. Ernst Behler (London and New York: Continuum, 1990).]

5. {Hegel's letter to the Restricted Heidelberg University Senate, 21 April 1818; and see also his letter to the Badenese Ministry of Interior, 21 April 1818.} [English translation: *Hegel: The Letters*, trans. Clark Butler and Christiane Seiler (Bloomington: Indiana University Press, 1984), pp. 381-82.]

has the passion of the optimistic improver of the world. A tremendous knowledge, together with a rare force of conceptual penetration and precision, of rich imagery, and of linguistic formation give his work a form that we cannot find elsewhere in our German philosophy.

As we said, we are *not* attempting a general presentation of the Hegelian system, say, by running through a general summary of the contents of his works and lectures. That would be nothing but a useless external observation. Instead, the point is to grasp the *inner movement* of the *questioning,* the outset and goal and the form of its coalescence into philosophical truth.

In turn, this *fundamental trend of questioning* must be found above all where Hegel's philosophy—and that means at the same time the tradition before him and up to him—sought the *core of philosophical labor.* That is the philosophical discipline that bears the ancient name *"metaphysics."*

§6. The concept of metaphysics and its transformation up to the time of classical modern metaphysics

a) The origin of the concept of metaphysics as a bibliographical title for particular Aristotelian writings (μετὰ τὰ φυσικά)

First we must get clear about this word "metaphysics" and the concept of it. True, in general it is familiar; at least, one can read in every standard textbook on the history of philosophy how the expression "metaphysics" arose. But for most people this is an irrelevant curiosity, whereas in truth the history of this word illuminates decisive segments of the history of the Western spirit.

It is put together from two *Greek* words: the preposition μετά and φύσις (φυσικός, φυσικά, the nominalization of φυσικός, τὰ φυσικά). μετά means with, amid (μέσος, between), after the one, before the other; μετὰ τά means *post,* spatially or temporally succeeding something else. Succeeding what? τὰ φυσικά: φύσις, nature, generally the present-at-hand beings that hold sway as such, that which arises and disappears without human interference. Fundamental character of motion; inanimate bodies, stars, heavens, and in addition living things, coming to be and passing away, the motion of animals—they are all φυσικά. So "physics" designates ἐπιστήμη φυσική, in a sense that is broader and more fundamental than the sense of "physics" today. φύσις: what makes itself on the basis of itself; θέσις: human positing and construction.

So it was, at the outset of the fourth century BC, when Greek philosophy passed its peak, at the time of *Aristotle.* His treatises and lectures were lost until the first century BC. When they were rediscovered and began to be put into order, those on τὰ φυσικά stood out among others and were easy to distinguish from them. But at the same time there were treatises that, although they seemed akin to those on τὰ φυσικά, did not coincide with them, and in fact differed from them according to remarks by Aristotle himself. Given this predicament—where to put them?—they were simply appended to the writings on physics.

In the meantime, another age had begun. The greatness and range, the uniqueness of creative questioning and conceptual formation had faded away, giving way to the business of the schools—still the words and concepts, but not the stimulating force of the thing itself anymore. So one found writings available, and tried to get one's bearings.

The writings that one really did not know what to do with at all were therefore placed behind and after τὰ φυσικά in the series of texts, μετὰ τὰ φυσικά. So μετὰ τὰ φυσικά is a stopgap title. Later, in the *Christian* age—we do not know exactly when and by whom, perhaps Boethius—this compound Greek stopgap bibliographical concept was brought together in Latin into one word and one name: *metaphysica,* or more fully, *scientia metaphysica.*

b) From the bibliographical title to the substantive concept. The
   Christian transformation of the concept of metaphysics:
   knowledge of the supersensible (*trans physicam*)

But this *unification* of the word *corresponds at the same time* to a *change* in its *meaning.* The change in meaning did not take place without a certain consideration of the content of the treatises that had been brought together earlier under the bibliographical title. It became clear that these treatises occupied themselves with what goes beyond the domain of nature in the broad sense: *non-nature.* But now, for the Christian way of thinking, the things of nature, the natural things, are fundamentally the creaturely things—that is, those created by God. What lies beyond nature is the *divine, God.* This being is not only outside the limits of nature, but also *higher in essence and rank* and thus beyond it, *trans.* The consideration of the content already shows a specifically Christian interpretation.

From this interpretation of the concept, non-nature in the sense of divine supernature, the word meta-physics acquires a changed meaning. μετά is no longer interpreted bibliographically in relation to the sequence of texts (*post*), but rather on the basis of the particular content of the texts in question, understood in a Christian way: *trans,* above and beyond nature. Nature is accessible to the senses, as distinct from the supersensible. But in contrast, *metaphysics is the knowledge of divine things, of the supersensible. The stopgap title becomes the name for the highest possible type of human knowledge.*

The compound word that was thus brought together into one word and name, and at the same time transformed in its meaning, thus became an extremely serendipitous and useful *title for designating the theological speculation of Christian thought about the world* in the coming centuries. And not just the Middle Ages, but the entire philosophy of modernity, including Hegel, maintained this concept, and no less the post-Hegelian period up to the present. The word's awkward origin was forgotten, and since then the word presents itself as if all along, it had been created especially as an expression of its substantive meaning.

Kant is of this opinion when, in a posthumously published text on the "progress of metaphysics," he says of the term "metaphysics":

> The old name of this science, μετὰ τὰ φυσικά, already gives a pointer to the kind of knowledge at which its aim was directed. The purpose is to proceed by means of it beyond all objects of possible experience (*trans physicam*), in order, where possible, to know that which absolutely cannot be an object thereof, and hence the definition of metaphysics, which contains the reason for advocating such a science, would be: It is a science of progressing from knowledge of the sensible to that of the super-sensible.[6]

Likewise in his frequently delivered lecture course on metaphysics: "Concerning the name of metaphysics . . . (a) to progress to, above, and over; (b) *higher* science, next in succession; (c) beyond."[7]

In all this, the *Christian* concept of *scientia metaphysica* holds sway. This indicates at the same time that the approach to and interpretation of the Aristotelian texts and fragments is no longer determined by these writings themselves, but by the methods and in the light of the *later* Christian concept of metaphysics. And not just medieval and later and contemporary Scholasticism, not only Kant and post-Kantian philosophy, but even philological, historical research on Aristotle in the present day still stands completely under the spell of this fixed tradition that has become self-evident. *Werner Jaeger* can serve as an example. Despite his quite different historical-philological insight into

6. {Immanuel Kant, "Über die von der Königl. Akademie der Wissenschaften zu Berlin für das Jahr 1791 ausgesetzte Preisfrage: Welches sind die wirklichen Fortschritte, die die Metaphysik seit Leibnitzens und Wolf's Zeiten in Deutschland gemacht hat?"} [English translation: "What Real Progress has Metaphysics Made in Germany Since the Time of Leibniz and Wolff?" trans. Peter Heath, in Immanuel Kant, *Theoretical Philosophy After 1781* (Cambridge: Cambridge University Press, 2002), p. 399.]

7. {*Vorlesungen Kants über Metaphysik aus drei Semestern,* ed. Max Heinze (Leipzig, 1894), p. 186.}

the "history of the development of metaphysics,"[8] he has a completely standard view of the content of metaphysics.

_____

§7. Kant's critical question regarding the possibility of metaphysical cognition and the classical division of metaphysics

a) On the influence of the Christianization of the concept of metaphysics

We have now drawn the basic lines and framework of the history of the word "metaphysics" and thus also experienced something of its meaning, and so of the thing that it means. In this regard we should say: the word "metaphysics" designates, in its transformed meaning, which is really definitive in history, a concept that is determined and fulfilled by Christian thought. Directly after its inception, Western philosophy becomes *un-Greek* and remains so, explicitly or not, until Nietzsche. The traditional concept of metaphysics, although it is a concept of philosophy, is a *Christian* concept through and through.

Now, the question is: how was this concept filled out in the course of its history? How was what it designates developed? We can most quickly gain the general answer if we begin by following the history of Western-Christian metaphysics at the point where it arrives at a new crisis, for both the first and the last time. That happens in and through the philosophy of Kant.

It is true that even this crisis of metaphysics and this transformation of its concept remain *within the framework of Christian thought;* and despite essential steps, the *question* that is *concealed* under the title of metaphysics could not be tied back to its origin and to the inception of Western philosophy. That is, even Kant was unable to awaken the *fundamental question of philosophy* in its originary power and develop it in its dangerous scope. The ancient world and ancient Dasein remained closed to him. The whole field of Kant's questioning is dominated by the Christian conceptual world. We will attempt to consider more closely which existentiell position determines the dominant understanding of Being.

Christian faith determined the question of beings as a whole in three essential respects. (1) The being that we know as "world" was created by God. (2) The being that we ourselves are, the human being as an indi-

_____

8. {Cf. Werner Jaeger, *Aristoteles: Grundlegung einer Geschichte seiner Entwicklung* (Berlin, 1923).} [English translation: *Aristotle: Fundamentals of the History of his Development,* trans. Richard Robinson (Oxford: Clarendon Press, 1934).] {Cf. also: Werner Jaeger, *Studien zur Entstehungsgeschichte der Metaphysik des Aristoteles,* Berlin, 1912.}

vidual, is considered in regards to the salvation of his soul, immortality. (3) The true and highest being, above the world and man, is God as creator and savior. In all three respects, reflection on what can be experienced through the senses sees itself led beyond into the supersensible, whether it is the afterlife of the soul, the limits and cause of the nature-world-whole, or the physical ground of the totality itself.

This conceptual world is still here today, even when it is no longer experienced on the basis of faith. In a pallid, washed-out form, pervaded by theory, it has become, as it were, the natural worldview within which everyday thinking moves. And philosophy has been confined to this field of vision.

b) The three rational disciplines of modern metaphysics and
Kant's question regarding the inner possibility and limits of
metaphysical cognition as cognition on the basis of pure reason

Object of "metaphysics": observation, or rather consideration, of the supersensible in these three respects is obviously, according to what we said earlier, the task of that cognition that bears the name "metaphysics." Therefore the cognitive task of metaphysics, as it develops and hardens, falls into *three domains:* (1) the *soul* of the individual human being, (2) the *whole of nature,* (3) *God.* A discipline is assigned to each of these domains: *psychology, cosmology, theology.* Insofar as these disciplines get at the ground of the domains, and do so on the path and with the means of human thought, of *reason* (not faith), that is, *ratio,* we have the disciplines of rational psychology, cosmology, and theology. Thus metaphysics is divided into these three disciplines. Three domains—three disciplines (free of all experience)—rational cognition—*pure* reason.

In each of these three regions we encounter the sort of thing of which we say "it is"—we encounter *beings.* What is common to all—soul, world, God—regardless of *what* they are in each case and *in what way* they are, is Being. From this Being, every being comes forth in some way. This Being in general is *ens in communi* [the being in general, or the being as such], on the basis of which the individual domain is distinguished. Being itself as being—*summum ens* [the highest being]. And thus the inquiry can aim in advance at what the being in a particular domain is in general, at *ens in communi.* This general foundation in *scientia architectonica* [architectonic science] is *metaphysica generalis* [general metaphysics]. In contrast to it, genuine metaphysics is *metaphysica specialis* [special metaphysics].

Kant toiled his whole life on metaphysics, understood and divided in this way. In the time *before* his main work, the *Critique of Pure Reason,* he tried to make improvements within traditional metaphysics, until he managed to *place the essence of this metaphysics itself into question* by asking *whether and how metaphysics is possible,* what it is *entitled* to, and what is *denied* it. To distinguish—κρίνειν/crisis—whether metaphysics knows what it *wants*, whether metaphysics understands what it *can* do: "the metaphysics of metaphysics."[9] Clarification of the title of the main work, *Critique of Pure Reason*. Pure reason, cf. above *metaphysica specialis:* rational psychology, cosmology, theology. Critique: to distinguish, to contrast, to set limits, to delineate possibility.

Which critical question? Cognition of the supersensible; becoming aware of something about it. *To this end: synthetic* knowledge; but not accessible in experience. *Free of experience,* before and without all experience, *synthetic a priori cognitions* from mere concepts a priori. *How* are these possible? The question itself and what it interrogates clarified in the course of the critical investigation: 1. In what sense are synthetic cognitions a priori possible (as ontological, not ontical)? 2. On what grounds? (transcendental unity).

Fundamental question really: *what is man? Metaphysics as natural tendency:* (a) constantly tending toward it, (b) at the same time a constant error (transcendental illusion).

But in spite of everything, [Kant's thought] remains in the received *Christian world. Today's Christianity* and its *theology*—traditional metaphysics and the decisive question? *The positive labor (ontological) is in itself restrictive, but at the same time regulative-practical.*

Kant's answer and solution to be pursued no farther; compare later to Hegel.

9. {Cf. Appendix I, addendum 11, [German] pp. 276-77.}

Chapter Two
The System of Modern Metaphysics and the First of Its Primary Determining Grounds: The Mathematical

§8. Preliminary remarks on the concept and meaning of the mathematical in metaphysics

a) The task: a historical return to the turning points in the concept of metaphysics

With this we have provided an *initially satisfactory* clarification of how the concept "metaphysics" was fleshed out in a decisive period of Western philosophy. The only thing we lack is the insight into the truly determining forces and driving powers of metaphysics, *into what wants to assert itself there as a claim and urgent need for human beings.*

So now we must ask about the *historical development* that preceded this hardening of the concept of metaphysics that we have discussed. The development embraces the period from the first collection of the Aristotelian treatises in the first century BC to 1800. We cannot master this entire period, and not only on account of the extent and fullness of the questions to be treated; much of it has not even been researched at all yet. Why then the amazing fact that there is still no real history of Western metaphysics—not of the concept and word, much less of the thing itself? On the other hand, this is not so amazing if one sees to what trivialities the century of history, the nineteenth century, could devote itself.

But for us now, what is decisive is not the completeness and seamlessness of the course of history, but the presentation of this course in its *essential effects* and *effective implications for the future.*

We are trying, going backwards from Kant, to hold firmly to some *characteristic turning points* in the history of the concept of metaphysics, with the initial intention of highlighting two points: I. The effects of both primary determining grounds that led to the development of the concept of metaphysics that we have presented. II. Allowing us to gauge how far this concept of metaphysics was driven away from the original Greek way of posing the question.

Both together can serve as a first piece of evidence for our assertion that the history of Western philosophy is an accelerating decline from its inception. This is not to deny that such philosophy brought forth great works; to the contrary, the greatness of the inception is only that much more powerful.

On I. The two primary determining grounds for the development of Western metaphysics: (1) the mathematical, (2) Christian theology (already highlighted). *But all with the fundamental intention of clarifying and directing our own historical Dasein.*[1]

The concept of metaphysics we have presented that Kant took as his basis (*metaphysica specialis—generalis*) was expressed *as an academic concept* by Christian Wolff[2] and Crusius,[3] as well as by Baumgarten and Meier,[4] whose textbooks Kant took as the basis not just of his teaching, but also of his own research. Both Baumgarten and Meier not only provided a *rigorous division* of the entire doctrinal content of philosophy into disciplines, but also viewed these as derived from underlying *fundamental disciplines* and as *rigorously, methodically constructed in themselves.* The ideal and standard for this was *mathematics,* mathesis in the broadest sense: fundamental concepts and principles and rigorous deduction. (Cf. Preface to *Ontologia,* so-called *Euclidea.*)[5] *The mathematical is here shown to be the sole determining ground in the law of the development and completion of modern Western metaphysics.* The significance of *metaphysica generalis* is not just as a "vestibule" but as a *foundation.* (Cf. Baumgarten's starting point, Wolff.)

But not simply taking over and promulgating a defunct doctrinal content—the doctrine was set in motion by *Leibniz;* hence the Leibniz-Wolff school. On Leibniz himself, cf. *De primae philosophiae Emendatione.*[6] Precisely for Leibniz, who himself was a productive mathemati-

1. Not forward to Hegel, but backward.

2. 1679–1754; Leipzig, Halle (mathematics), Marburg, Halle; extensive educational and writing activity.

3. {Christian August Crusius, 1715–1775.}

4. {Alexander Gottlieb Baumgarten, 1714–1762; Georg Friedrich Meier, 1718–1777.}

5. {Christian Wolff, *Philosophia prima, sive Ontologia, methodo scientifica pertractata, qua omnis cognitionis humanae principia continentur* (Frankfurt and Leipzig, 1729), Praefatio.}

6. {G. W. Leibniz, "De primae philosophiae Emendatione, et de Notione Substantiae," in *Die philosophische Schriften von Gottfried Wilhelm Leibniz,* ed. C. J. Ger-

cian, mathematics became, as it was for Spinoza and Descartes before him, the *prototype of all scientificity* and thus also of the *cognitive character* of philosophy.

To be sure, it is a great *error*, and one that is still definitive everywhere today, to believe that this *predominance* of mathematics and mathematical thinking in the seventeenth and eighteenth centuries was restricted only to the external construction of philosophical systems, the articulation of their concepts, and the ordering and sequence of their propositions. The only thing correct in this opinion is this: the mathematical must be understood here in a broader, more fundamental sense, not as the particular methodology of some particular mathematical domain.

b) The Greek concept of the teachable and learnable (τὰ μαθήματα) and the inner connection between the "mathematical" and the "methodological"

When Spinoza titles his main work *Ethica more geometrico demonstrata*, the geometrical method here does not mean, say, the procedure of analytic geometry; Spinoza is thinking of Euclid's procedure in his *Elements*, and of this procedure in its general formal sense, not as restricted to definite spatial elements and forms. The mathematical as μάθημα, the teachable as such, that which can be learned in a preeminent sense; μάθησις, learning, μανθάνειν.

And what is that? Here we can see more clearly if we investigate how the Greeks, to whom we owe the word μαθήματα and thus the discovery of the matter itself, distinguished the μαθήματα from other things. Within the whole domain of beings and of that which can become an object in this or that way, the Greeks are familiar, among other things, with (1) τὰ φυσικά (cf. above), that which arises, grows, and passes away on its own; (2) τὰ ποιούμενα, what is produced by manufacture; (3) τὰ χρήματα, things insofar as they are in use in a particular sense; (4) τὰ πράγματα, the things we have something to do with (πρᾶξις). All four domains are distinguished by the fact that the *objects that belong to them in each case* become *accessible in a particular way of experiencing and dealing with them,* and only in this way. Threatening and favorable natural phenomena, tools, weapons, means of nourishment and exchange, raw materials, and the like—all this is always encountered only in particular experiential contexts, according to particular directions of human concerns, in a particular historical situation in each case.

hardt, 7 vols. (Berlin, 1875–1890), vol. 4 (Berlin, 1880), pp. 468–70.} [English translation: "On the Correction of Metaphysics and the Concept of Substance," in *Philosophical Papers and Letters,* 2nd edition, ed. Leroy E. Loemker (Dordrecht: D. Reidel, 1969), pp. 432–33.]

Now, in contrast to this, what does τὰ μαθήματα mean? When we speak of the "mathematical," we run the *risk of misinterpreting* the Greek concept. For with the "mathematical" we initially and exclusively think of number and numerical relations, of the point, line, plane, solid (spatial elements and forms). But all this is called mathematical only in a derivative sense, insofar as it satisfies precisely what *originally* belongs to the *essence of the* μαθήματα; the μαθήματα are not to be explained through the mathematical, but vice versa.

And what belongs originally to the essence of the μαθήματα? Teaching, what is taught, what can be taught and learned. And what does that mean? The terms above are words for the use of the present-at-hand, for production, for presence at hand in itself. Now we have a word [i.e., μαθήματα] for *appropriating* and *communicating* (taking and giving), without characterizing the content of these acts at all. This word clearly concerns what can be received and communicated in a preeminent sense. What distinguishes it is that it deals with the reception or communication of what is *known* and *cognized* as such, *truths* as such, for precisely that is *learning and teaching*. With this, again, we have not said *what* is known in each case.

There are certain items of knowledge and notions that man does not somehow gain in dealing with and using things, on the basis of experiences and dealings, but which he comes upon wholly on his own, quite apart from the extent, ground, and manner of his other experiences—a kind of knowledge with its own way of taking and giving. The most striking, but not the only such knowledge, is the knowledge of numerical and spatial relations. We acquire such knowledge insofar as we "recollect" precisely only what we already know by ourselves; ἀναλαβὼν αὐτὸς ἐξ αὑτοῦ τὴν ἐπιστήμην [getting the knowledge himself from himself] (Plato, *Meno*, 85d4).[7] A *reception* in which I communicate (give) *to myself* what I already fundamentally have, a *communication* in which I allow *the other* to receive only that which he gives to himself.

The cognitive procedure as such provides itself with its own objects and possible data that it can come to know, insofar as it first *forms* them, as it were. They first arise in learning and teaching; μαθήματα are given and acquired in a preeminent way—knowledge-forming procedure. In these objects the *activity that first of all forms them* is especially prominent. The mathematical is "experienced," if at all, *in and through the activity itself.* This procedure itself creates its own *rules* for the way in which it attains and develops its knowledge; it expresses and fixes itself in propositions.

7. {*Platonis Opera. Recognovit brevique adnotatione critica instruxit Ioannes Burnet* (Oxford: Clarendon Press, 1899–1907), vol. III (1903).}

The mathematical is what can be taught and learned in a preeminent sense. It *begins* with *principles* that everyone can attain on his own; it *develops* into *inferences* whose progression also unfolds in itself. The mathematical bears within it the beginning, progression, and goal of an activity that is contained within itself; that is, it is in itself a *way*, that is, a *method*. As such a way, (1) *it secures* the distinction of the true from the false, and (2) in its course, it brings to knowledge everything that can be known in the domain at hand.

From this essence of method we must then derive the *two fundamental conditions* that a procedure must satisfy in order to be a genuine method:

> *At si methodus recte explicet, quomodo mentis intuitu sit utendum, ne in errorem vero contrarium delabamur, et quomodo deductiones inveniendae sint, ut ad omnium cognitionem perveniamus, nihil aliud requiri mihi videtur ut sit completa, cum nullam scientiam haberi posse, nisi per mentis intuitum vel deductionem, iam ante dictum est.*

> But if our method properly explains how we should use our mental {immediate} intuition to avoid falling into the opposite error, and how we should go about finding the deductive inferences that will help us attain this all-embracing knowledge, then I do not see that anything more is needed to make it complete; for as I have already said, we can have no knowledge except through mental intuition or deduction.

The sentence is taken from a text by Descartes (1596-1650): *Regulae ad directionem ingenii* (second comment on rule IV).[8] According to this text, the two main elements of method are *intuitus* and *deductio*. This means: (1) the immediate *vision* of and insight into the principles and what is posited in them, principles which as such cannot be derived from anything further; (2) this very *deduction* of further propositions from the fundamental propositions or principles.

This distinction of the fundamental elements of every method goes back in its content and concepts to *ancient philosophy;* there, in particular in Plato, the distinction between νοεῖν and διανοεῖσθαι was determined on the basis of a reflection on the "mathematical" in the broadest sense. Then Aristotle saw the main elements in an essentially clearer way, and one that is definitive for posterity as a whole: ἐπαγωγή

---

8. {*René Descartes's Regulae ad directionem ingenii. Nach der Original-Ausgabe von 1701 herausgegeben von Artur Buchenau* (Leipzig: Dürr, 1907). Heidegger's personal copy.} [English translation: "Rules for the Direction of the Mind," trans. Dugald Murdoch, in *The Philosophical Writings of Descartes,* trans. John Cottingham et al. (Cambridge: Cambridge University Press, 1985), p. 16 (trans. modified).]

and ἀπόδειξις. Descartes's entire reflection on the essence of method circles around these two main elements.[9]

For evidence, let us simply give the text of rule V:[10]

Tota methodus consistit in ordine et dispositione eorum, ad quae mentis acies est convertenda, ut aliquam veritatem inveniamus. Atqui hanc exacte servabimus, si propositiones involutas et obscuras ad simpliciores gradatim reducamus, et deinde ex omnium simplicissimarum intuitu ad aliarum omnium cognitionem per eosdem gradus ascendere tentemus.

The whole method consists entirely in the ordering and arranging of the objects on which we must concentrate our mind's eye if we are to discover some truth. We shall be following this method exactly if we first reduce complicated and obscure propositions step by step to simpler ones, and then, starting with the intuition of the simplest ones of all, try to ascend through the same steps to a knowledge of all the rest.

The return to the immediate view of and into the simplest propositions and concepts: but this fundamental rule of the method—the mathematical method—now becomes at the same time the instruction to build up a science, or rather *the fundamental science,* in accordance with this rule, a science that with a view to everything in general that can possibly be known prepares the fundamental propositions and simplest fundamental concepts for immediate insight. Descartes designates the most universal fundamental science with the term *mathesis universalis.* Leibniz, who took up the idea, termed it *characteristica universalis* [universal characteristic] and *scientia generalis* [general science], the fundamental elements of method as analysis and synthesis. *Est autem methodus analytica, cum quaestio aliqua proposita tamdiu resolvitur in notiones simpliciores, donec ad eius solutionem perveniatur. Methodus vero synthetica est, cum a simplicioribus notionibus progredimur ad compositas, donec ad propositam deveniamus* (Couturat, p. 179).[11]

9. [νοεῖν and διανοεῖσθαι are usually interpreted as immediate and discursive understanding. The standard translations of ἐπαγωγή and ἀπόδειξις are "induction" and "demonstration."]

10. Cf. text and translation. {Text and translation added by editor.} ["Rules for the Direction of the Mind," p. 20.]

11. {In Louis Couturat, *La logique de Leibniz d'après des documents inédits* (Paris, 1901), p. 179; also in *Opuscules et fragments inédits de Leibniz,* ed. Louis Couturat (Paris, 1903), p. 572.} [This passage reads: "Now, a method is analytic when any proposed question is resolved into simpler notions until its solution is reached. A method is synthetic when we progress from simpler notions to composite ones until we attain the [solution of the] proposed question."]

But the fundamental and universal science at the same time serves as the *paradigm of all science and scientificity*.[12]

---

§9. The precedence of the mathematical and its advance decision regarding the content of modern philosophy: the possible idea of knowability and truth

We have seen that the mathematical[13] is not determined by its relations to experience. It manifests its content on its own, *for* every experience and apart from experience. Everyone ἀναλαβὼν αὐτος ἐξ αὐτοῦ τὴν ἐπιστήμην of what becomes learnable in this way, "everyone gets the knowledge of it himself from himself" (Plato, *Meno* 85d4). This does not mean from the arbitrary preference of the individual, but from the human essence. Insofar as he exists as one who knows, an ordered manifold of relationships in number, size, and space displays itself to him. The order is such that it yields propositions about these relationships that must be laid at the foundation of all propositions in the domain—fundamental propositions, principles, which develop themselves in fundamental concepts. Thus the mathematical is this experience-free order in which derivative propositions are grounded on fundamental ones.[14]

Because this form of knowledge appears to have the *highest universality,* and even coincides with the fundamental form of human thinking in general (cf. logic, the doctrine of inference), it is easy and was easy from early on to assimilate all knowledge, and precisely philosophy as the most essential knowledge, to this form of knowledge (cf. modern philosophy).

But, as we have already noted, it is an error to believe that the mathematical here is just an external form of the articulation and ordering of propositions and concepts that are not touched by the mathematical in their content. Instead, the *content* of philosophy is *affected by the mathematical so thoroughly* that the mathematical and its precedence decides *in advance* and in general *what can be known* philosophically and *how it should be known*. The mathematical form of knowledge is, for modern philosophy up to Hegel, not a mere external framework

---

12. Today's crisis of foundations [in the philosophy of mathematics]: intuitionism—formalism; neither of the two. Question inadequate.

13. The inner connection between the "mathematical" and "methodical" and hence a definite concept of "method"; cf. Descartes, *Regulae.*

14. On method in general, and in particular the mathematical as method and logic, cf. Summer Semester 1929. {Martin Heidegger, *Der deutsche Idealismus (Fichte, Schelling, Hegel) und die philosophische Problemlage der Gegenwart* (GA 28), ed. Claudius Strube (Frankfurt am Main: Klostermann, 1997).}

for the presentation of the system, but the *inner law* that determines the *substantive starting point* of philosophy and at the same time the *idea of truth*. But despite all this, philosophy was unable to gain insight into the scope and fatefulness of this law; to the contrary, in ever repeated attempts, philosophers felt a real passion to satisfy the law, to "raise philosophy to the rank of a science."

Now we must actually show that and how the mathematical constituted not just the external framework of the system, but an essential *determining ground of modern metaphysics*. This shall be shown in two decisive stages of its history: (A) in its modern inception, (B) in the stage that Kant takes up in his critique.[15] Then we shall show what these considerations *imply* for a proper understanding of Hegelian metaphysics.

§10. Modern metaphysics in its illusory new inception with Descartes and its errors

a) The usual picture of Descartes: the rigorous new grounding of philosophy on the basis of radical doubt

The usual picture of this philosopher (1596–1650) and his philosophy is as follows. In the Middle Ages, if philosophy subsisted at all on its own, it stood under the *domination of theology* and declined ever further into the mere dissection of concepts, without any closeness to reality or confrontation with it—a *school knowledge* that neither affected the individual human being nor illuminated reality as a whole from the ground up. Philosophy was torn away from this unworthy situation by Descartes, after a general *resistance* to medieval Scholasticism had arisen in the *Renaissance*, although without leading to a new grounding of philosophy as a whole.

This achievement was reserved for Descartes. With him, a completely *new* age of philosophy begins. He dares to philosophize *radically*, for he begins with *universal doubt* about all knowledge, and seeks and finds in his questioning the indestructible foundation on which the edifice of philosophy and all science is to be erected in the future.

I doubt everything, I put all knowledge in every domain and of every kind out of commission. But *insofar as* I am doubting, and the more and the longer I doubt, what is indubitable is precisely this doubting of mine; the *me dubitare* [the fact that I am doubting] is evident and *can never be doubted away*, so it is *indisputably* present at hand in advance. I as doubter—I am present at hand, *my own presence at hand* is the primal certainty and truth. *Dubito*, I doubt, I think of something,

---

15. {Cf. below, [German] pp. 46ff.}

cogito. Cogito—ergo sum; id quod cogitat, est. [I think—therefore I am; that which thinks, is.] (Major premise?)

This *ergo* [therefore] does not mean an inference here. Descartes does not infer from the fact that he is thinking the further fact that he is; instead, I am thinking, therefore I must accept what is *given in advance along with* the presence at hand of my thinking: my presence at hand, *sum* [I am]. The *sum* is not a conclusion and inference, but *to the contrary, the ground,* the *fundamentum absolutum et inconcussum* [absolute and unshakeable foundation].

Inasmuch as Descartes forces human beings into doubt he also leads them to themselves, each to his own I as the reality that is ultimately indubitable and thus becomes the ground and site of all questioning. Man in his I-ness moves into the center of philosophy, the "subject" and subjectivity gain a decisive priority over the object and objectivity.

At first only the Being of the subject is certain, the Being of objects is uncertain—but now at the same time we have reached the *sole point of departure* for posing and then answering the question of the presence at hand of beings *outside me,* in Latin, *extra me.*

Descartes appears as the paradigm of the radical thinker, who finally stakes everything on one card and also provides the directive for a completely new construction of all science. He embodies modernity and its awakening ("liberation") from the obscurity of the Middle Ages.

True, it has lately been noted that this Descartes is not completely independent of his forerunners; they are precisely the medieval Scholastics. One is rather proud of this discovery, which after all rests only on the fact that until now one was ignorant of the medieval Scholastics; but one does not think any further after discovering this connection between Descartes and Scholasticism, but instead uses the discovery in order to declare with satisfaction that even a thinker of Descartes's rank is in some way dependent on others.

This Descartes, viewed in this way, with his universal doubt and simultaneous "emphasis" on the I, is the favorite and most customary topic for tests and examination papers called philosophical in German universities. This custom that has endured for centuries is just *one* sign, but an unmistakable one, of the thoughtlessness and irresponsibility that has spread throughout the universities. We would never have reached this state of spiritual bankruptcy among students and examinations if the teachers themselves had not fomented and allowed it.

b) The illusion of radicalism and the new grounding in Descartes under the predominance of the mathematical conception of method

If we now *destroy* this usual picture of Descartes and his philosophy, and deprive philosophy in the future of the right to appeal to Descartes's metaphysics as an actual inception, this is not supposed to mean that now you should present this new picture, say, on the occasion of your examinations; it means that you should know and understand how completely philosophy lies outside the domain of examinations and of what can be tested in the usual sense.

With the intention of actually determining the position of Descartes in the history of Western philosophy in regards to its fundamental questions, and thus bringing out the decisive predominance of the mathematical conception of method, I assert:

1. The radicalism of Cartesian doubt and the rigor of the new founding of philosophy and of knowledge in general is an illusion, and thus the source of fateful delusions that are hard to root out even today.

2. Not only is there no such thing as the supposed new inception of modern philosophy with Descartes, but this is in truth the beginning of a further essential decline of philosophy. Descartes does not bring philosophy back to itself and to its ground and basis, but drives it still farther away from the asking of its fundamental question.

α) Methodical doubt as the way to what is ultimately indubitable.
The simplest and most perspicuous as fundamentum

What we must do now is prove these assertions in connection with one another. At the same time, this project is the *first advance* of our general attack that aims at *Hegel*. But first we must characterize Descartes's position still more exactly, and above all, we must see *one* point: how his procedure of doubting and laying a new foundation completely corresponds to his *guiding methodical thought*.

Cartesian doubt is often called "methodical" doubt. What one means by this is that the doubt is not supposed to be an end in itself—doubting for the sake of doubting—but that it is carried out with the intention of reaching something indubitable. The doubt serves only as a path to certainty.

But Descartes's doubt is also "methodical" in a completely different and *deeper* sense—namely, insofar as doubting occurs in the sense and *in the service* of what Descartes understands *by method in general*, that is, what we characterized as "mathematical" method. This means that insofar as Descartes subordinates philosophizing to this guiding thought, this sort of method, it is *decided* in advance through this thought what must be the character of that which alone can come under consideration as the secure basis for any knowledge. It must be something that is *simplest, simplicissima propositio* [the most simple proposition], and thus something *purely perspicuous* (*intuitus*).

β) The process of doubt as an illusion.
The substantive advance ruling in favor of something indubitable
that has the character of the present-at-hand

Yet in itself, it is not at all obvious why, precisely, the foundation of philosophy should be something purely simple, and even purely perspicuous. This demand is justified only if one presupposes that the knowing and questioning of philosophy is subordinate to the "mathematical" method. But this is an arbitrary presupposition that Descartes does not ground in any way. Descartes does not even make an attempt to ground it. He lacks every motive for such an attempt. *The rigor of his process of doubt is a mere illusion,* and not, as it were, just because he comes to a secure standpoint afterwards, but because *behind* the process of doubt there stands the completely ungrounded opinion that the method of philosophical questioning and grounding is the "mathematical" method. This presupposes a prior decision that the basis on which all knowledge of philosophy is to be grounded can only be what has the character of the *indubitably present at hand.*

γ) The fundamentum *as the I*

But it is not just the general, sole possible *character of the fundamentum* that is determined in advance and in general by the predominance of this mathematical conception of method; through this method, it is also decided in advance and in particular *what* the only thing is that can come under consideration as such a foundation.

Dedicating oneself, once and for all, to the method means seeking out what is simplest and most perspicuous, that is, indubitable. To begin with, the doubt has the character of doing away with or putting out of commission everything that is incapable of resisting it, that is, whatever is not a *mathematical object* in the broadest sense. Away with everything that is doubtful at all and in any way. When such doubtful things are cut out altogether, what is left over is, in principle, *only the sheer doubting* itself. Doubting leaves only itself untouched; but doubting is a kind of thinking in the broader sense, *cogitatio.* What can be encountered in general as the indubitably present at hand that is sought must have the character of *thinking.* But every thinking thinks *with* the thinker who thinks; thinking knows about itself as the *I* think. What is indubitably present at hand is the *I* that thinks.

δ) The I as self. Self-reflection as a delusion

So this is the source of the first, simplest proposition—the assertion of the presence at hand of the *I.* The *I* of the thinking human being thus moves *into the center of what can truly be humanly known.* But first of all, for the individual human being, the I means *what he himself* is, that within which he has *his self as his own*. The radical return to the I acquires the character of originary self-reflection.

Yet the return to the I by means of the process of doubt is only *the illusion* of originality and radicalism (behind and above it there stands the dogma of the priority of the mathematical method). Just as the return is an illusion, the *rigor of the self-reflection is a delusion*. For it has not been settled in the least whether man attains his self by thinking of his "I" at all, whether the *human self* is not something far *more originary* and is missed precisely through the I. So the supposed self-reflectiveness of Descartes is a delusion, because it never arrives at this question.

And now, two essential pieces of evidence for the extent to which the fundamental Cartesian line of thought *misses the human self* by grounding itself on the I.

ε) The essence of the I (self) as consciousness

Since Descartes, the *essence of the I* has been seen, above all, *in consciousness*. The I is the sort of thing that knows of itself; this self-consciousness determines the Being of the self. The natural consequence of this determination of the I is that the I dissolves into a bundle of representations, which remain even if one assigns them all to a so-called I-pole from which they radiate. Neither action nor decidedness, much less the characteristic of historicity and of man's essential connection to those who are being-here with him—a characteristic that lies at the ground of decidedness—enter into this approach to the self. This point-like, ahistorical, and spiritless character of the Cartesian I corresponds completely to what a priority of mathematical thought decides in advance about its possible object.

The *consciousness* of the I and its form determine here the *Being of the self*. In the Hegelian system we will see how fatefully this *priority of consciousness over Being*, which arises completely arbitrarily from a predominance of the mathematical method, worked itself out in the period following Descartes. The I: the understanding and the understanding will, but not spirit; the later concept of spirit is not yet there.

ζ) The self as I and the I as "subject." The transformation of the concept of the subject

There is a second piece of evidence for the extent to which the conception of the human self was pointed in a certain direction by the Cartesian thought of the I: through Descartes, the I is really made into the subject, and it has been called the subject since then. Just as one believes the term "metaphysics" was coined quite originally and especially to designate the rational knowledge of the supersensible, one also thinks that "subject," "subjective," and "subjectivity" have meant I, I-like, and I-ness from time immemorial. Subject in contrast to *ob-*

ject. But the "subject" *originally,* and still throughout the entire Middle Ages, does not have the least to do with the concept of the I and self of the human being. Quite the contrary. *Subjectum* is the translation of the Greek ὑποκείμενον, and this means everything that already lies before us in advance, that we run into and come upon—that is, when we set about determining something about beings, and for the Greeks this means asserting something about them.

The fact that beings are characterized here as what we run into in our asserting is not accidental and stands in the most intimate connection with the essence of the inception of philosophy, that is, with the question of beings as a whole and as such. To begin with, let us note only this: *subjectum* originally designates precisely what we call an object today; and *objectum,* to the contrary, means in the Middle Ages what we grasp as represented and opposed to us in mere thought, what is intended subjectively in today's sense. But now, how could the word *subjectum* take on precisely the opposite meaning, so that it no longer means what lies at hand over against the I, but the I itself, and only this?

If we have grasped the preceding account of Descartes's procedure, the answer cannot be difficult to reach. For under the spell of his method, Descartes seeks something that lies at hand as indubitable and that cannot be doubted away again. But this thing that lies at hand is the "I" of the doubter himself. *Thus the I is a subjectum in the old sense.* But now, because the I is not just any *subjectum,* but the fundamental thing that lies at hand, the *subjectum* receives the fundamental meaning of "I." The I is not only a *subjectum* simply, but also and for this very reason, the *subjectum* is originally "I." From now on, "subject" becomes the term for the I. (The I as something present at hand = *subjectum.* The subject as a preeminent *subjectum. Subjectum* = I.) And now we understand that it is not an innocuous term; behind it there stands the entire way in which the priority of the mathematical method has been worked out in philosophy.

c) The substantive consequence of the predominance of the mathematical conception of method: the failure to reach the authentic self of man and the failure of the fundamental question of philosophy. The advance decision of mathematical certainty regarding truth and Being

The first piece of evidence, according to which the self was taken as I, and the I was taken as *consciousness,* is joined now by the conception of the self-qua-I as *subjectum:* something present at hand. And if the later efforts of German idealism aim so passionately at *not* allowing the I to appear as a thing, this proves only that the original approach to the I as *subjectum* forces one in advance to make these efforts—that the effort must acknowledge precisely what it wants to deny. But the *thing-character* of the I and self is not overcome as long as its *subject-character* is not removed in advance, that is, as long as the fatefulness of the Cartesian approach is not grasped and overcome from the bottom up.

This shows that the process of doubt that leads to the I as foundation has only the illusion of originality. This illusion is at the same time the source of a fundamental deception, as if such a contemplation of the I were self-reflection. Instead, it obstructs in all possible ways every path to the human self.

Secondly, we said that this supposed radicalism not only was *not an actual inception* of philosophy, but even was just the beginning of a *further decline.* For Descartes does not bring philosophy back into its fundamental question, but brings it out of this question once and for all, albeit with the illusion of a new inception. However, these statements can actually be proved only when the *fundamental question* has been found and is asked, for only on that basis can one assess to what degree and to what extent the age of philosophy that Descartes inaugurated is a decline.

However, we can already give a few indications, based on what we have said in an introductory way. Descartes's founding of philosophy is guided by the mathematical-methodical idea of *knowability* and *certainty in general.*[16] This idea of certainty pre-delineates what can and cannot be true. The essence of truth is determined by certainty. But *truth* says what and how beings are. Therefore, the idea of mathematical certainty decides in advance what is truly being and what may be addressed as genuine Being. But to investigate what beings are and what Being is, is the intention of the fundamental question. In Descartes, not only is this question not posed, but assertions are laid down in advance that presuppose an answer.

In accordance with the priority of the I-qua-consciousness, *consciousness determines the essence of Being.* That of which one is conscious, in a particular mode of mathematical indubitability, "is"—and this consciousness is genuine Being. One does not see and does not want to see that in this *Being*-conscious, a quite definite concept of Being is presupposed, yet in such a way that it is not first subjected at all to a question of doubt, much less given a foundation.

But this implies that the *necessity* of this question is not recognized at all, the question itself *remains forgotten. The predominance of the mathematical conception of method nips the fundamental question of philosophy in the bud.* Modern metaphysics begins with Descartes by *neglecting its fundamental question,* and by covering up this neglect with the *illusion of mathematical-methodical radicalism.*

16. Certainty → truth → beings—Being.

§11. The predominance of the mathematical conception of method in the formation of metaphysical systems in the eighteenth century[17]

In order actually to show the predominance of the mathematical conception of method in modern metaphysics, we choose as a piece of evidence the stage of this metaphysics immediately preceding Kant. We already drew our general characterization of the structure of metaphysics in its disciplines from this period. Now we have the opportunity to bring that rough depiction to life—with a view to the task we have mentioned.

Let us recall the structure and division of metaphysics.[18] We had emphasized how here, *metaphysica specialis* was pervaded by *Christian thought*. Summit and center: *God as creator. Metaphysica generalis* constructed in advance. Wolff, *Ontologia,* 1729.[19]

Now, where and in what form does the predominance of the mathematical method become visible here? Anyone who knows the works of this period, particularly German metaphysics of the eighteenth century, even at a distance and superficially, will immediately refer to two points: first, the frequent appeal to Euclid's *Elements,*[20] long seen as the *model* of the structure and derivation of mathematical knowledge, and then the construction of the works.

These works exhibit, first of all, a closed and pervasively *systematic character,* and at the same time a *didactic, textbook-like* manner of handling the material; here there is a *conscious recourse* to the *summae* of medieval Scholasticism, although these noticeably lack the closed continuity of the train of thought and, above all, the rigor of a coherently organized derivation. (Backgrounds: 1. the mathematical idea of knowledge is not [present in Scholasticism] with this degree of rigor, 2. the extensive consultation of authorities and exposition of others' views.) Works of Wolff and his students: simple, strict. Terse sections containing the definitions of the fundamental concepts and the main propositions; all subsequent sections always refer back to the earlier ones.

17. {See above, [German] pp. 29, 36.}

18. {See above, [German] p. 25.}

19. [See note on German p. 30, above.]

20. {Euclid (the mathematician), *Stoicheia.* Didactic collection in thirteen books, ca. 300 BC in Alexandria.}

§12. Introductory concepts from Wolff's *Ontology*. The point of departure: the philosophical principles of all human cognition

We take our first indications from the introductory concepts of Christian Wolff's *Ontology* (1729), in particular from (1) the title, (2) the *Dedicatio* [Dedication], and (3) the *Praefatio* [Preface].

1. Title: *Philosophia prima sive Ontologia, methodo scientifica pertractata, qua omnis cognitionis humanae principia continentur.*
   (a) Terms: *philosophia prima—ontologia* [first philosophy—ontology] (Clauberg),[21]
   (b) *methodo scientifica pertractata*—thoroughly treated according to the scientific method (what does *scientifica* mean? cf. Descartes's *scientia*);
   (c) *omnis cognitionis humanae principia continentur*—in which the "principles," starting points and foundations of all human cognition, are contained; not epistemology, much less psychology, but the knowable and what pertains to it. Definition in Baumgarten, *Metaphysica*,[22] §1: *Metaphysica est scientia primorum in humana cognitione principiorum.* [Metaphysics is the science of the first principles in human cognition.]
2. *Dedicatio*
   (a) *manus . . . emendatrix* [correcting hand]—error-free procedure of seamless proof (*deductio*) lacking until now.[23]
   (b) As Euclid brought the principles of all mathematical cognition into a system so that its unshakable truth could be displayed and lie open, in this way, *eius exemplo*, according to his example, *simile coegi* [similarly I have gathered] the first principles of all human cognition in general into a *systema*.
   (c) These principles are already included in those from which Euclid borrowed the insight for his own. This system contains the *fundamenta omnis scientiae, ipsius etiam mathematicae* [foundations of all science, even of mathematics]. Indispensable to expound the principles first, only, and

21. {Johannes Clauberg, *Metaphysica de ente sive Ontosophia* (1656).}

22. {Alexander Gottlieb Baumgarten, *Metaphysica* (Halle, 1739; 7th edition, 1779).}

23. ["Antiquity knew nothing greater than philosophy that was given to the human race by immortal God, but philosophy is still awaiting a correcting hand so that mortals may perceive its excellent fruits" (Wolff, *Ontologia*, Dedicatio).]

properly according to the "mathematical" method in the broadest sense, but no longer just "mathematical" objects in the narrower sense. The *Praefatio* makes this clear.

3. *Praefatio*

Here one can gather that Wolff *opposes* Descartes in a certain way. To be sure, not in the sense that he resists Descartes's mathematical method; to the contrary, Wolff finds that, precisely through his principles, Descartes brought *philosophia prima* into disrepute and left the simplest fundamental concepts undefined.

Wolff recognized that the *certainty and rigor* of the mathematical in the narrower sense goes back to the *philosophical* principles and fundamental concepts; but these, for their part, may not be entrusted to a simple *intuitus,* but are subject to a demand for *most rigorous definition.*

But here is also the real reason why the Wolffian system and the systems of his school display a *different character* from the system of Descartes. Distinctive of Descartes's system: starting with the *ego sum* [I am], beginning with the process of doubt. Wolff begins with the *primal concepts* of first philosophy, but both follow the mathematical method. What Wolff emphasizes at the very start of his major philosophical work is only confirmed by the *form* of all his writings and works.

But—with all this we still have not grasped the dominance of the mathematical method in this age of "metaphysics." To the contrary, what we have said could even serve to confirm the thesis that the mathematical is just an external form for dividing and arranging a present-at-hand doctrinal content. So what we must do now is prove *that and how* the mathematical determines the *inner structure* and the *claim to truth of this entire metaphysics.* In this we must show how the fundamental shape of Hegelian metaphysics was prepared here, the metaphysics in which both *Descartes's starting point* in the subject and *Wolff's point of departure,* the fundamental concepts of metaphysics, join together into *one* system that is determined by Christianity and theology from first to last.

Until now, the *scope of the mathematical method* within the content and the claim to truth of modern metaphysics has been underestimated, and one has let oneself be deceived by the fact that the same objects and concepts are treated everywhere.

It would be of great significance, pedagogically and substantively, if we could draw out the distinctive features of the Wolffian system in a *comparative study,* looking back to medieval Scholasticism and forward to Hegel. Yet that would demand that we run through Wolffian metaphysics, at least, without any gap. Here we cannot manage this.

We will resort to an alternative: first, we will restrict ourselves to the metaphysical system of Wolff's most significant student, Alexander Gottlieb Baumgarten; furthermore, we will consider even this metaphysics only in its fundamental trait, its inception, and its end. (*Metaphysica*, 1739; 2nd edition, 1743ff.)[24] Kant treasured this work especially, and used it as a basis for his teaching throughout his life.[25]

24. {Cf. also [German] p. 48, note.}

25. Cf. Kant, *Prolegomena*, §§1-3. Cf. also the report on the organization of Kant's lecture courses in the Winter Semester 1765-1766, in *Werke*, ed. Cassirer, vol. II, pp. 317ff. [English translation: "M. Immanuel Kant's Announcement of the Programme of his Lectures for the Winter Semester 1765-1766," in *Theoretical Philosophy, 1755-1770*, ed. David Walford, with Ralf Meerbote (Cambridge: Cambridge University Press, 1992), pp. 287-99.]

Chapter Three
Determination by Christianity and the Concept of Mathematical-Methodological Grounding in the Metaphysical Systems of Modernity

§13. The two main tasks that frame modern metaphysics: the grounding of the essence of Being in general and the proof of the essence and existence of God

Metaphysics is the *knowledge of beings as a whole.* God—according to the tradition the highest being, *summum ens*—rules and determines all beings. But in another sense, *Being* is also *comprehensive,* that which belongs to every being as such, *ens in communi.* "God," taken in the light of the most universal concept of Being, is only one being among others, albeit the highest.

Now, if we are right in our thesis of the *predominance of the mathematical method* in the *inner* construction and claim to truth of this metaphysics, then obviously this construction must begin with the simplest concept and its grounding deduction, and in such a way that on the basis of this inception all other beings are derived—both *what* they are and *that* they are. That applies above all and ultimately to the *summum ens.* So what is at stake here is nothing less than deriving the essence and existence of God as *summum ens* from the *universal essence of Being* in a step-by-step deduction.

This project *demands two things* if it is to become properly possible. First, the concept of God must be grasped in such a way that its *specifically Christian content,* as viewed from the end and conclusion of this metaphysics, remains intact, while its mathematical derivation from the concept of Being becomes possible: *to mathematize* the Christian concept of God. But then, from the point of view of the *inception* of this

metaphysics, the question arises: whence the *ens in communi*? If everything is subject to deduction, and if even and precisely the simplest
concepts are to be subjected to a deductive definition, *whence and how
do we arrive at the ens in communi?*

The *entire structure* of this metaphysics is *framed* by these two main
tasks, the proof of the essence and existence of God and the grounding
of the essence of Being in general—and so much so that these tasks are
not even expressly named at all. They are *taken for granted* as the *point of
departure* and goal of the whole, and they mutually determine each
other. Behind this framework stand *two powers,* powers of the history of
Western humanity: the Greek question concerning beings and the
Christian faith in God.

But both have already also lost their edge and their dangerousness.
The question concerning Being is now nothing but a search for a way
to define it, and faith has been made "rational" in the age of Enlightenment. The proof of this is precisely what this metaphysics now
strives for in its construction and claim to truth: the *mathematical.*

The rigor of this thinking and defining does *not* grow from *strength*
and from the *struggle* to *overcome an urgent need,* but results and flows
from a secured position of Dasein that, certain of what it possesses,
would like to shape it in an unassailable way that is accessible to everyone. But precisely *this* is the *presupposition* for the fact that then,
later on, with Hegel, the whole of this metaphysics can return in a
changed way, and as something that has been surpassed in a certain
sense. This means: we must learn to grasp Hegel on the basis of the
connections we have now elucidated, and to set aside the perspective
that has become usual in recent times, the perspective that tries to
grasp Hegel only *on the basis of Kant.*

---

§14. The mathematical character of the system at the basis of Baumgarten's metaphysics

a) The concept of *veritas metaphysica:* the agreement of what *is* with the most universal principles

Now let us try to achieve an actual insight into the inner construction
of the entirety of Baumgarten's metaphysics, (1) on the basis of its
starting point and goal, and (2) at the same time on the basis of the *inner
connection* of both, in order thus to support our assertion about its
mathematical character. To this end, we first need to clarify a question. If it is the case that the inner construction of this metaphysics,
not just its external framework, is mathematical, then this must be
apparent above all in the *concept of truth* under which the knowledge

that is being claimed here is placed. In brief: what does metaphysical truth, *veritas metaphysica,* mean here?

Baumgarten answers this question in §92: *veritas metaphysica potest definiri per convenientiam entis cum principiis catholicis.* Metaphysical truth can be defined as the agreement of what *is* with the universal "principles," the grounds and the grounding propositions.

This definition of metaphysical truth is unintelligible at first and must remain so, as long as we do not say what is meant by principles here, and in general by the agreement of beings with them. Now, *convenientia* [agreement] consists in the fact that *ens conformiter his principiis determinatur* (cf. ibid.), that what is (as such) is determined in accordance with these principles. That is just a reformulation in other words! What does it actually mean?

It is a matter of determining what beings in general are, and what they are in their main realms; this must be determined in conformity with the *most universal principles.* But what kind of principles are these? How do they come to be principles? Why is it that principles play such a definitive role here in the first place?

Principium, ἀρχή: that on the basis of which something is, becomes, and in general is determined. Here it is not a matter of arbitrary principles, but of the most universal, *catholicum:* what concerns the whole, beings in general and as a whole; it is something that determines what beings are; it is something that *every* being, insofar as it is a being, *must fit into* in advance.

It was already clear what is expressing itself in this demand: nothing other than the idea of the mathematical, of the grounding return to a first starting point and of the determining deduction from this point. The *mathematical* has accordingly entrenched itself in the concept and essence of metaphysical truth from the beginning. What is metaphysically true is only what satisfies this essential demand.

b) Preliminary considerations on the principial character of the principle by which the *ens in communi* is supposed to be determined

But let us think this over: *what* is being demanded here? Something that determines what beings as beings are, from the ground up and from the inception on! What determines beings to be what they are as beings, we call *Being.* Being is the essence of beings. The essence—what beings are, the What—is a "principle," should be determined by a principle or vice versa. Being must coincide in its essence with the most universal principle. The principle is always what is higher and more universal than the *principiatum,* that is, what stands *under* the principle.

Under which principle, then, can *Being* be put? Is there anything that stands even *above* Being, that accordingly is *non*-"Being"? What could that *be?* Can such a thing still even *be* at all? Obviously not, for *if* it still *is,* then it is a *being,* and *as* a being it *stands beneath* Being. But the principle is supposed precisely to stand *above* Being, and *not* be referred back to Being. What does *not* stand beneath Being, what has nothing in common with Being, is the *nothing.* So if one wanted to be serious about the demand to trace beings and Being back to a still higher principle and derive Being from this principle, then this would mean positing the nothing as the principle of Being.

If this should succeed, then a *fundamental demand of the method* would be fulfilled: the *ens in communi* would not simply be accepted, but would itself be further delimited and defined.

But can the nothing be grasped as the principle of Being at all? Can *anything* be delimited by the nothing? One would like to counter this in advance by pointing out that *if* the nothing is grasped at all—however it may be grasped, if it is simply *grasped at all*—then it is already something, and never is nothing. But inasmuch as the nothing is *not* graspable *at all,* then the question of *through what* and *how* it should be grasped also *becomes superfluous.*

Yet in the end, these very reservations against the nothing as the principle of Being are all too obvious for them to mean anything here. In any case, we do not want to let our questioning be lured away from its task any further by such formally logical and apparently clever objections. We will now simply investigate two points. *1. Does the fundamental concept of general metaphysics, the* ens, *depend on something more originary? 2. What then is the principle by which the* ens *is determined?*

---

§15. Baumgarten's starting point as the *possibile* (what can be) and the logical principle of contradiction as the absolutely first principle of metaphysics

The *first question* is easy to answer. The presentation of *metaphysica generalis* has as its immediate task the exhibition and derivation of the *praedicata entis interna universalia,*[1] what pertains in general to every being in itself. The *first* characteristic of beings turns out *not* to be Being—which would provide the *definitive* elucidation of the *ens*—but instead, all metaphysics begins with the analysis of the *possibile* (the possible, or better, what *can* (*be*)).

But the presentation of the *possibile* in paragraphs 7-18 is still not followed by the *ens* [what *is*], but by the *rationale* [rational],[2] what is *grounded* (*grounding*), in paragraphs 19-33. And only now, as section III, does *ens* follow in paragraphs 34-71.

1. Baumgarten, *Metaphysica,* caput I (title).
2. Ibid., sectio II: Connexum (rationale) [Connection (rational)].

In retrospect this fully supports our assertion that the *ens* is *not* set up as the *initial concept,* although it does delimit the only true theme of *metaphysica generalis.*

As for the second question: *what is the principle by which the* ens *is determined?* This second question changes now that we have answered the first; for *ens* has been related to *rationale,* and this to *possibile* [possible]. Accordingly, we now have to ask: on what basis (principle) is the *possibile* determined? To ask the question differently, on what basis is the meaning of *possibilitas* [possibility] delimited (defined)? In other words, what is the *absolutely first principle* for metaphysics *as a whole,* the *principium absolute primum* [absolutely first principle]? Answer: the *principium contradictionis,* the *principle of contradiction.*[3]

That sounds strange at first, and strange altogether. In fact, here we are running into a *main part of the foundation of Western metaphysics.* This foundation was laid by Aristotle—after the long preparatory work of Greek philosophy. And this very part of the foundation returns in a particularly significant place, in the philosophy of Hegel.

But before we take a look at *this* principle in its various aspects, we want briefly to sketch its position in the metaphysics of the Wolffian school, which we are now considering, and at the same time provide the answer to a question we posed earlier, namely, how the *nothing* could serve *as the principle of Being.*

Contradictorium est A et non-A; praedicatorum contradictoriarum nullum est subjectum; nihil est, et non est,[4] that is, the *contradictorium* is the *nihil;* hence there is nothing to find! The *non contradictorium = possibile,* possible = can be = the kind of thing that does not contradict itself. So here, in fact, the nothing (*contradictorium*) serves as the principle of Being. *Contradiction and Being. Contradiction* and *lack of contradiction* decide about the incapacity to be and the capacity to be, the impossibility of Being and the possibility of Being, "Being."

----

§16. Remarks on the grounding of the *principium primum.* The principle of contradiction and human Dasein: the preservation of the selfsameness of the selfsame

How does "contradiction" attain such dominance and authority? (Familiar in the "principle of contradiction," cf. Leibniz.) We must try, as far as the context demands, to penetrate this principle.

----

3. Ibid., §7, last sentence: Haec propositio *dicitur* principium contradictionis et absolute primum. [This proposition *is called* the principle of contradiction and the absolutely first principle.]

4. [The contradictory is A and not-A; there is no subject of contradictory predicates; it is nothing, and it is not.] Ibid., §7.

Showing that the law of Being expressed by the principle of contradiction is unprovable and indisputable leads us back to a *quite unexpected ground*—unexpected for the entire conception, interpretation, and treatment of the axiom up to now. This ground in which its validity is grounded is *human Dasein;* and not that of man in general, but of *historical* man in the language- and people-bound, spiritually determined being-with-one-another of those who belong and are obligated *to* each other.

The dominant *fundamental reality* of this *being-with-one-another* is *language.* But language is not at all a tool that, as it were, is subsequently attached to a sum of initially isolated human beings so that they may find their way to each other with the help of this tool. To the contrary, the individual, if he ever somehow isolates himself into his own individuality, is releasing himself in each case on the basis of the shared world and spiritual community of the already *dominant language* and is speaking "in" language. Language can be a tool of communication only because in advance and in its origin it is what *preserves and increases the world* into which a people exists in every case.

But in language, as understood and as holding sway in this way, *beings* as a whole *reveal themselves* according to the powers that hold sway in them. But language could not be, that is, it could be neither spoken nor kept silent, if the speakers as such could not relate to beings *as such.* And they could not do this if they did not understand something like Being in general, and this means what belongs to the essence of Being, among other things.

And this includes, for example, the *selfsameness of the selfsame* as something that is understood in general. If such a thing were not preserved and maintained, then it would be impossible to come to an understanding about one and the same thing in being-with-one-another, and even the individual would be unable to relate himself on his own to a being, to something that remained selfsame, that is, *he would be unable to be human.* The *inevitability of the preservation of the selfsameness of the selfsame*—and this means the conservation of the Being of beings—is not inevitability pure and simple and absolutely, but is *subject to the condition that man exist.*

But what the principle of contradiction expresses, and only in a negative form, is nothing other than this *inevitability of the law of Being in the sense of the preservation of selfsameness.*

Aristotle expresses this briefly as follows: if what is said in the axiom did not hold, then human beings would sink down to the level of a plant, that is, they could not exist at all in language and in the understanding of Being.[5] So *behind the persistence* and the *recognition* of the *first law of Being* there stands the *decision* of whether human beings

5. [Cf. Aristotle, *Metaphysics* IV, 4, 1006a15, 1008b10.]

will to exist as human or not; this means, whether they elevate λόγος[6] to the rank of the dominant *power* of their Dasein or not, whether they stand up to this essential possibility or not!

Yet this decision also brings with it the *step over into the realm of non-Being,* of the null, the contrary and erroneous. Only where there is all this, and where it is conceived as *necessary,* only there is there also greatness, what is to be affirmed, the noble and true. The animal and plant know neither the one nor the other—nor their opposition.

The principle of contradiction, as a particular conception of the fundamental law of Being, is no empty proposition of logic on which cleverness may practice, but is *a fundamental element of the existential structure of our Dasein in general.* The *truth* that pertains to this principle is a *primally distinctive* one—and so far we have no concept of it at all; and much less do we possess the adequate form for its conceivability.

This is just a new proof of how far our usual logic is removed from the things that are essential; and that implies not just some logical inelegance, but a *fundamental lack* in our thinking that prevents dominant thought from facing up to new realities and proving itself fit for them; instead of this, it only puts restrictions and reservations into play—and in this it even takes itself to be "spiritually" superior.

Here we have to forego developing the entire essential ground from which the principle of contradiction arises. Let us just point out one thing: namely, the *distance* between the form of the principle at its origin and its treatment in later academic philosophy. First, a brief assessment according to the aspects we mentioned earlier.[7]

In Baumgarten and Wolff, the principle of contradiction stands quite without question at the *outset* of the entire deductive structure of metaphysics. The only question concerns *the proper ordering* of the propositions that are *to be deduced.* The *fundamental principle* is correspondingly understood in *this* role. Admittedly, a part of its content, the mathematical, thereby attains an emphatic importance, such as it already has in Aristotle, in accordance with the matter at stake, although it is not yet explicitly expounded with a view to derivation; *contradiction,* or more precisely the *lack of contradiction,* emerges *as a determination of the essence of the capacity to be,* of possibility.

In contrast, we search *in vain* for the *sheer originality of questioning* through which the principle should be grasped *as such* and grounded in its *essential content.* Everything stands there in *unquestioned self-evidence.* And so it has been for a long time—really since Aristotle concerned himself with the axiom. Only Leibniz brought movement once

---

6. [Ordinarily λόγος means speech, account, or reason; for Heidegger's own interpretation of this Greek word see below, German p. 114.]

7. {Cf. above, [German] pp. 37ff.}

again into the long-calcified doctrine, admittedly without unfolding the entire context of the question in a sufficiently radical way. He was too strongly bound to the *academic tradition* for that.

If the principle and the way of treating it have been moving for a long time within a nearly unassailable self-evidence, this may not be taken as a definitive unquestionability pure and simple; rather, we must consider that this fundamentally thin veneer of the self-evident will one day *break apart* and that *we* will then *break through* into the *groundless,* at least at first.

In Aristotle the questioning circles precisely around the fundamental concepts and fundamental principles; more precisely, these are not yet settled, but everything remains close to the substantive essential connections that they indicate. And accordingly, we also seek in vain for a system, or even for the mere basic outline of one. Such a representation of Aristotelian philosophy is *completely un-Greek* and arose only later, in the time of the Middle Ages, through Arabic-Jewish and Christian philosophy.

But in contrast, for Wolff and Baumgarten *everything* is clear and unquestionable in the fundamental principles and fundamental concepts; and accordingly, the construction of a total system of genuine knowledge, that is, metaphysics, comes about without friction, as it were. And *in* metaphysics the *highest claim to knowledge* is put into effect, insofar as one undertakes to derive the *summmum ens* in its what-Being and that-Being starting from the fundamental principle.

A preliminary overview of this construction:

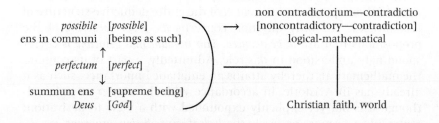

§17. The mathematical-logical determination of the starting point, goal, and deductive method in Baumgarten's metaphysical system

The principle of contradiction holds sure and steady here, in its unassailable self-evidence. It is also a *grounding* principle here in its own way; it posits the grounding, fundamental concept of Being and thus the fundamental rule for deducing the determinations of beings. This grounding principle stands at the outset of all metaphysics and dominates it as a mathematical principle. This means that (1) everything is deduced from it and what it delimits; (2) every deduction, in the sequence of its steps, must observe the law of the fundamental principle, the rule of the *avoidance* of contradiction, or *preservation of the lack of contradiction.*

But metaphysics comprises and exhibits the essential whole of genuine and highest human knowledge, it includes in itself and concludes itself as a whole as knowledge of the highest being, *summum ens.* The grounding construction of metaphysics as a whole thus includes as its main task the *mathematical* deduction of the essence and presence at hand of the highest and truest being from the most universal and emptiest concept of what *is,* as such—to obtain the richest fullness and definiteness from the greatest emptiness and indefiniteness in a mathematically rigorous deductive sequence.

How is the chasm between *ens in communi* [beings as such] and *summum ens* [the supreme being] to be bridged? This much is clear from the start: the concept of the *summum ens* must be conceived in such a way that its determination and deduction can be subordinated completely to the mathematical-metaphysical method; only then is there a prospect of mathematically reaching the highest concept from the most universal concept.

a) The summum ens as perfectissimum.
The belonging of the perfectum to the concept of Being and
its suitability as leading to the highest being

And how is the concept of the *summum ens* conceived? As *ens perfectissimum* [the most perfect being]. The decisive characteristic consists in *perfectio* [perfection].[8] But that does not mean much at first, if we remember the tradition and know that Christian thought thinks of God as the most perfect entity, as the *summum bonum,* the *highest good.* What remains decisive is *how* the concept of *perfectio* and of the *perfectum* [the perfect] itself is conceived.

If this metaphysics understands itself and its intention at all, then the concept of the *perfectum* must be conceived in such a way that it proves to be an *essential determination of Being in general,* for only then is there any possibility of deducing the concept of the highest being from the most universal concept of Being. But this means that the determining ground of the concept of *perfectio* must lie *there* where the concept of Being also arises, in the *principium primum absolutum* [absolute first principle], in the *principle of contradiction.* But precisely this concept of the *perfectum* that belongs to the *ens in communi* must also be suited to serve as the transition to the *summum ens.*

---

8. {Cf. Baumgarten, *Metaphysica,* pars IV, caput I: Conceptus Dei, sectio I: Existentia Dei, §§803ff., esp. §§803, 810, 811.}

Hence two things must be shown: (1) The belonging of the *perfectum* to the concept of Being in general. (2) The suitability of the *perfectum* to serve as a guide that leads to the true highest being.

First we must say what is understood by *perfectum.* Answer: *consentiens,* agreeing. But agreement is in itself *consentiens ad unum,* agreeing in and to a unity.[9] That is the formal concept of the *perfectum;* we must see how it is defined more precisely.

But just one question first: in what way does this perfection involve a characteristic of the *ens in communi,* a connection to the *ens in communi,* and how does it thus have its *source* in the fundamental axiom, the *primum principium absolutum?* That can be shown most clearly if we retrace the main steps in the construction, beginning with the fundamental axiom, in order to see whether and where we run across the *perfectum* in this procedure. With this, we can clarify what is distinctive about the *foundation* of this entire metaphysics.[10]

b) The main steps in the construction of the metaphysical system

α) Beginning with what is thinkable in thought as judgment (assertion) and the principle of sufficient reason

Metaphysics begins with the *nihil,* the nothing, and *thus creates the impression of a complete lack of presuppositions* and simplicity; yet this nothing is conceived on the basis of *contradictio.* Accordingly, behind *this* inception of metaphysics there stands *dictio,* saying (cf. κατάφασις—ἀπόφασις) in the sense of assertion, λόγος. Precisely here, more sharply and clearly than anywhere else, we see how the predominance of thinking as "logic" emerges.

Now, if we observe that this inception of metaphysics is striving to delimit and define the *ens in communi,* then what we have indicated means that *the essence of Being is defined by reverting to thought as judgment,* and not just in the sense that the concept of Being is thought—every concept *as a concept* is thought—but the *content* of the concept

---

9. {Cf. ibid., pars I, caput I, sectio VII: Perfectum, §94: consensus ipse est *perfectio,* et unum, in quod consentitur, *ratio perfectionis determinans.*} [Agreement itself is *perfection,* and the unity in which it agrees is the *determining reason of perfection.*]

10. Nihil—possibile—rationale—ens—realitas—essentia—unum—verum—perfectum. Verum—perfectum: cuius determinationes sunt inseparabiles (ibid., §73). Veritas metaphysica est ordo plurium in uno (ibid., §89): in ordine coniunguntur plura eidem rationi conformiter (ibid., §86). [Nothing—possible—rational—being—reality—essence—one—true—perfect. True—perfect: that whose determinations are inseparable (ibid., §73). Metaphysical truth is the order of many in one (ibid., §89): many are combined in an order in conformity with the same reason (ibid., §86).]

"*Being,*" the essence of Being, is defined as something *thought-like*. The *thinkable as the measure for the capacity to be*—what is unthinkable *cannot* be. For the counter-concept to the *nihil,* the concept that grasps what in a certain sense eludes the nothing altogether yet is still close to it, namely the *capacity to be* or the *possible*—this concept means nothing other than the *thinkable*. This, as expression of the *possibile*, takes it as *in se spectatum* [viewed in itself]. Opposed to this *in se* is the *in nexu,* what stands in connection with something else. That which is a *possibile in nexu* has its capacity to be *with* and *on the basis of* the other, that is, it is grounded in the other, it has its ground or *ratio* there; hence the *possibile in nexu rationale est* [what is possible in connection is rational] (cf. ibid., §19). And from this there follows the proposition *omnis possibilis est ratio* [everything possible is a ground (reason)], or to put it the other way around, *nihil est sine ratione* [nothing is without a ground (reason)] (this is the *principle of sufficient reason*) (cf. ibid., §20).

Whatever supposedly can be must first pass through this tribunal of thought—and not only that.

β) The logical delimitation of the ens.
Possibilitas as essentia (what-Being): compatibility of
the internal and simple determinations

Now, insofar as something is not only put in relation with something other in general, but is related to it in such a way that it somehow either is or is not the other, it is *determined, determinatur.*[11] And just this, that which *in aliquo objecto ponitur* [is posited in some object] in such a manner of determining, is its *determinationes* (ibid., §36). For *determining* is just the *asserting form of dictio as praedicatio* [utterance as predication], and this *ponere* and *determinare* [positing and determining] are either attributive (positive) or delimiting (negative).

A determination that is *attributed to* the subject in such a way that this attribution is *true* is called *realitas, thinghood;* in the determination, something is meant that belongs to the essence of the thing, positively contributes to its content as a thing. The counter-concept to *realitas* is *negatio;* this is to be translated not as negation, but as true *negatedness*.

(One of the main reasons why neo-Kantianism could so miss and misinterpret the problem of Kantian philosophy is its complete unfamiliarity with and lack of understanding for these metaphysical, ontological fundamental concepts that play a central role in Kant's way of posing the question, and that, at the time of the *Critique of Pure Reason,* underwent, as did all metaphysical categories, a peculiar transformation and new grounding.)

---

11. *Terminus*—limits traced, what it is and is not.

Those determinations, *determinationes*, that as completely simple make the pure thing possible by themselves, constitute the *possibilitas* of the thing; this is also called the *essentia*, the *what-Being* of a being, its essence (cf. ibid., §§37 and 39). *Possibilitas* does not simply designate mere possibility in the sense of freedom from contradiction, but the *compatibility* of the simple and internal determinations. These determinations that constitute the essence of the thing stand in a *nexus universalis* [universal connection] (cf. ibid., §§47 and 48). These *determinationes* are the *affectiones* (ibid., §48).

But what is possible in this internal way does not yet have to "be" in the sense of the *actually present at hand, compossibilis existens*. But something possible that also properly contains the possibility of *existentia* in itself is what *is*, by definition. So the *ens* [what *is*] is *more than the aliquid (non nihil)* [something (not nothing)], but *less than the existens* [what exists]; *existens* as *complementum essentiae sive possibilitatis internae* [the complement of essence or of internal possibility] (ibid., §55) (*existentia* itself is a *realitas*, ibid., §66).

γ) *The* relatio ad unum *of* essentia *as* perfectum.
The mathematical sense of the concord of the perfectum

The question of the conceptual delimitation and relation of *essentia and existentia* is old and controversial; in its traditional form, it simply cannot be solved. In the context at hand it remains significant that *existentia* is considered as a *complexus affectionum in aliquo compossibilium* [complex of compossible affections in something] (ibid., §55). This means, in brief: *existentia is conceived in principle in the framework and with the means of essentia, determinatio, praedicatio, and dictio* [essence, determination, predication, assertion]. *Existentia* itself is a *realitas*. So here we see the *inner* dominance of the *mathematical*.

Essentia, compatibility, agreement (*perfectum*) means: *plura simul sumpta unius rationem sufficientem*, [many] taken together constitute the sufficient ground of a unity. This *relatio ad unum* [relation to a unity] is essential for *consensus qua perfectio* [agreement as perfection],[12] the *grounding-grounded* oneness, belonging-together.

There likewise belongs to *consensus* the moment of the *plura*, the many. But *both* moments just betray in a higher and more definite development what is already intended in a quite empty and general way in the freedom from contradiction of the emptiest possibility of togetherness, of nonexclusion: (1) the emptiest possibility of togetherness, (2) *first grounding* of unity qua belonging-together.

12. {Cf. ibid.: . . . consensus ipse est *perfectio*, et unum, in quod consentitur, *ratio perfectionis determinans*.} [Agreement itself is *perfection*, and the unity in which it agrees is the *determining reason of perfection*.]

The *perfectum* is thought completely in the *mathematical sense of concord*, of what can be deduced as belonging together, and not, say, in the moral sense, that is, the *perfectum* linked to *voluntas, bonum* [the will, the good]. (*Bonum* as one of the transcendentals, (1) to willing in general, (2) to *Deus* [God]. Nothing *here* about either; and that is necessary for the *strictly mathematical* construction. Leibniz!) *Thus the concept of the perfectum is a mathematical concept.*

δ) *The suitability of the* perfectum *as leading to the* summum ens:
the mathematically-logically necessary capacity of
the perfectum *to be increased to the* perfectissimum

How, now, is *this* concept of the *perfectum* suitable to lead to the *summum ens?*[13] Both moments make it possible to think the concept of the *perfectum* as *capable of being increased.* But *this possibility* that belongs to the concept of the *perfectum*, the possibility of being thought out in terms of increase, becomes a *necessity* as soon as it is thought in the context of derivation and deduction and implication,[14] and this context, as *mathematical*, is the *guiding* fundamental context for all metaphysics. Hence it is only an *internal consequence* of the mathematically thought concept of the *perfectum* that the concept of the *perfectissimum* is *thought out as lying within it.*[15] The *perfectissimum* would be the greatest and highest that can be combined in agreement, to the greatest and highest degree, among all possible beings.

ε) *The* summum ens *as* perfectissimum *and the*
inherent determinations of its Being

Ens perfectissimum est ens reale [the most perfect being is a real being] (§806), in fact *realitas tanta, quanta . . . potest; ergo ens realissimum* [(it has) as much reality as can be; therefore (it is) the most real being] (cf. ibid.); *omnitudo realitatum* [totality of realities] (§807), *nulla realitas tollenda* [no reality to be subtracted] (cf. §809). *Existentia est realitas . . . compossibilis. Ergo ens perfectissimum habet existentiam* [existence is compossible reality; therefore the most perfect being has existence] (§810). (With the intent of mathematically-logically grounding the necessity of the existence of God as thought in a Christian way.) *Deus est perfectissimum ens* [God is the most perfect being] (Christian!). *Ergo deus actualis est* [therefore God is actual] (§811).

The nonexistence of God is impossible in itself. If God did not exist, then something impossible in itself would be the case, that is, some-

13. (Procedure of *thinking out!*)
14. 1. fulfilled togetherness, 2. highest unity.
15. *Ens perfectissimum* cf. §§803ff.—In Crusius ontology is immediately followed by theology.

thing most perfect that nevertheless lacked something. But if something impossible in itself were the case, then the *primum principium absolutum* would *not* be valid; in order that it may be and remain true, God must exist. The nonexistence of God would be a *logical contradiction*. God is the *essential ground* of the principle; the principle is the *epistemic ground* of the knowledge of God.

With this it has become clear how the mathematical concept of the *perfectum* itself brings about the mathematical-deductive *connection* between *possibile* and *Deus*. But at the same time this shows how *the entirety of this metaphysics* stands under the determining power of the mathematical. But this entirety itself is delimited and articulated *in its content* by the *Christian* concept of the world and determined by the Christian concept of God.

Chapter Four
Hegel: The Completion of
Metaphysics as Theo-logic

§18. Transition to Hegel

We have now fulfilled the task that we initially set ourselves—the exhibition of the two determining powers of Western, and in particular
modern, metaphysics: (1) the worldview of Christian faith, (2) the
mathematical in a sense that is broad in principle and that we have
explained earlier, the mathematical as the propositional derivation of
propositions from fundamental principles and fundamental concepts,
the mathematical in the broader sense of the "logical."

We can now distinguish the two determining powers of modern
metaphysics from each other still more clearly with a view to the
sphere in which they are determined. The concept of the world that is
based on Christian faith concerns *the substantive What* of beings as a
whole and their division. The mathematical-logical concerns beings
not so much in their What as *in their How,* that is, *Being,* insofar as
Being is determined on the basis of the principle of the *primum principium absolutum.* And if we take the *concept of metaphysics* in the sense of
the knowledge of beings as such and as a whole, then we easily see
how the whole concept—what it essentially grasps in itself—is determined precisely by the powers we named.

But the point was to display these powers for *actual insight,* in order
to secure the most necessary preparation for understanding the shape
of Western metaphysics in which this metaphysics finds its completion, *the philosophy of Hegel.*

But between the developments we traced and Hegel there stands
Kant and his critique of this very metaphysics. Yet even this Kantian
critique of metaphysics stands under the domination of those pow-

ers—no matter how much, within this subjection, it transforms what came earlier. And so it is no wonder that the Kantian critique is followed right away by a new approach to the entirety of metaphysics, an approach that brings these two determining powers to their highest development, in part precisely *with the means* that Kant made available for the first time through his critique.

Now we must indicate the fundamental character of Hegelian metaphysics, and with this show at the same time how it must be seen as the completion of Western metaphysics. (Cf. Hegel lecture 1930[1] and Winter Semester 1930–1931.[2])

Let us anticipate our account of the fundamental character of Hegelian metaphysics with the statement: *Hegel's metaphysics is theo-logic, and as such it is the completion of Western metaphysics.* The statement is to be justified by answering the two questions that are included in it.

I. In what way is metaphysics for Hegel *theo-logic?*
II. In what way does Hegelian metaphysics *as* theo-logic become the completion of Western philosophy?

§19. The fundamental character of Hegelian metaphysics. Metaphysics as theo-logic

In what way is it "theo-logic"? *In general:* what does that mean? *Negative:* it does *not* mean "theology." Theology has as its task the knowledge of God, divine things and their relation to man and world. "-Logy": *system of assertions* about. Thus theology is a particular *kind* of cognition with a special *domain of knowledge* and its own *standards* for knowledge—and this in a double sense: (1) as *natural theology,* based on reason alone and the natural cognitive powers of human beings; (2) as *revealed theology, on the basis of* faith and *for* faith and the community of a church. *Theology* delimited in this way from physiology, geology, biology, philology.

Positive: theo-logic, thus *logic,* in such a way that it is essentially related to and *grounded* in θεός, *the Christian God.* Hence our question is divided in two: (a) in what way is Hegel's metaphysics *logic?* and (b) in what way is this *theo*-logic?

1. {Martin Heidegger, "Hegel und das Problem der Metaphysik." Lecture at the scientific convention in Amsterdam, 22 March 1930. Projected to be published in volume 80 of the *Gesamtausgabe* [*Vorträge (1915–1967)*].}

2. {Martin Heidegger, *Hegels Phänomenologie des Geistes* (GA 32), Freiburg lecture course, Winter Semester 1930–1931, ed. Ingtraud Görland (Frankfurt am Main: Klostermann, 1980; 3rd edition, 1997).} [English translation: *Hegel's Phenomenology of Spirit,* trans. Parvis Emad and Kenneth Maly (Bloomington: Indiana University Press, 1994).]

a) Hegel's metaphysics as logic

α) The science of logic as authentic metaphysics

In what way is Hegelian metaphysics "logic"? (Cf. text of the lecture.[3])

1. The *title of the main work,* which leads into, supports, and determines the system, reads *Science of Logic.*[4]
2. Hegel says in the preface to the first edition (III, p. 6)[5]: "the science of logic which constitutes *metaphysics proper* or purely speculative philosophy, has hitherto still been much neglected."
3. With such facts little is gained, as long as with the title "science of logic" one thinks immediately and exclusively of the received "school logic"; "for its structure and contents" have "remained the same throughout a long inherited tradition, although in the course of being passed on the contents have become ever more diluted and attenuated . . ." (III, p. 5).[6]
4. Logic as science should adopt a *higher* standpoint and thus attain a *completely changed shape.* (Cf. introduction, Lasson p. 24.[7])

Quite generally: authentic metaphysics is "logic," but in a higher shape.

β) Metaphysics as logic in its higher form.
The logic of the logos as logic of the pure essentialities

5. "Logic" in a higher form—how should we approach it? It cannot be represented, (a) not now, (b) not at all; we can only participate in enacting it. *Solution: examining the inception* [of Hegel's logic], then seeing what is *higher and distinctive* in comparison to the lower and earlier logic.
6 *Earlier logic;* Wolff's definition, Kant's definition. *Wolff: scientia dirigendi facultatem cognoscitivam in cognoscenda veritate* [the science of directing the cognitive faculty in the truth that is to be

---

3. {Martin Heidegger, "Hegel und das Problem der Metaphysik." See note, [German] p. 70, above.}

4. {*Wissenschaft der Logik, von D. Ge. Wilh. Friedr. Hegel,* 2 vols. (Nürnberg: Johann Leonhard Schrag, 1812-1813, 1816).}

5. {*G. W. F. Hegels Werke: Vollständige Ausgabe durch einen Verein von Freunden des Verewigten,* vols. I-XIX (Berlin: 1832-1845, 1887); vols. III-V: *Wissenschaft der Logik,* ed. Leopold v. Henning (1833-1834; 2nd edition, 1841); here vol. III (1833), p. 6. Heidegger's emphasis.} [English translation: *Hegel's Science of Logic,* trans. A. V. Miller (London: Allen & Unwin, 1969), p. 27.]

6. {Ibid., preface to the 1st edition, *Werke* III, p. 5.} [Cf. *Science of Logic,* p. 26.]

7. {G. W. F. Hegel, *Wissenschaft der Logik,* ed. Georg Lasson (Leipzig, 1923), intro., p. 24: "it is time . . . that this science were grasped from a higher standpoint and received a completely changed shape."} [Cf. *Science of Logic,* p. 44.]

cognized].[8] *Veritas, ordo, connexio* [truth, order, connection]: *mathematical*. *Veritas metaphysica est ordo plurium in uno* [metaphysical truth is the order of many in one][9] . . . *secundem principium contradictionis* [according to the principle of contradiction].[10] (Baumgarten, §§78ff.[11]) *Kant:* we call logic the science of the necessary laws of the understanding and of reason (judgment, concept, inference) or what is the same, the science of the mere *form of thought*.[12] That is, not about what is *thought* in its substantive What and How, but concerning the ways in which something can be thought; but that is in every case *beings in their Being*. Precisely *this* {substantive What and How} is *excluded in principle and forever* from *logic*.

7. How does Hegel's logic begin? Precisely with Being. "Being is the indeterminate immediate."[13] Being in this indeterminate immediacy is the nothing (and this is pure Being) and yet is not the nothing—transition from Being to the nothing: *becoming.* Both the same, each disappears into its opposite, is overcome—becoming.

So Hegel's "logic" does not deal with "thinking," but with *Being, nothing, becoming,* determinate Being [*Dasein*], existence, possibility, actuality, necessity, ground, cause—primordial concepts of metaphysics.

8. But in the "Introduction" to the *Science of Logic* (Lasson, p. 23 [Miller trans., p. 43]) it is stated explicitly that the object of logic is "thinking," or more precisely *conceptual* thinking, thinking that grasps the "concept." *Concept* for Hegel is not the universal representation of something and mere opinion, but the fundamental determination of the concept (not complete) is what is *conceived* in the *thing as such,* its *thinghood—realitas,* essence, essentialities, *essentia.* The pure essentialities constitute the con-

---

8. {Christian Wolff, *Philosophia rationalis sive Logica* (Frankfurt and Leipzig, 1790), pars II: Philosophiae rationalis sive Logicae Prolegomena, §1: Definitio Logica.}

9. {Alexander Gottlieb Baumgarten, *Metaphysica* (Halle, 1739), §89.}

10. {Ibid., §90.}

11. {Ibid.}

12. {Cf. *Immanuel Kants Logik: Ein Handbuch zu Vorlesungen, zuerst herausgegeben von G. B. Jäsche* (1800), 3rd edition, ed. W. Kinkel (Leipzig: Meiner, 1904), p. 14: "Now this science of the necessary laws of the understanding and of reason in general, or what is one and the same, of the mere form of thought as such, we call *logic.*"} [English translation: *Lectures on Logic,* trans. and ed. J. Michael Young (Cambridge: Cambridge University Press, 1992), p. 528.]

13. {Hegel, *Wissenschaft der Logik* (Lasson), p. 66.} [Cf. *Science of Logic,* p. 81.]

tent of logic. (Cf. Preface, *Werke* III, p. 8.[14]) Concept "logos" in this sense. Hence "it is least of all the logos which should be left outside the science of logic" (Preface to the second edition, Lasson, p. 19 [Miller trans., p. 39]).

9. *Logic: science of logos*, that is, of the essentialities of things, that is, "metaphysics."—But as such, just another name, or an ancient name, for a discipline that has long been ontological? Already in Aristotle λόγος for εἶδος!!!

γ) The higher logic as logic of reason

10. *Higher logic:* that is, *logos*, reason, and concept *higher*, more comprehensive in their essence. αα) *essence of reason*—as *stage of consciousness*, ββ) *truth of reason as spirit*.

αα) The essence of reason as self-conscious knowing

Reason grasped as a stage of consciousness (in Kant: faculty of principles), *form and way in which consciousness comes forth. Phenomenology!*

(1) Consciousness—immediate representing of the given, the object, of which one is conscious; immediately bound to it, "in itself."

(2) *Self-consciousness*—consciousness's turning back on itself and thus itself for-itself, in a certain separation from the in-itself.

(3) Negation of both—neither only the one nor only the other, but the one *insofar* as it is the other. The object of consciousness is thus known as it is in self-consciousness, the in-itself also "and" for-itself.

ββ) The truth (the self-knowledge) of reason as absolute spirit

But the truth, the essence, that is, the *possibilitas* of reason is *spirit*, which makes possible the self-knowledge of reason itself as a whole.

Spirit is above and beyond every isolated relationship—the relationship of the subject to an object, of the subject to a subject, of the subject to an object only in the subject. The making-possible of this relativity, that is, the *ab-solute* in which all "oppositions" are superseded. Not merely the negative concept of the *ab*solute, that is, not what lacks all relations, but what has superseded all relations.

But this does not mean against opposition as such—this is a "factor of life"—but against the absolute fixation of the opposition and its members; against merely persisting in contra-diction, instead of conceiving the unity of the contradiction in something *higher*. Cf. above Being—

14. {Cf. ibid. (Lasson), Preface to the 1st edition, p. 7: ". . . pure essentialities which constitute the content of logic."} [Cf. *Science of Logic*, p. 28.]

nothing. Not the same A ≠ not-A; but not just ≠, also =; insofar as each is distinct from the other, the same in the "not."

Higher logic: logos as the absolute. Fundamental law of "logic," principle of contradiction, *superseded.* (*Tollere*—to take away, not to let it rest; *elevare*—to raise; *conservare*—to take up, to preserve.)[15]

b) Logic as the system of the absolute self-consciousness of God: theo-logic

In what way is this "logic" "*theo*-logic"? This answer has already basically been given, inasmuch as "logic" is the science "of" the absolute.

(1) But we must characterize the *Hegelian* concept of the *absolute* more precisely, with a view to clarifying in what way the science of logic, as science "of" the absolute, is *metaphysics,* that is, *science of the Being of what is as such,* that is, of the *infinite whole of its essentialities.*

(2) The absolute as *absolute "identity."* Concept of "identity" in German idealism! Fichte, Schelling. *Identitas* in transcendental logic is the empty uniformity of the selfsame! Already Leibniz—identity: belonging-together of what belongs together. What belongs together in idealism: I and not-I, intelligence and nature, subject and object.

Absolute identity: not just the belonging-together of subject and object, but making this belonging-together possible; the *absolute* has its *actuality* precisely *in this making-possible.* The becoming of what is, in the whole of its Being, and according to the essential laws of becoming that belong to its essence.

Absolute identity is the making-possible of the absolute *actuality of the actual. Absolute actuality* is the essential whole of the essentialities, that is, of the concepts of essence as *thought absolutely.* Hegel explicitly tells us in the introduction to the *Logic:* "Accordingly, logic is to be understood as the system of pure reason, as the realm of pure thought. *This realm is truth as it is without veil, in and for itself.* It can therefore be said that this content is the *exposition of God as he is in his eternal essence before the creation of nature and a finite spirit.*"[16] This realm (of pure thought) . . . is *omnitudo realitas* [totality as reality] in the *absolute logical* sense.

Metaphysics as science of the Being of beings is "*logic*" and this logic is the logic "of" the absolute, that is, God. Genitive consciously ambiguous! Not just a *genitivus objectivus:* exhibition of God, but also *genitivus subjectivus:* the *essence* of God as *he essentially unfolds as absolute spirit.*

---

15. [The parenthesized phrases explain the various senses of the word *aufheben,* a crucial term in Hegel that we are rendering as "supersede."]

16. {Ibid. (Lasson), p. 31.} [Cf. *Science of Logic,* p. 50; trans. modified.]

Logic is the system of the absolute self-consciousness of God; it is essentially related to God and grounded in God. *Hegel's metaphysics is logic in the sense of theo-logic.*

---

§20. The completion of Western philosophy in metaphysics as theo-logic and the questionworthiness of this "completion"

In what way is Hegelian metaphysics as this theo-logic the *completion* of Western philosophy?

Completion here means *no higher,* the absolute *fully known.* But this already in pre-Kantian metaphysics! Regress? No, there *only finite,* theoretical-speculative knowledge. Kant: finite practical knowledge.

Now *infinite knowledge,* not in relationships, finitudes. Now one gets serious about the *perfectum* (mathematically: *consentiens* [in agreement]): absolute identity; *perfectissimum* as absolute spirit. Metaphysics *absolute* in the *What* (God) and *How* (principle of contradiction). Knowing as absolute equates itself with absolute Being; by creating absolute Being, it knows it and just simply is it.

Western philosophy

in the inception	*at the end*
deepest urgency of questionworthiness in the struggle with the unmastered powers of truth and errancy. Philosophy as the highest power that arouses the people and clarifies its Dasein. Realm of decision, moment of decision.	*highest blessedness of the supersession of all oppositions;* powerlessness of mere conceptual oppositions; failure and dying-out of all questioning. Empty eternity of the decisionless.

Conclusion

§21. Confrontation and engagement

What con-frontation[1] is not and what it is. Not a formal refutation, demonstration of mere incorrect points, but *scission*—and that only on the basis of decision. *Decision* only as engagement in Dasein; the decision *for.*

Engagement as steadfastly letting fate hold sway. Wisdom—knowing—knowing that we do not know—*questioning.* The innermost and broadest history is neither left to accident nor left to the *placidity* (our people will once again want science) *of the customary.*

Knowing that *we do not know;* not as an ascertained fact, but as insight into the necessity of having to *act.* This acting as *questioning* is not for the sake of questioning, but is an *answer;* the answer is *engagement:* seizing a necessary possibility, exposing oneself to the *necessity* of fate, complying with the freedom of a resolution. The engagement itself as the knowing questioning of *willing to know;* the engagement itself as *teaching.*

"Engagement" a guiding word and slogan; it is good to grasp what it signifies, and that means what it demands.

When I spoke emphatically four years ago, at the end of my inaugural lecture,[2] of the engagement of existence in the fundamental possibilities of Dasein, I was indignantly repudiated on every side. Metaphysics {?}, so it was said, was not at the mercy of subjective whim; personal mood

---

1. [*Aus-einander-setzung:* literally, "setting out and apart from one another." Heidegger goes on to explain this concept in terms of *Scheidung* and *Entscheidung,* rendered here as "scission" and "decision."]

2. {Martin Heidegger, *Was ist Metaphysik? Antrittsvorlesung, gehalten am 24. Juli 1929 in der Aula der Universität Freiburg i. Br.* (Bonn: Cohen, 1929; 14th edition, Frankfurt am Main: Klostermann, 1992).} [English translation: "What is Metaphysics?" in Martin Heidegger, *Pathmarks,* ed. William McNeill (Cambridge: Cambridge University Press, 1998).]

was being made into the measure of truth. I have until today avoided answering this "criticism"; truth itself will make its nullity apparent.

Engagement in the possibilities: that is, in the essentially uncertain. It is *not an engagement* if, when everything has been secured and made ready in advance, I give it my all and manage to achieve something, pulling it off without anything ever happening to me. But it is just as little an engagement when one runs off blindly—without any regard to whether one will succeed or not. Instead, engagement involves the *will* that the attempt succeed; but also the courage to stand there when it does not succeed, that is, to *learn;* not in order to speak from then on with caution and in opposition, but in order to rein in one's strength and thus to bring it into play all the more securely and courageously, and to extend the courage of action as far and as long as possible.

There are still a good many of our contemporaries, in all the domains of our political Dasein today—even among those who today wear party insignia and the like—for whom in their existence and fundamental attitude, not the least thing has changed. One comports oneself as follows: (1) one declares one's readiness to cooperate, (2) but one waits to see how things develop; (3) while waiting, one hopes that things may once again become as they were earlier, just that now everything is called National Socialist. (4) This attitude then convinces itself that it is superior and rational and realistic.

Example: it is said that "the new German state is not yet here." Then one takes this negative assertion only in this interpretation: nothing at all has yet come of the whole movement, and it is highly questionable whether anything will come of it—and perhaps, quite in secret: we hope nothing will come of it. But the deeper interpretation is: it is not yet here, but we will and shall create it, and have already taken hold of it and will not slacken, but will bind ourselves to it all the more strictly.

But this whole attitude, as well intended as it may be, completely excludes itself from the authentic happening and from its inner demand.

The German people does not belong among those peoples who have already lost their metaphysics. The German people has not yet lost its metaphysics, because it cannot lose it. And it cannot lose its metaphysics because it does not yet possess it. We are a people that must *first gain* its metaphysics and *will* gain it—that is, we are a people that still has *a fate.* Let us see to it that we *do not oppose* this fate, but *measure the distance we have traveled in* and *with* this fate.

ON THE ESSENCE OF TRUTH

Winter Semester 1933-1934

Introduction
The Question of Essence as
Insidious and Unavoidable

§1. The question of the essence of truth and the
willing of what is true in our Dasein

We are asking about the essence of truth. To begin with, this means that we want to find out what truth "in general" is, what such a thing "really consists in." So this questioning about the *essence* of truth is obviously a "profound" and "important" undertaking. Or does it only seem to be? Let us consider what it means to think about something like the essence of danger, to provide an extensive discussion of the universal concept of danger—and meanwhile to overlook actual dangers and to be no match for what is dangerous. What about this: to set out on a profound contemplation of the essence of honor, diligently to work out the universal concept of honor—and at the same time to be without honor and to act without honor? And this: to chase after the essence of truth, to fight keenly over the structure and content of the concept of truth—and meanwhile to fail to recognize and to neglect what is true?

Is this not a highly insidious procedure? To brood over the essence of things and to think behind the cover of concepts—and abstract oneself from the things themselves? To evade reality through the semblance of profundity?

It seems a completely baseless and idle undertaking to ask about the essence of truth, when the urgency of our Dasein assails us and the *only* thing that *matters* is that we ourselves *be true* and *remain in the truth*. Who would hesitate here for even a moment, when the choice stands before us either to think through the general concept of truth or to grasp and bring to fulfillment what is true in our being and acting? Who then still doubts the insidiousness and idleness of the question about essence?

So let us drop it; let us not seek the essence of truth in general, but instead let us grasp what is true, the true that is the sole law and support for our Dasein here and now. This *true*—how is it recognizable so that we can set it apart immediately and certainly from the untrue? This true— how is it certified *as* the true? Who or what can vouch that this true is not a great, singular error? Can we achieve and hold firm to the true without being sure that we are not actually falling victim to the untrue?

How could we be sure of this, if we do not decide and have not decided between the true and the untrue? How can we decide here, if we do not distinguish the true from the untrue? And how can we distinguish here, if we do not know what makes the true true and the untrue untrue?

And how can we do that, when we do not know what truth is and what untruth is, and what their essence consists in? Precisely when we want, in the highest and unique passion, only what is true in our Dasein, we are unable to do without knowing what truth is and what distinguishes and divides truth from untruth. As insidious, grandiose, and empty as the question of essence sounds, knowing about the essence of truth is nevertheless *unavoidable*.

Accordingly we were entirely in the right with our plan to ask about the essence of truth; for we are asking about it in order to know what truth in general is. But then on the other hand, the point still stands that we will lose ourselves in the universal concept, that we will be chasing after a mere idea, or, in plain language: we will remain stuck with the look that truth in general offers us, we will re-present this look (which surely is something) and set it up before us—hence the talk of intuition of essences. In asking about essence, we become onlookers and forget both acting and actuality.

As unavoidable as it is to know about essence, we must take into the bargain the insidiousness, as well as the risk of baselessness, of every question of essence. So it seems, and so has it seemed for a long time, since Plato defined the essence of things as "Idea."

But the first question is whether essence as such is attained by this definition, or whether this conception of essence as "Idea" was not the starting point for a great, centuries-long error. That is a question; that is, it is by no means settled that the essence of a thing—for example, the essence of truth—should be sought in what we think of as the concept of truth in general, whether essence should be located in the Idea and sought there.

But if this question must remain open, then there is suddenly something different about the insidiousness of the question of essence.[1]

---

1. We *must* ask about essence. Accordingly, the questioning as such is not insidious. What, then? *Essence?*

Then in the end, it is not asking about essence *per se* that is insidious, but rather simply and solely the customary *way* in which one determines the *essence of essence* in advance, precisely as the *representation of something* in general—as *concept and Idea.*

Therefore everything hinges upon *how* we pose the question of essence, that is, *what* we *really* understand by the essence of something and *what kind of understanding* this is. This gives us a clear and simple indication of how we should proceed: before we ask about truth in its essence, we should thoroughly and firmly establish how matters stand with the *essence of essence.*

Admittedly, there still remains the suspicion that we are now really losing ourselves in the highest heights of so-called abstraction, where there is no more air to breathe. Essence of truth—that at least still seemed somewhat definite in content. But essence of essence? Now everything evaporates; it really borders on empty wordplay.

---

§2. The question of the essence of essence.
Presuppositions and beginning

a) Dasein's becoming essential in authentic care for its ability
to be and the putting to work of the essence of things.
The how of essence

We begin to characterize essence as such when we say: *essence essences,* and when we explain this as follows:

The essence of our *people* is what rules throughout our doings from the ground up and as a whole, insofar as we have come to ourselves.

The essence of our *state:* what impels and secures our people as a whole to the structure of an enduring Dasein that answers for itself and takes action.

The essence of *labor:* what permeates the achievement of gaining power over the world in its smallest and greatest facets, as the empowerment of our Dasein.

The essence of the *world:* what assails our Dasein as a whole, in its depth and breadth; what either drives us away from ourselves or lifts us out beyond ourselves into the greatness of our fate.

The essence of *human Dasein:* that into which we are thrown and bound; what we in our Dasein conquer or what defeats us; our occasions for joy or cowardice.

The essence of the world and the things of the world, and the essence of human Dasein in the world: both are *one* as the essence of beings as a whole. This essence cannot be brought together in thought and represented in empty concepts and displayed in a conceptual system. Because this essence of beings as a whole rules beings through and through in many forms, ruling all beings in accordance with their ways of Being, it can be exhibited only when human beings—peoples in their power relations, in their works, in the manner in which they bear their fate—*transform the spirit of the earth.* The essence of beings comes to the light of day only when human beings, rooted in their heritage and vocation, *put* essence to *work.* The *essence* of things *is put to work* through the *confrontation* with beings, insofar as we rise to the essence of things in this confrontation or are destroyed in it. How the essence of things is put to work depends on how and how far we ourselves as a people, and each individual among the people, become *essential* in our Dasein. Essential: that means bound into the law and structure of beings.

The fundamental achievement, through which alone our Dasein can become essential, is the awakening of the courage for ourselves, for our Dasein in the midst of the world. The courage for one's own originary Dasein and its concealed powers is the fundamental precondition for every working-out of the essence of things. This courage first forges our disposition, the fundamental moods in which Dasein soars out to and back from the limits of beings as a whole. Essence does not make itself known through a casual notion, does not take shape through a "theory," does not display itself in doctrine. *Essence opens itself up only to the originary courage of Dasein for beings as a whole.* Why? Because courage moves forward; it releases itself from what has been so far, it dares the unaccustomed and makes the inevitable its concern. But courage is not the mere wish of a spectator; rather, courage anchors its will in clear and simple tasks; it compels and harnesses all forces, means, and images.

Only insofar as the one care of human Dasein, the care concerning Dasein's ability to be and its having to be, becomes care pure and simple, is the human venture into the world fulfilled. Only in this way does the world's mastery hold sway and display itself in law, organization, deportment, and work. Only thus does what is as a whole, as well as each individual thing, open up in its essence.

In the ordinary hustle and bustle, a human being—indeed, often an entire people—chases and hastens after arbitrary objects and opportunities, through which they are transported into greater and lesser moods in which they want to be confined. And human beings are surprised when they see themselves compelled to devise and supply ever new means of stimulation and excitement. They do this instead of grasping that the reverse is needed from the start: to create and to awaken *fundamental moods* through *originary courage*—that then all things become visible, decidable and durable. I repeat: this is the courage for what is originary as one's own.

Yet if *this* is how things stand with essence, then not only is the question about essence not insidious, but it is the very questioning that unrelentingly holds us in actuality and impels us to a decision there. Essence is not what can be grasped representationally, for all representation is setting-aside [*alles Vor-stellen ist weg-stellen*]. We do not want to set essence aside but to come to grips with it, and we want to do so in the resoluteness that reaches forward by acting together, in courageously coming to grips with essence by *reaching forward.*

And if we now want to grasp the essence of truth, that is, work it out, then this means that, through our acting, we must experience and demonstrate how much truth we can endure and withstand. This is the measure by which truth displays itself to us on each occasion, namely, as that which makes our Dasein sure, bright, and strong in its Being.

But in contrast, if we were to arrive simply at a pedantic so-called "definition" that brought together all the familiar features of truth, then that would lead us astray.

b) The question of the what of essence.
Harkening back to the Greek inception

We may now have clarified *how* essence essences, but not *as what.* So far, the innermost content of the essence of beings as a whole has not been determined. To ask about this—that is, to want to figure out what the Being of all beings consists in—is sheer arrogance. And yet we may not evade this question. If it must remain without an answer, then we must also actually experience this, and in the experience of this failure, come to fathom our Dasein.

The essence of beings essences. But what does it really consist in? This is not a question raised by an individual, although it may in each case be an individual who raises this question in language, in a sentence. The question itself resonates in our Dasein—and it has done so for generations, since our Dasein received its fundamental orientation through the inception of Greek philosophy. Since then, the question and the attempts at answering it have persisted. Since then, everyone who asks this question must listen to its inception just in order to arrive at the right context for the resonance of the question as such. This does not mean turning back to antiquity and making it out to be the rigid standard for all Dasein. If we *hearken back* to this Greek inception, this is *not an arbitrary whim* or just some pedantic habit, but rather the deepest necessity of our German Dasein.

This means learning to grasp that this great inception of our Dasein has been cast out over and past us as what we have to catch up with—again, we do this not to complete Greek civilization, but rather fully to draw on the fundamental possibilities of the proto-Germanic ethnic essence and to bring these to mastery.

We must grasp that our Dasein, with all its progress and achievements, lags behind as measured against the inception—and has run off course and lost itself.

§3. The saying of Heraclitus.
Struggle as the essence of beings

When we, with the originary courage of our Dasein, directed forwards, hearken back to the voices of the great inception—not so as to become Greeks and Greek-like, but rather to perceive the primordial laws of our Germanic ethnicity in their most simple exigency and greatness and to put ourselves to the test and prove ourselves against this greatness—then we can hear that saying which gives the first and the decisively great answer to our question about what the essence of beings consists in and how it essences: πόλεμος πάντων μὲν πατήρ ἐστι, πάντων δὲ βασιλεύς, καὶ τοὺς μὲν θεοὺς ἔδειξε τοὺς δὲ ἀνθρώπους, τοὺς μὲν δούλους ἐποίησε τοὺς δὲ ἐλευθέρους.[2] (Heraclitus, fragment 53, Bywater XLIV.[3,4])

How forgotten, misunderstood and debased this saying has become is proved precisely by its relatively frequent employment. War, struggle is the father of all things—one does not know what more to say. One cites this fragment mostly on occasions when one is, as it were, apologizing for the fact that there has been any conflict. And the sense of it, then, is that struggle (unfortunately?!) just happens.

This is not the occasion to undertake a formal and comprehensive interpretation, but simply to interpret the fragment in view of our immediate question, which is also our guiding question, our broader and proper question.

a) The first part of the saying. Struggle as the power of
generation and preservation: innermost necessity of beings

One word stands great and simple at the beginning of the saying: πόλεμος, war.[5] This does not mean the outward occurrence of war and the celebration of what is "military," but rather what is decisive: stand-

2. [A conventional translation would be: "War is both the father of all things and the king of all things, and on the one hand it shows forth the gods, on the other, human beings; on the one hand it makes slaves, and on the other hand, the free."]

3. Only one fact about Heraclitus has been handed down with relative certainty: he stemmed from the noble lineage of masters in the sixth or fifth century BC.

4. {Hermann Diels, *Die Fragmente der Vorsokratiker. Griechisch und deutsch*, 4th edition (Berlin, 1922), vol. 1, p. 88: Heraclitus, fragment 53. *Heracliti Ephesii reliquiae*, ed. I. Bywater (Oxford, 1877), fragment 44.}

5. The two major parts of the saying: 1) up to καί; 2) to the end.

ing against the enemy. We have translated this word with "struggle" [*Kampf*] in order to hold on to what is essential; but on the other hand, it is important to bear in mind that it does not mean ἀγών, a competition in which two friendly opponents measure their strengths, but rather the struggle of πόλεμος, war. This means that the struggle is in earnest; the opponent is not a partner but an enemy. Struggle as standing against the enemy, or more plainly: standing firm in confrontation.

An enemy is each and every person who poses an essential threat to the Dasein of the people and its individual members. The enemy does not have to be external, and the external enemy is not even always the more dangerous one. And it can seem as if there were no enemy. Then it is a fundamental requirement to find the enemy, to expose the enemy to the light, or even first to make the enemy, so that this standing against the enemy may happen and so that Dasein may not lose its edge.

The enemy can have attached itself to the innermost roots of the Dasein of a people and can set itself against this people's own essence and act against it. The struggle is all the fiercer and harder and tougher, for the least of it consists in coming to blows with one another; it is often far more difficult and wearisome to catch sight of the enemy as such, to bring the enemy into the open, to harbor no illusions about the enemy, to keep oneself ready for attack, to cultivate and intensify a constant readiness and to prepare the attack looking far ahead with the goal of total annihilation.

πόλεμος, struggle (to stand up against the enemy) encompasses and permeates πάντα, all; πάντων—beings collectively, all as a whole. From this we derive from the start the scope of the saying: it does not only deal with struggling as a human activity; it deals with *all* beings. And struggle is furthermore *not* just a mere epiphenomenon (something pervasive, to be sure, but only accessory), but rather what determines beings as a whole and determines them in a crucial way. It does this in every case in two distinct forms.

πατήρ—βασιλεύς ["father . . . king"] does not just mean that in addition to the "father," progenitor, there is also the ruler as well; instead they are sharply distinguished and yet at the same time brought into a relation by the μέν—δέ ["both . . . and"]. Accordingly, "father" has a deepened meaning. The first thing this means is that struggle does not just allow each being to go forth into what it is, it does not just direct and control the emergence of beings. Instead, struggle also rules their persistence; beings are in their constancy and presence only if they are preserved and governed by struggle as their ruler. Therefore, struggle in no way steps back from things as soon as they have wound their way into actuality, but rather precisely this *subsequent* persisting and being actual is authentic only in struggle. Through this, the full domain of the power of struggle first becomes clear; it becomes clear how in all beings, insofar as they are, struggle already constantly holds sway from the start, that is, constitutes beings in their Being.

In holding sway, struggle pervades the whole of beings with a double power: as power of generation and power of preservation. It hardly needs mention that wherever no struggle reigns, standstill, leveling, equilibrium, mediocrity, harmlessness, decline, fragility and tepidity, decay and collapse, in short: passing-away sets in on its own.

This means that the powers of destruction and ruination have their home *in* beings themselves; in struggle and through struggle they are only subdued and bound. And even then, these powers are still understood too negatively and not in the Greek sense, for these powers fundamentally break forth as the unbridled, the unrestrained, the ecstatic and wild, the raving, the Asiatic. We must be on our guard against devaluing these powers according to the Christian standards of evil and sin and thereby casting them into denial. Neither does struggle, then, mean picking fights arbitrarily; struggle is the *innermost necessity* of beings as a whole and therefore the confrontation with and between the *primordial powers.* What Nietzsche characterizes as the Apollonian and the Dionysian are the opposing powers of this struggle.

So much for the interpretation of the *first major part* of the saying, up to the καί [and]. In brief: 1) the essential power; 2) the domain of power; 3) the double character of power (generation and preservation); 4) the two as belonging together.

b) The second part of the saying. The sway of the double power of struggle and the decisive domains of power

This is now explained by the *second major part,* which begins with καί, and here we experience two things: 1) in what manner the double power of struggle holds sway; 2) which domains of power count as the decisive ones and what this means. Furthermore (to elaborate): the *generating and preserving sway* in all beings is of the following kind.

Of πόλεμος it is said: ἔδειξε—ἐποίησε; we translate this as: "it displays, it lets come forward" (and we elaborate this as follows: "into openness"). The customary and "correct" translation is: it "engenders," it "makes." Our translation, by contrast, is meant to clarify the genuinely Greek sense of the words. Accordingly, what matters is not simply that struggle has some result—or the reverse, that some actuality points back to struggle as its cause; but what is above all being said here is the sense in which the Greeks understand in advance the manner by which beings come to Being through struggle. The meaning of Being implies this: having been placed on display—as stamped, limited, subsistent shape—placed into *visibility,* or better, *perceptibility.* Whatever is displayed and directed into its belonging to "beings," "is."

And ἐποίησε means the same thing; in this, one should not so much see the mere completion of a making, but rather that making, *setting-forth*, accomplishes the fundamental task of setting something, as finished and at rest in itself, into availability and perceptibility. For the Greeks, then, a being is whatever is stamped within limits and thereby present, and in such presence, constant. *Being: stamped subsistent presence.*

So above all it becomes clear how immediately struggle, in the holding sway of its power, pervasively reigns over the Being of beings as such. For struggle proves to be setting things into Being and holding them there, by making them emerge yet holding them fast. *Origin of Being.*

We are now asking about what is expressed in the second major part of the saying: which domains of power count as the decisive ones, and what this means. This part speaks of gods, human beings, servants, and masters. Obviously these are not just any arbitrary areas within the whole of beings, but rather beings as a whole are decisively determined precisely by these.

How so? Could not other domains serve just as well? Why not animals and plants, land and sea, fire and air, the living and the dead? Why is it restricted to the human and the divine? But this is asking the wrong question. How so? Because we are not holding onto the fundamental content of the saying. What this means is that it has nothing to do with naming certain regions of beings as examples, but rather with making the *fundamental modes of Being* visible in their origin from the essence of Being: *being* god, *being* human, *being* servant, *being* master.

And furthermore, it is not sufficient to take these fundamental modes of Being simply as a list of various types, but rather they must be taken only *in their originary character.* This means: the essence of Being is struggle; every Being passes through decision, victory and defeat. One is not simply only a god or just a human being, but rather in each case a decision takes place in struggle, and thereby struggle is transposed into Being; one is a servant not because there simply are servants, in addition to other types, but because this Being contains in itself a defeat, a denial, a deficiency, a cowardice—indeed, perhaps a will to be lowly and base.[6]

It is now clear that struggle sets things into Being and holds them there; it constitutes the essence of Being, and in such a way that struggle *permeates* all beings with *the character of decision,* with the constant sharpness of the either-or: either them or me; either to stand or to fall.

---

6. Confrontation and decision in struggle are what is essential in Being; this *fundamental character modifies itself,* and in each case the domains of Being are modified in accordance with it. But then is even Being anthropomorphic!? Yes and no! Question!! In brief: from these modes of power only the immediate indication of *Being*—exhibited in these modes of power most proximately and vividly.

This decision in struggle that characterizes all Being imparts a *fundamental mood* to beings: victorious jubilation and will at the same time as the fearsomeness of unbridled pressure (resistance), grandeur and fury united—something that we are incapable of saying with one word, but for which the Greeks have a word that recurs in the great poetry of the tragedians: τὸ δεινόν [usually translated as "the terrible" or "wondrous"].[7]

The saying of Heraclitus is therefore, taken as a whole, precisely a saying and not a mere assertion that would establish something or other; it is not a scientific proposition, but a *philosophical* declaration that speaks from the highest fullness, in the greatest simplicity, and in a definitive form. And we must listen to this declaration appropriately, put ourselves at its command, and allow ourselves to be sobered by the self-ruling gravity of this primal declaration.

§4. On the truth of the Heraclitean saying

a) Two traditional meanings of truth. Truth as un-concealment (ἀ-λήθεια) and as correctness

In the interpretation of the saying of Heraclitus, we said *how* and *as what* essence essences: as struggle. Now, right away someone might want to ask: on what basis is the *truth* of this saying grounded—how does this truth prove and demonstrate itself?

In the end, the "truth" of such a saying is precisely of such an exceptional kind that, from the start, it would be a mistaken requirement to demand a *proof* in the ordinary sense here.

In other words, we cannot really understand this saying at all, if we know nothing about the manner of truth that is appropriate to it in particular; and how are we supposed to know this, if we do not know about the *essence* of truth and the possible forms of truth? On the other hand, this saying is supposed to give us an indication of what the essence of essence (Being) consists in, so that we know sufficiently what we are asking about when we ask about the essence of truth. It is becoming clear that we are going around in a circle here: first we seek

---

7. Angst in its deepest depth! Not "anxiousness" and fear. Angst as only the great and heroic human being knows it! And whoever says that he does not know authentic angst has not yet proven that he is courageous, but only that he is dull and stupid. (Philosophy of angst—rationalism.)

"In our days, angst rightfully enjoys very little popularity."—What then is resoluteness other than the precondition for great and essential angst, otherwise it would indeed be useless and idle play and would have nothing of greatness and strength.

the truth about essence in order next to grasp the essence of truth. You can't have one without the other.

But this remarkable abyss in our questioning, which now we see, is always the unmistakable sign that we are asking about something that is *first* and *last*, that is, we are standing in the midst of a philosophical question.

But how to find a way out of this circle?[8]—Not at all! For then we would be giving up the proper standpoint. So all we can do is move in a circle—but how? A first response might be: as we did before with the truth of essence, we will now seek to grasp the essence of truth in such a saying, and so we will go back to the inception of philosophy in order to be on the lookout for a corresponding declaration about the essence of truth.

But this is entirely superfluous, for precisely *the same saying*, the one that speaks of the *essence of essence*, *also* tells us about the *essence of truth*. The saying certainly does not seem to be talking explicitly about truth at all. But it only seems this way.

In order to see that the same saying is in fact speaking about truth as well, we need only *remember* the Greek word for what we call truth: ἀ-λήθεια, which is aptly translated as unconcealment. Admittedly, not much is gained by this, as long as we do not transpose ourselves into the full strength of this word's meaning and thus make it clear to ourselves that at issue here is not just another explanation of the meaning of just another word.

We understand the meaning of the Greek word for truth in a provisional yet unambiguous way: unconcealed, not veiled and not covered over. And then how does it stand with the word "truth" [*Wahrheit*] in our own language? So what do we really mean by it when we say it? If we don't want to fool ourselves, we must readily admit that for the most part we fumble around, as it were, with a highly imprecise meaning of the word. In any case, the meaning of this word is not as unambiguous and simple as that of the Greek word; for the German meaning is *non-visual* and *non-sensory* and therefore has no immediate perceptual counterpart.

On the other hand, however, the word "truth" is not just a meaningless sound; we "think" something by it and use it, correspondingly, for specific things and, accordingly, not for other specific things. For example, with respect to the factual situation that we call "sickness," we say precisely sickness and not truth; with respect to the factual situation that we call "bravery," we say bravery and not truth, because we mean something else with this word.

---

8. Indeed we must, otherwise we commit the elementary logical error of deriving b from a and in the same breath a from b. Nonsense!—according to vulgar thinking! Not so in this questioning about the first and last.

Yes, fine! But *what* do we mean, then, if we do use the word with such certainty? What do we understand, then, by truth in the first place?

We usually proceed very securely with questions of this sort. We refer to examples. To clarify what truth itself means, we cite this or that truth. And how does this happen? We say, for example: "2 and 1 is 3"; "The earth orbits the sun"; "Winter follows fall"; "On the 12th of November the German people will cast the vote that determines its ownmost future";[9] "Kant is the greatest German philosopher"; "There is noise on the street"; "This lecture hall is heated."—These are *individual truths.*

How are these truths? I mean to say, these are *propositions, assertions.* Certainly—but they each contain something "true," a truth. Yet *"where"* is this true contained? Where is it hiding, then? And above all—what does the "true" that these sentences contain consist in, then? In what way, for example, is this "proposition" true: "This lecture hall is heated"? But why bother to explain such obvious things? The proposition is true precisely because it says *that* which *is.* It's the simplest thing in the world. The proposition reproduces what we find in front of us: the fact that this lecture hall is heated. In other words, the proposition agrees with how things stand, with the state of affairs. And precisely this *agreement* is its being-true, what is true about the proposition. The assertion agrees with reality in the sense that, in what it says, it *directs* itself toward reality. The being-true of the sentence consists in its *correctness.* With this we have grasped what we initially think in an indistinct way with the word "truth." And "correctness" also contains something perceptual. *Truth means correctness.*

Our concept of truth and the Greek concept of truth take their *perceptual intelligibility* from *entirely different domains* and *relations.* ἀ-λήθεια, unconcealment, is taken from the factual situation of *concealing, veiling,* or in turn, unveiling and unconcealing. "Correctness" is taken from the factual situation of the *directedness of* something *towards* something, from the factual situation of gauging and measuring. "Unveiling" and "measuring" are entirely different factual situations.

Let us leave it at that. We are not yet asking whether, in the end, these two entirely different concepts of truth might nevertheless be

9. [On 12 November 1933, a plebiscite was held to affirm Germany's withdrawal from the League of Nations. For Heidegger's speeches on the plebiscite, see "Aufruf zur Wahl" and "Ansprache am 11. November 1933 in Leipzig," in *Reden und Andere Zeugnisse eines Lebensweges: 1910-1976* (GA 16), ed. Hermann Heidegger (Frankfurt am Main: Vittorio Klostermann, 2000), pp. 188-93. For translations, see "German Men and Women!" and "Declaration of Support for Adolf Hitler and the National Socialist State," in *The Heidegger Controversy,* ed. Richard Wolin (Cambridge, Mass.: MIT Press, 1993), pp. 47-52.]

connected to one another and in what way—and indeed whether they *must* go together. There is something more important for us now.

b) The indeterminate prior knowing of truth
and the superior power of Being

We have just made clear for ourselves, by taking an entirely unartificial path, what we really mean when we ordinarily use the words "truth" and "true," namely: correctness and correct. But with this, we have brought an entirely different factual situation into view, namely: that we *already understand in advance what truth and true mean.* By no means have we just now learned and experienced for the first time that truth amounts to correctness; rather, at most we have now noticed for the first time that we *always already fundamentally* knew this *in advance,* even if indistinctly, that we automatically, so to speak, and constantly hold onto this knowledge.

A remarkable situation, this! For it relates not just to the meaning of the words "truth" and "true," but also others: house, river, animal, space, mountain, people, time, and so on—indeed, the whole of language! We think of something with these words. We understand animality in advance—and only because of this can we speak of something that we encounter *as an animal;* we understand the birdlike—and only because of this can we speak of something as a bird; we understand spatiality—and only because of this can we speak of something as situated "in" space; we understand the mountainous . . .

By understanding such things, we are, as it were, out beyond in the "real"—as we call it: the individual, present-at-hand animals, birds, spaces, and mountains. Indeed, only to the extent that and because we understand animality, the birdlike, spatiality, and the mountainous, can we encounter the real, the individual—each this and that—*as that which it is.*

A remarkable situation? No! A provocative one—presuming that we are not dulled and too enslaved by the tyranny of the self-evident. As if this situation were self-evident. But let us once seriously attempt to exist while giving up our understanding of animality, spatiality, thingness, and so on—would animals, space, things, or indeed any being whatsoever still be given to us? No. Perhaps some hazy rush of some unbearable confusion—which could only be endured in madness.

But madness certainly exists; and therefore precisely what we, in our good bourgeois and presumably superior manner, call the "normal" is not "normal" at all but something tremendously unique, a uniqueness that can be endured only if one constantly forgets and falsifies it into some everyday thing.

So *before* which—or better, *in* which—fundamental situation do we stand, then? We comport ourselves and maintain our Dasein in the midst of the multiplicity of beings; yet we are not first and properly delivered over to beings, but rather first we are bound *to that* which in each case this individual, multiplicitous being *is, what* and *how it is: its Being*. If this Being were not in power over us and, consequently, in our knowing, all beings would remain powerless. Only because human beings *are transposed into the superior power of Being and have in some manner mastered that power,* only because of this are human beings capable of holding themselves up in the midst of beings as such. *This bond to the superior power of Being* is for us the *deepest essence of human beings*.

<hr>

§5. On truth and language

a) The human bond to the superior power of Being and the necessity of language

Because and *only* because human beings are of this essence, they exist *in language,* and indeed there *must* be something like human *language*. The animal does not speak because it cannot speak. And it cannot because it does not need to speak. It does not need to speak because it does not have to. It does not have to because it does not find itself in *the urgent need* to speak. It does not stand in such a need because it is not *compelled by need*. It is not compelled because it is *closed off to the assailing powers*. Which powers? The *superior power of Being!*[10]

It follows that the fact that the human being is exposed and open to the superior power of Being, and the fact that we speak, are one and the same fundamental fact in the essence of human beings. In turn, what it means to remain shut out from the capacity for speech is something one can see in a cow or a chicken, or indeed any animal. And at the other extreme, it is just as impossible for a god to "speak" (the "word" of God).

Initially, our explication of the word ἀ-λήθεια, "truth," yielded only this point: that in language, words already contain a certain intelligibility of things. But then we saw that language has a place in the essential constitution of human beings. This is so because human beings can *exist* only because they are bound to the superior power of Being. To exist: to be a being oneself such that this being, as a being, "is" in the midst of beings as such and as a whole.

We could content ourselves with the point that obviously language as well as other "phenomena" characterize the particular essence of human beings, but that here we are not dealing with the essence of human beings but rather with the essence of truth. Certainly—but it is not yet settled whether the question of the essence of truth is not the

---

10. The other way around! {Heidegger's presumably later addition.}

same as the question of the human essence, and furthermore, whether precisely in this whole constellation of questions the question about the essence of language must not play a preeminent role.

From an external standpoint the answer is not immediately clear, above all not as long as we persist in the usual notions and opinions about language. On this subject we will now make only the most provisional remarks.

b) The logical-grammatical conception of language

The dominant approach to individual languages and to language in general is passed on to us through what we call *grammar*. By this we understand the theory of the elements, structures, and rules for structures in a language; separate groups of sentences, individual sentences, and sentence types; analyzed into groups of words, individual words; words into syllables and letters, γράμμα. Hence the name.

The *grammatical* conception of language is taken for granted in the customary notion of language, especially in linguistics and in the so-called philosophy of language. Moreover, this view has taken hold in a centuries-long tradition and can claim for itself a certain semblance of naturalness. For what is more accessible and tangible than just this analysis and ordering of the otherwise completely unmanageable amalgam of a living language in sounds, letters, syllables, words, word-constructs, and sentence structures?

But it is important to recognize the provenance of this reigning *grammatical* representation of language. It derives from the *Greeks;* it developed in the age of Greek sophistry and rhetoric and found its authoritative form in Plato and Aristotle. At the basis of this is the experience that speaking, discourse, is speaking with one another, public transaction, advising, assemblage of the people, judicial proceedings; speaking of this kind is having a public opinion and consulting, deliberating, and *thinking.* And in connection with the question of *what* thinking and opining and understanding and knowing are, contemplation arrives at *discourse,* speaking, as what is immediately accessible and in reach of the senses. Discourse is *given* and *is,* just as are many other things; it "is" as the Greeks understood the Being of beings: the available, stamped, durable presence of something. Language is something present at hand, and as such gets taken apart and put together in determinate parts and structures. Accordingly, the emphasis is on exhibiting what is at all times the most constant and the most simple and enduring fundamental structure, in the sense of the Greek conception of Being.

As such a fundamental structure of discourse, after long and difficult consideration, there finally emerges in Aristotle the notion of the simple sentence that has the character of discourse: "The stone is hard," and the like. Discourse is therefore that in which something present-at-hand has something else present-at-hand asserted of it. Assertion: ὄνομα, ῥῆμα: κατηγορεῖν [name/noun, utterance/verb: predication]. Hence the categorical, simple sentence counts as the fundamental structure of discourse; λέγειν—λόγος (see below).

What deals with and knows about (ἐπίστασθαι) λόγος and what λόγος is, is ἐπιστήμη λογική [knowledge or science of λόγος]—"logic." As we said, the real occasion for considering discourse was the power that discourse has to define, instruct, and seduce, insofar as in discourse, *thinking and contemplation* are at work. But because *engaging in discourse* is simply thinking out loud, thinking that is made public, that is generally accessible, reflection on *discourse* (λόγος) becomes the *form of the theory of thinking, "logic."* In other words, it is by no means obvious that "logic" should be the theory of thinking; rather, this has its unique grounds in the character and course of Greek philosophy.

But contained in this fact that the theory of thinking and knowing developed as "logic" is another essential fact. Since thinking constitutes the area of questions for logic, reflection on λόγος as the theory of *language,* that is, *grammar,* is dominated at the same time by logic as the theory of thinking. In other words, all fundamental grammatical concepts concerning linguistic structures and word-forms derive from logic, that is, from the theory of thinking, a thinking that is conceived as comprehending beings (what is present at hand). *Substantivum, verbum, adjectivum* [noun, verb, adjective]—these names for word-forms go back to forms in which beings are comprehended in their Being by thought. In brief: *grammar comes under the dominion of logic,* and indeed of a very particular *Greek logic,* one that lays the ground for a very particular conception of beings in general. But *this* grammar dominates the manner in which language is represented. And with this arises the more or less explicit representation of language as if it were primarily and properly the *verbal expression of thinking* in the sense of the *theoretical* observation and discussion of things.

One easily sees that this is *a monstrous violation of what language accomplishes;* consider a poem or a living conversation between human beings: the tone of voice, the cadence, the melody of the sentences, the rhythm, and so on. It is true that later, as well as in the present day, people have sought to supplement this theory and to hold the logical-grammatical conception of language in check; nevertheless, the old grammatical-logical representation has endured. And it will endure so long as (a) the mode of thinking and representing endures as it has been accepted in Western thinking by way of Greek logic, and (b) the question concerning the essence of language is not at long last developed from the ground up.

But this task can be carried out only by way of a simultaneous deconstruction of the grammatical-logical mode of representation, that is, by leading this mode back to its concrete, particular starting point, that is, by *destabilizing the grammatical representation of language.* Here we have to be led by a *positive* determination of the essence of language.

c) The characterization of language as sign and expression

In this task, the first thing that must be decided is the following set of questions: To which "category" does something like language belong? Is it even possible to subordinate language to a more universal concept, or is it something ultimate in itself, which cannot be derived from anything else? If it is something ultimate, *how* is it then to be understood *on its own terms?* Into which equally originary context can it be integrated?

To clarify: already in the inception of the logical-grammatical conception of language, a characterization of language came to light that has maintained itself to the present: discourse makes thinking public, and accordingly discourse is the *expression* and *sign* of thinking. With the phenomena of expression and sign, one believes one has finally found those characteristics by which language may be classified and subordinated. Like gesture, for example, language is a form of expression. The meaning of the term *language* has also been correspondingly determined: we speak of "body language," "the language of flowers," "the language of nature," and by these we always mean the giving of signs, expression. Language is a way of giving signs, and so it is classified according to a general phenomenon. At the same time this means that the other phenomena that are indirectly connected to language as a sign are also conceived in this way. In other words, sounds and letters, or a group of these as a word, are signs for what the word means. For its part, this meaning of the word, that which we understand by it (in hearing and reading it), is the expression and sign for the thing that the meaning signifies. So one recognizes three levels: the sound of the word, the meaning, and the thing—which stand in a relationship that is designated by the sign. This particular conception of linguistic forms was also already developed among the Greeks, above all in Aristotle (φωνή, νόημα, πρᾶγμα [sound, thought, thing]). Later, νόημα and πρᾶγμα were taken up by logic, and φωνή was assigned to physiology and psychology (phonetics!).

d) Toward a positive delimitation of the essence of language

What subsequently developed as *linguistics*, or *the science of language,* is a mixture of these entirely different questions and programs of inquiry. Doubtless it will bring ever new facts to light for us, but only by way of a path that is hopelessly misguided. For it is certainly not possible that an originary and essential conception of the essence of language could emerge from the *science* of language, because for its part the *science* of language already assumes such a conception. First a real insight into the essence of language must be gained through more originary contexts of experience, and then science can build upon this ground.

But this essential insight must now pass through a decision on this question: does language stand under the higher and broader characterization of it as gesture and expression and sign, or is it precisely the reverse: are human gesture and expression and sign given only because *human beings exist in language*? And what then is language, if not expression and sign? Something ultimate? But not for itself, but rather *in* the essential context of human Dasein?

Do human beings speak only because they want to designate and offer information about something—a thing, a being—so that language is a tool for the designation and presentation of information? Or do human beings in general have something to give information about and to give a name to because and insofar as they speak, that is, are able to speak? Is language an imitation—albeit a richly developed one—of beings as a whole, or are these beings as a whole, as beings, *made powerful and unfolded only in and through language*?

Do human beings speak because they want to declare and communicate something, or do human beings speak because they are the entities who can keep silent? In the end, is the originary essence of language the *ability to keep silent?* And what does that mean? Is keeping silent merely something negative, not speaking, and simply the outward appearance of noiselessness and quiet? Or is keeping silent something positive and something deeper than all speaking, whereas speaking is not keeping silent and no longer keeping silent and not yet keeping silent?

Whoever has not experienced and asked these questions from the ground up lacks all the preliminaries for access to the essence of language. Such a person immediately falls victim to conventional and very correct opinions. Unless we work through the above questions, there can be no adequate knowledge from which a science might first grow.

The ability to keep silent is therefore the origin and ground of language.[11] All speaking is a breach of keeping silent, a breach that does not have to be understood negatively.

e) The ability to keep silent as the origin and ground of language

In order to further clarify our conception of the essence of language we should now characterize the ability to keep silent. Here we come

11. {Cf. Martin Heidegger, *Sein und Zeit* (Tübingen: Niemeyer, 1953), §34, pp. 164-65.} [English translations: *Being and Time,* trans. John Macquarrie and Edward Robinson (New York: Harper & Row, 1962), p. 208; and *Being and Time,* trans. Joan Stambaugh (Albany: State University of New York Press, 1996), p. 154.]

again to that philosophical situation that we have already encountered: circularity. This circularity makes itself known now in that we are supposed to speak about keeping silent—and this is highly problematic. For whoever discourses about keeping silent is in danger of proving in the most immediate way that he neither knows nor understands keeping silent.

On the other hand, with the remark that one should not speak about keeping silent, one could sell oneself short all too cheaply and relegate keeping silent, as a dark and "mystical" thing, to the so-called emotional premonition and intimation of its essence. So long as we are engaged in philosophy, this must not be. But we also must not believe that with the help of a "definition" we have come to grips with keeping silent. What is at stake for us now is the minimally necessary clarification that will allow us further to unfold the question about the essence of truth.

The attempt to trace back the essential origin of language to keeping silent seems at first to run contrary to everything that we said at the start about human beings and language when we distinguished the human being from the animal. The animal cannot speak, because it does not have to speak. So the animal is in the happy position of being able to keep silent, and the facts show this quite evidently. Animals certainly do not talk; therefore, they keep silent—indeed, they are silent all the time. In fact, just as the human being, if not simply mute by birth, cannot keep silent at all, we must say, on the grounds of our conception of the ability to keep silent as the essential origin of language, that the animal is prepared for and capable of speaking to a much higher degree, because it can keep silent more—indeed, constantly.

The animal, according to our position, must really have a higher capacity for language than the human being. This is obviously not the case. So we arrive at a remarkable and absurd state of affairs: the entities that have the higher capacity for language are unable to speak, and those (human beings) that have the lesser capacity, because they can hardly keep as silent as the animals, are able to speak, indeed they are even able to construct the most elaborate languages. Human language arises from the inability to keep silent, and consequently from a lack of restraint. The *miracle* of language is therefore based on a *failure*. Something has gone wrong here! Let us reconsider!

We came to these remarkable results on the basis of the following assertions: (a) the ability to keep silent is the origin and ground of language; (b) animals are able to keep silent, because they do constantly keep silent—in contrast to human beings. *But can animals really keep silent?* A superfluous question: animals demonstrate that they can at any given moment. They simply don't talk. But in order to keep silent, is it enough simply not to talk? Does the window somehow keep

silent? No! But it does not talk, either! Certainly! But likewise, it cannot keep silent either. Therefore *only the entities* that can talk have the
capacity to keep silent. Keeping silent is a mode of the ability to talk.
Hence even a mute is unable to keep silent, even though he says nothing. He cannot even provide proof that he is able to keep silent, because for that, he would have to be able to talk.

So by no means is keeping silent simply not talking, which applies
even to a window and the like. But neither is keeping silent simply
being mute. The window is not mute; for that, it lacks the capability to
vocalize. Even animals are unable to be mute, although they have the
capacity to vocalize: roaring, bleating, barking, twittering. For us, to be
struck dumb in the broader sense is of course to cease vocalizing; in the
narrower, proper sense, vocalization is the vocalization of speech.
Someone mute by birth can therefore be mute only because and insofar
as he has the drive to speak—and in a certain manner is able to speak
inwardly and does "speak." But even being mute is not yet a keeping silent, because keeping silent is not-talking in the sense of being unwill-
ing to talk, whereas the mute would precisely like to talk. This indicates
that the mere lack of vocalization—whether vocalization is impossible
(as in the case of the window), or simply not actual, as when one is
struck dumb or is mute—is not equivalent to keeping silent. This con-
firms our earlier proposition that keeping silent can by no means be
conceived as a mere negation. Keeping silent is indeed a not-talking, but
not every not-talking is keeping silent. Keeping silent is rather, at the
very least, the not-talking of someone who can talk. As we said before,
it is a definite, exceptional way of being able to talk. This is already evident in the fact that by keeping silent we are often able to say something
much more definite than by the most longwinded talking.

So much for now to clarify keeping silent. But by clearly delimiting
it against an inadequate characterization of it as not talking, we have
clarified ourselves right into a difficulty. Our *guiding proposition* ran as
follows: *keeping silent is the origin and ground of language.* But now we are
saying exactly the opposite: keeping silent is a definite possibility of
the ability to speak and the ability to talk. Whoever is able to talk—
and only such a person—is essentially able to keep silent. *Whoever keeps
silent is able to talk and must be able to talk.* Accordingly, being able to talk
is the precondition, the ground for the possibility of keeping silent, but
not the reverse, as we asserted at the outset. Yet we did not just assert
this at the outset, but we even assert it now: the ability to keep silent
is the origin of language.

Note that with this proposition, I pass decisively beyond what is
said in *Being and Time,* §34, page 164 and following. There, language
was indeed brought into an essential relationship with keeping silent;
the *starting point* for a sufficiently originary conception of the essence

of language was also laid down, in opposition to the "philosophy of language" that has reigned until now. And yet I did not see what really has to follow from this starting point: keeping silent is not just an *ultimate* possibility of discourse, but discourse and language *arise from* keeping silent. In recent years, I have gone back over these relationships and worked them through. This obviously cannot be explained here. Not even the different manners of keeping silent, the multiplicity of its causes and grounds, and certainly not the different levels and depths of reticence. Now only as much will be communicated as is needed for the advancement of our questioning.

Whoever keeps silent and whoever wills to keep silent must, as one puts it, "have something to say." But what does that mean? Certainly not that he must *really* talk in the sense of speaking. What we *have* to say, we *have* and *maintain in an exceptional sense*. We have it and keep it with us in advance. But it is not as simple as having information about something or other that others just don't have. True, this *keeping things to oneself* is a mode of Being in which we close ourselves off against the public, letting nothing out. But this is not what is decisive, as it also applies to the distrustful, the underhanded, and the "deranged."

The above-mentioned mode of keeping things to oneself suggests being constrained, narrowness. But authentic keeping things to oneself is something *positive*: that mode of Dasein in which the human being is not "buttoned up," but rather is *opened up* to beings and to the superior power of Being. Not opened up in the sense, though, that one chases after every random attraction and incident and disperses oneself in their diversity. Rather the reverse: it is *the openedness* for beings that is *gathered in itself.*

Gathering, for its part, is not obstinate egocentrism and mere navelgazing: compared to essential {?} Dasein, these too are no less ways of being lost and dispersed. In fact, they are even worse, because they still offer the semblance of being concerned with the self.

Keeping silent is gathering, the gathering of one's entire comportment so that this comportment holds to itself and so is bound in itself and thereby remains properly oriented and fully exposed to the beings to which it relates. *Keeping silent: the gathered disclosedness for the overpowering surge of beings as a whole.*

Everything great and essential—and this belongs to its essence— always has beside it and before it its non-essence as its semblance. Keeping silent therefore looks like keeping oneself closed off, and yet it is fundamentally the opposite, so long as it maintains its authentic essence.

Keeping silent thus turns out to be the *happening* of the *originary reticence of human Dasein*, a reticence by which Dasein brings itself— that is, the whole of beings, in the midst of which it is—into words.

And the word is then not a replica and facsimile of things, but rather the binding formation, the bound holding-itself-together of that gathered disclosedness and of what is disclosed within it. The next step is to show how this *fundamental mood of reticence* gives voice to sound and vocalization.

The word breaks silence, but only in such a way that it becomes a witness to that reticence and remains a witness, as long as it remains a true word. The word can fade away into mere words, discourse can fade away into mere idle talk; this is *the non-essence of language,* whose insidiousness is as great as the miracle of language.

We now see this much:

1. Keeping silent is nothing negative.
2. It should not simply be understood externally, in terms of vocalization, as the interruption or lack of vocalization (mere quiet, "silence in the forest").
3. Neither does keeping silent pertain to the so-called mineness of human beings, to gathering oneself together in the sense of isolating oneself.
4. Rather, keeping silent is the distinctive character of the Being of human beings, and on the ground of this Being, human beings are exposed to the whole of beings. Keeping silent is the bound gathering of this exposure.
5. So neither does keeping silent mean saying nothing as a form of submission, as evasion and flinching, as incapacity. Such modes of keeping silent are only forms of its non-essence, whereas the essence of keeping silent as the bound gathering of exposure is superiority, that is, power. It is that power that both empowers vocalization into word and language and also empowers us to set ourselves against the superior power of Being and to maintain our position in it—and this means to speak and to be in language.

The ability to keep silent as reticence is the origin and ground of language. It must be noted that what has been said here can offer only a rough indication of the essential character of language. But this indication must do in order to make it clear that although the grammatical representation of language is not accidental, it remains superficial and inadequate; that above all, language and the question of its essence are very tightly interwoven with the question about the *essence of the human being.* The conception of language becomes a yardstick for how originary and broad the question of the human essence is. But *both* questions of essence now concern us *only* because—as we have asserted—they are connected to the question of the essence of truth.

f) Language as the gathered openedness
for the overpowering surge of beings

How is the question of the essence of *language interwoven* with the question of the essence of *truth*? So far, we know two things about this: ἀλήθεια = unconcealment; truth = correctness. But we have never asserted that we have definitively reached and fully circumscribed the essence of truth with this clarification of the meaning of a word. Rather, from the word's meaning, we draw an *indication* of the essence. So far, from the explanation of language and of the word, we know nothing about whether a word's meaning, as such, immediately informs us about the essence of a thing; in fact, it could also be the case that the meaning of a word only gives a hint concerning a *particular aspect* of the essence of the thing, and therefore might just as well harbor the danger that we grasp the *non-essence* of the thing.

Be this as it may, explanation of words is not comprehension of essence; but neither is it irrelevant, for even if the explanation hits upon the non-essence, the explanation still always contains an indication of the essence. Of course, what is called for here is an appropriately thoroughgoing critique. For very specific reasons, philosophy has up to now developed no critique of the cognition of essence. The meanings of *alētheia* and truth that we have derived are only signs of the fundamental factual situations of concealing and measuring. It remains an open question whether with these, the essence of truth is exhausted or even adequately ascertained. We raised the question: does the essence of language stand in relation to the essence of truth, and in which relation?

Language *breaks silence,* that is, it brings it to word. And keeping silent turned out to be the gathered disclosedness for the overpowering surge of beings as a whole. The word does not simply eliminate keeping silent. Rather, the word brings silence along within itself, that is, for its part, the word becomes the disclosure that communicates itself, whether a listener is there or not. Every word is therefore spoken *from* the disclosedness of beings as whole, however narrow and indeterminate this sphere of disclosure may seem to be.

The word itself is not coined as the sound of a word; rather, the coining of the word arises from the prior and originary minting of the disclosure of beings. We must be on guard against taking the derivative distinction among the sound of the word, its meaning, and the thing it refers to, and reading this distinction back into the originary, creative speaking; we must be on guard against understanding this speaking as giving signs. In addition, the creation of language and language as a tradition are not the same and involve completely different ways of speaking. In historical language, the two interpenetrate.

In the word, in discourse, beings exhibit themselves in their disclosedness. Neither is there just a being and next to it a word, nor is there a word as a sign without the being. Neither of the two is separate, and neither is attached to the other in a one-sided manner; rather, both are attached to *the being in the word*.

Above all, the originary gathering of keeping silent loses itself, disperses itself, and displaces itself in the multiplicity of words and their organization. But it is not as if everything drifts apart into individual things; rather, because they arise from keeping silent, word and discourse remain tied to silence and operate as the bond that stamps—as gathering, in a secondary sense. And *this* is the character of language that the Greeks experienced directly and named with the names λόγος, λέγειν, selecting, gathering. What these words express is that the human being, as a discursive being, stands by that very fact in confrontation with beings, and wills to become powerful in the face of multiplicity and obscurity and boundlessness through the simplicity, clarity, and stamping force of *saying*. This gathering in the λόγος puts what is talked about together and thereby exhibits it. In such exhibition beings are gathered as what they are and are thus *revealed*, δηλοῦν.

g) Language as lawgiving gathering and revelation of the structure of beings

Earlier we heard that *Being* is οὐσία for the Greeks, *stamped, subsistent presence* of something; not-Being is simply the absence of οὐσία. The broader sense of presence implies that if beings are a multiplicity, then this being *and* that being are insofar as they have *co-presence*. Hence we encounter this characteristic of Being early on: the co-presence of the one with the other. Strictly speaking, there simply cannot "be" something single, something solitary in itself as a being. For a being as single—for itself—already lives, as it were, by excluding all that is absent and therefore in a relation to it: ὄν [that which is] is always ξυνόν [common, being with], οὐσία [Being] is always παρουσία [Being present].

In Heraclitus, we find a saying that teaches us something about this: διὸ δεῖ ἕπεσθαι τῷ ξυνῷ . . . τοῦ λογοῦ δ' ἐόντος ξυνοῦ ζώουσιν οἱ πολλοὶ ὡς ἰδίαν ἔχοντες φρόνησιν.[12] "Therefore it is necessary to follow the co-present . . . Although discourse {as gathering} pertains to co-presence {of the one with the other}, the human crowd behaves as if each had in each case his own understanding."[13] This saying contrasts the masses with—whom? The difference is not between the

---

12. Heraclitus, fragment 2 (92); loc. cit. (Diels, 4th edition), p. 77.

13. [A conventional translation would be: "Therefore it is necessary to follow what is common . . . while reason is common, the many live as if they had an understanding of their own."]

many and the few in number, but rather in their manner of Being and discoursing. The masses are undisciplined; they let themselves get caught up in whatever is going on, disperse themselves in arbitrariness, and blather about all sorts of possibilities and impossibilities, even though discourse and language pertain to the gathered, that which belongs together, the constant, and the delimited.

Whoever wishes to hold himself apart from the arbitrariness and unrestraint of opinions must inquire into the connectedness of beings. That is, he must fit into and take shelter in the structure and law of things and, accordingly, stand in the discipline of language. Such a person should not debase discourse and abuse it in blather.

We take from this saying a threefold lesson:

1. On the essence of λόγος: it is gathering, and it pertains to the With and the Together of beings.
2. On the essence of Being: it is ξυνουσία, co-presence of the one and the other, structure and assignation.
3. λόγος, as what gathers, relates to nothing other than beings; and precisely because of this—because it gathers in itself the structure or jointure of beings—it enjoins beings, it contains the rules, and thereby itself becomes the measure and the law.[14]

Language is the law-giving gathering and therefore the openness of the structure of beings. We now see without difficulty the connection between language, λόγος, and truth, ἀλήθεια. The setting-out and setting-fast that collects is a setting-forth, and thereby makes things visible and reveals them. Consequently, it is a happening in which something previously inaccessible and veiled is torn from its concealment and set into un-concealment, ἀλήθεια, that is, truth.

h) Language as λόγος and as μῦθος

Here we must take notice: λόγος as such means, for its part, only a very particular experience and conception of the essence of language. The Greeks also know a second and older one: language and word as μῦθος.

But here the word does not have the collecting force, the force that, as it were, braces itself against beings and stands firm against them. As μῦθος [usually translated as "myth" or "story"], the word that comes upon human beings is that word that indicates this and that about the entirety of human Dasein. It is not the word in which human beings give their account of things, but rather the word that gives them a directive.

The word as μῦθος gives clues and indicates; the word as λόγος takes hold and brings itself and human beings into the clear. Language

---

14. N.B.: λόγος, "reason"—apprehensibility of essence, νοῦς; Parmenides.

first becomes λόγος through and with philosophy, that is, in the moment when human beings, bound and suspended in the midst of beings, step forth *against* beings as such and address them on their own, with respect to what beings are. But the originary λόγος of philosophy remains bound to μῦθος; only with the language of science is the bond dissolved.

We saw that language as breaking silence and language as λόγος show in each case the inner essential relation to truth in the sense of ἀλήθεια (unconcealment). This shows us what connection exists between concealment (the fact of truth) and language.[15]

---

§6. The double sway of the struggle (ἔδειξε–ἐποίησε) as indication of the connection between Being and truth

But all this should serve us only as a preparation for coming to grips with our leading task at this time. That task is indicated in our assertion that fragment 53 of Heraclitus, which gave us insight to the *essence of Being*, at the same time also gives us insight to the *essence of truth*, even though it apparently does not specifically and literally talk about ἀλήθεια.

We are now in a position to prove this assertion. According to the saying, the essence of essence (the essence of Being) is *struggle*—in its double role as progenitor and ruler. The second part of the saying clarifies the manner in which struggle holds sway: ἔδειξε–ἐποίησε. In our introductory interpretation, we already deliberately emphasized that we do not get to the decisive point with the usual, so-called literal translation. Instead: ἔδειξε—sets out; ἐποίησε—lets come forth. These translations are meant to indicate that a being comes into Being, in and through struggle, when it is set out. Set out—into where? Into the *visibility* and *perceptibility* of things in general; but this means into *openness*, unconcealment, truth. Likewise, ποιεῖν is not just a making; rather, it is the letting-go-forth in which the *forth* means forth out of the previous absence and concealment, into *the state of being set forth*, so that beings stand in openness, that is, *"are."*

Struggle brings beings into *Being*, and this means at the same time: struggle sets beings out into *unconcealment*, into truth. Therefore we really must expand the translation, always in keeping with the sense: struggle sets out and lets come forth—that is, into openness (truth).

If one understands truth as correctness or as some other characteristic, then certainly one will search the saying in vain for something about truth. But if we understand truth in a *Greek* way—that is, in the only way that is at all suitable for this archaic Greek saying—then it becomes

---

15. Correctness—measuring? Cf. later {[German] p. 121}.

immediately clear that it is "also" a discourse about truth. And we will have to ask: is this by *accident* or *inner necessity*? Presumably the latter, for the saying does not speak of πόλεμος as the rise of Being and then in addition about openness. Rather, the characterization of struggle as holding sway *is in itself discourse* about *setting out into openness*. What is this saying? *The essence of Being (of essence) stands in an inner connection with the essence of truth and vice versa*. But then our question, the guiding question of the essence of truth, is *in itself* and *necessarily* the question of the essence of Being.

And more than this. At the beginning of our work, when we were merely preparing the question, we already received an answer to the guiding question. And, as will be shown, this answer is the decisive one, namely, that the *essence of truth is essentially one with the essence of Being itself.*[16]

---

§7. The historical transformation of the essence of truth and Dasein

We are still far from measuring the full scope of this insight. But this realization allows us to grasp for the very first time what is happening with us today, with our people—and with human beings in general on this earth. This grasp of our history that we are striving for here has nothing to do with a philosophy of history that hobbles behind reality and dissects it after the fact. Instead, this grasp of Being compels us into struggle and transposes us into decisions that grasp out into the future and prefigure it.

But we must first conquer this realization about the essential connection of truth and Being and prepare the conquest through the corresponding questioning. With this in view, our interpretation of the saying of Heraclitus was only a first encounter with truth, which has only apparently sunk back into the nothingness of the past.

But above all, in order to really take part in knowing the essential connection of truth and Being, we must overcome the *great obstacle* that opposes a genuine insight into the essence of truth. And this obstacle is nothing less than the entire history of Western Dasein up to now, a history in whose tradition we stand, whose power now becomes all the more obstinate as the *great transformation of human Dasein* arises in a more originary and irresistible manner.

At this point, it is getting embarrassing that there are more and more people who believe they have discovered that liberalism must be refuted. Certainly it should be overcome, but only when we comprehend

---

16. Truth of the saying, and *each Dasein that* understands *this saying.*

that liberalism is just a marginal epiphenomenon, a very weak and late one at that, rooted in great and still unshaken realities. And there is the danger that the overzealous killers of liberalism will quickly turn out to be so-called "agents" of a liberal National Socialism, which just drips with the naive and upright innocence of the youth movement.

The question of the essence of truth has nothing to do with pitting some scholarly theory of the concept of truth against some other theory, nor with supporting some philosophical standpoint against another. We have neither desire, nor time, nor need for this. Rather, the question has to do with this alone: actively coming to grips, or failing to come to grips, with the moment of world history into which the spirit of this earth has entered. Everything else is superfluous, a waste of time.

But if this is how things stand with us, and we leave aside all the paraphernalia that pertain to a lecture like this on philosophy, according to the customary notions and expectations, and we contemplate that which we cannot attain without a struggle in our labor, then we see that we are under the power of, and entangled in, a tradition that sweeps over us in a manner that is as great and rich as it is petty and empty.

Our first encounter with Heraclitus gave us an indication of how to construct our questioning and move forward. This should tell us from now on that we will not and cannot think up the essence of truth from nowhere using empty concepts, or snatch it out of thin air without any standpoint. We will put the essence of truth to work only if we *put* our *own Dasein to decision* in its essence, that is, in the whole of its rootedness, commitment, and choice.

We can do this only if we know where we stand, what surrounds the place where we stand, *what tradition* rules over us without our knowing—and indeed rules over us so thoroughly and decisively that we believe that the usual conception of the essence of truth must have always been valid and above all remain valid.

----

§8. The disappearance of truth as un-concealment in the traditional transmission of the concept of truth

And what is this conception? We pointed it out before: truth grasped as *correctness*. It should be emphasized again and again that this characterization of the customary conception of truth is not complete, although it does indicate its fundamental framework.

a) The long-accustomed conception of truth as correctness. The agreement between proposition and thing

Correctness: to direct oneself by, to measure oneself by; the factual situation of measuring. Completely different is the factual situation of concealment. The latter at the inception; the former at the end. Today, no more ἀλήθεια. How did it come to this? Do the two have any connection at all? Or parallel to ἀλήθεια, a different concept? But then *how* are they still the same? And which conception of the essence of truth will be decisive for us in the future: ἀλήθεια or correctness, or both, or neither of the two? How do things stand with the concept of truth as correctness, and where does it come from?

1. Correctness = *agreement;* true propositions; correct: "This coin is round." *Agreement between proposition and thing*—that's as clear as it gets.

2. Likewise, this always comes up, entirely independent of the so-called philosophical standpoint: this concept of the truth is, so to speak, *the fundamental feature of a healthy common sense;* and thinkers of entirely different kinds have agreed on this point, for example, Kant no less than Thomas Aquinas.

Kant	"The explanation of the term truth, namely that it is the agreement of cognition with its object, is granted here and presupposed" (*Critique of Pure Reason*, A 58/B 82). Truth is "agreement of our concepts with the object" (ibid., A 642/B 670).
Thomas Aquinas	*Quaestiones de veritate*, question I.
Aristotle	*On Interpretation*, chapter 1. σημεῖον, σύμβολον; ὁμοίωσις [sign, symbol; likeness].[17]

These are not just three stages but three worlds—and yet in each case, there is *this fundamental notion of measuring up* that has a peculiar power from which human Dasein finds it hard to extricate itself.

All the more necessary, then, to go deeper into this conception of the essence of truth. This happened by way of a simple example: this coin is round. (Notice: earlier: truths—propositions.)

1. *The "aporia" of agreement.* A proposition is "correct," it "agrees," that is, it agrees with the thing. *Agreement:* a connection, a *relation*— and one of *difference.* Even equality is possible only between different things, even if this difference is only numerical (metaphysically). For example, two coins are equal, they agree with one another, they coincide in the same what-Being and appearance. Likewise, a truth: a true *proposition* as true "in agreement" with the thing. *Proposition and thing:* there is no question of their difference. The round coin that is made of

17. {On the traditional determination of truth, see also Appendix II, addenda 7-8.}

metal—the assertion that is nothing material at all. The coin is "round"—the proposition has no spatial form whatsoever. I can buy something with the coin—the proposition isn't legal tender at all.

So then, given this complete difference between proposition and thing, how is one supposed to agree with the other? By the way, one might say, if pressed, that every proposition, say, when it is written down on the blackboard, is after all something extended in space, that is, the letters and words. But this just makes it all the more clear *how little* one can talk here about "agreement" between something like a "proposition" and a thing like a "coin."

But obviously no one means the written form of the proposition as what must stand in agreement, but rather what the proposition *means*. Sure—but where is that, then? And does it have anything at all to do with the "coin"? Just as little as with a window, tree, street, sky, triangle or any other random thing.

As soon as we inquire into this just a bit more decisively and persistently, one difficulty after the other shows up, and what seemed clear and within our grasp, is completely dark and incomprehensible.

2. *The characterization of truth as correctness displaces truth into the proposition.* The statement is precisely that which is true or false. This conception is already found in Aristotle. This conception has, in the most recent times, developed into the notion of truth as "validity." *The proposition is valid.* In part, this is a way out from the difficulties of the theory of agreement; but it is a way out that really leads way off—a way not to be followed. It still insists that *the location of truth is the proposition;* the Being-true of the proposition is equivalent to and decides about the Being of things. The meaning of beings is nothing other than the Being-true of valid propositions about them. This is a last reflection of the essential relation between truth and Being, but now turned exactly on its head: truth is not based on Being, but Being on truth.

b) The last struggle between the earlier (inceptive) and later concept of truth in the philosophy of Plato

But these considerations regarding the reigning conception of truth have persuaded us that this concept is really very old, reaching far back into a tradition, all the way back to the Greeks—that is, into the time in which the other conception of essence prevailed. Why was this inceptive conception forgotten and driven back? What happened there? Is the later conception the deeper and more tenable one? Or is it the reverse: is the later conception the lesser one? Is its ascendance based on the fact that the inceptive and originary conception lost its power and became ineffective? And why?

Therefore, we are not so much asking when and with whom the reigning concept of truth qua correctness first arose; rather, we want to know what happened there, such that the reign of the inceptive and perhaps more originary concept of truth was dissolved by the concept that has long since become the customary one. We want to know this, not to enlarge our expertise for the exam in the history of philosophy, but rather to experience what powers are reigning over our Dasein when that Dasein stands under the dominion of the customary concept of truth.

How did the reigning concept of truth come to its reign? How did it repress the earlier one? What happened here? Is this happening still in effect today? In what way? And why is it that we seem to know nothing about it anymore? We want an answer to *these* questions with the intention of knowing how things stand with the *essence of truth*.

We will now trace the rise to power of the concept of truth that is customary today and its confrontation with the earlier concept. We will follow this most directly at the point where *the earlier and the later concepts collide, as it were, in a final struggle. That* happens in the philosophy of Plato. This philosophy is, as it were, nothing other than this collision. But we do not want to present this philosophy as a system, which it is not; we especially do not want to relate what Plato professed in logic, ethics, and the philosophy of nature, history, and religion. Fortunately, he did not yet philosophize in these academic categories.

We will come close to him only if we talk with him in the form of conversation in which he himself composed his work: in dialogues. In the course of one semester we might be able to come to terms with a single one of the many Platonic dialogues with some degree of thoroughness—and we would then have to set aside our guiding question. Therefore, we choose a solution that is in a certain way prescribed for us.

§9. The start of the investigation with the myth of the "allegory of the cave" as the center of Platonic philosophy

A passage is found in one of the great Platonic dialogues, the *Republic* or *Politeia*, at the beginning of book VII, that could really have a place in any Platonic dialogue. It presents, so to speak, *the single center of Platonic philosophizing*. First and foremost, this is not some arbitrary discussion and certainly not a disputation. Rather, it is the telling of a μῦθος, the μῦθος of the underground cave, known by the name of "the allegory of the cave."

Here we also have an opportunity to see how, in later Greek philosophy, μῦθος once again thrusts itself forward beside the λόγος that is really appropriate to philosophy. This can only be a sign that we stand in a decisive transition here, *decisive for two thousand years*. Plato always speaks in μῦθος when his philosophizing wants to say something essential with the greatest intensity.

The μῦθος speaks of a story—and in order to understand it, it is essential that we actually go through the story ourselves. I will not go into the usual interpretations of the μῦθος. Above all, we will not get caught up in technicalities of interpretation. It is clear that this interpretation cannot be achieved without real knowledge of the language, without mastery of Platonic philosophy, and without intimate familiarity with Greek Dasein in general. For us, it is not a matter of introducing the techniques and mastering the methods for interpreting Platonic dialogues; rather, it is a matter of *awakening and carrying out the question of the essence of truth.*

Therefore, for you, the authentic understanding of the μῦθος does not depend, in the first instance, upon whether you understand Greek well or badly or at all; it does not depend on whether you know much or little or nothing at all about Plato; rather, it depends on this alone: whether you are ready to take seriously the fact that you are sitting here in the lecture hall of a German university—that is, whether something unavoidable, something that has an enduring effect, speaks to you in the story of the underground cave that is to be interpreted.

PART ONE

Truth and Freedom:
An Interpretation of the Allegory of
the Cave in Plato's *Republic*

Chapter One
The Four Stages of
the Happening of Truth

§10. Interpretive procedure and the structure
of the allegory of the cave

Our answer to the question of the essence of truth had to pass through a decision. We cannot, as it were, think up the essence of truth in an indifferent rumination. Instead, what is at issue is the confrontation in history with the tradition of two fundamental conceptions of the essence of truth, both of which emerged among the Greeks: truth as unconcealment or truth as correctness. The *originary* conception as unconcealment gave way.

Here we cannot decide without further ado whether it was the inner superiority of the latter conception (correctness) that gave it the upper hand over the originary concept, or whether it was a mere inner *failure* that led to the predominance of the conception of truth as *correctness*. We must begin *at the point* where the two conceptions are still engaged in *struggle*.

Plato's philosophy is nothing but the struggle between these two conceptions of truth. The outcome of this struggle determined the spiritual history of the millennia to come. This struggle is found in Plato in *every* dialogue, but in its highest form it is found in the *allegory of the cave.*

The fact that we put the allegory of the cave into *this* context, that we see the struggle between the conceptions of truth in the story that the allegory tells, indicates a quite definite conception. The interpretation of the myth of the cave leads into the heart of Platonic philosophy.[1]

The story of the cave in Plato's Republic is found in book VII, 514a–517b. We cite the text of the Platonic dialogue by the edition of Henricus Stepha-

---

1. {Recapitulation at the beginning of the session of 5 December 1933, reproduced from the lecture transcript of Wilhelm Hallwachs. Cf. note 4, below.}

nus, 3 vols. (Paris, 1578), whose page numbers, and usually also the five subsections a-e, are printed in the margin of modern editions.[2]

We divide the text into *four sections*—and this means that we divide the whole story into *four stages*.

I. Stage 514a-515c.
The situation of the human being in the subterranean cave.
II. Stage 515c-e.
The liberation of the human being within the cave.
III. Stage 515e-516c.
The authentic human liberation into the light.
IV. Stage 516c-517b.
The look back and the attempt to return to the Dasein of the cave.

We proceed in such a way that we will elucidate each stage *on its own*, while attending from the start to the fact that the individual stages on their own are not what is essential, but rather what lies between them: the *transitions* from one to the next. This means that what is decisive is the whole course of the happening; our own Dasein should participate in completing this course, and should thus undergo movement itself. When, for instance, the first stage has been elucidated, we may not set it aside as something over and done with; we must take it along with us into the transition and the subsequent transitions.

At first I will always supply the translation of the text of the whole section, and then the interpretation will follow. It would be more convenient to refer you to the text or to one of the usual translations. But this is ruled out by the very fact that every translation is an *interpretation*.

The μῦθος is presented in such a way that Socrates tells the story of the cave to Glaucon, with whom he is conversing.[3,4]

2. {The basis for the text here is Heidegger's personal copy of *Platonis Opera*, ed. Ioannes Burnet (Oxford: Oxford University Press, 1899 sqq.), vol. 4.}

3. Cf. for what follows Winter Semester 1931-1932.

4. {Martin Heidegger's handwritten text for the lecture course of Winter Semester 1933-1934 ends here. For the main part of the course—i.e., the interpretation of the allegory of the cave and the *Theaetetus*—no new text was prepared. According to Heidegger's note above, the lectures that follow were delivered on the basis of the handwritten text of the lecture of the same name from Winter Semester 1931-1932. (See Martin Heidegger, *Vom Wesen der Wahrheit* (GA 34), ed. Hermann Mörchen. Frankfurt am Main: Vittorio Klostermann, 1988.) [English translation: *The Essence of Truth: On Plato's Cave Allegory and "Theaetetus,"* trans. Ted Sadler (London and New York: Continuum, 2002); this edition includes the German pagination.] Due to both textual and conceptual deviations from the text of 1931-1932, the following text of the lecture course of 1933-1934 is reproduced from the transcription by Wilhelm Hallwachs, which Heidegger preserved among his records. For more details, see the editor's afterword at the back of this volume.}

A. The first stage (514a-515c)
§11. The situation of the human being
in the subterranean cave

SOCRATES: Make an image for yourself of human beings in an underground, cave-like dwelling. Upwards, toward the daylight, it has an entrance that extends along the length of the whole cave. In this dwelling, human beings have been chained since childhood by the legs and neck. Hence, they remain in the same position and look only at what is *in front of* them {as we would say: what is present at hand before them}. {They can neither leave their place nor turn their heads.} They are unable to move their heads around because of the chains. But light {brightness} comes to them from behind, from a fire that burns far above. But between the fire and the prisoners {behind their backs} there runs a road along which, imagine, a little wall has been built, like the partitions that entertainers set up in front of an audience and over which they show their tricks.

GLAUCON: I see {I represent that to myself}.

SOCRATES: Now see, along this little wall, human beings carrying all sorts of implements that poke up over it: statues and other sculptures made of stone and wood, as well as all sorts of equipment designed by human beings. Some of the people carrying these things are talking, as is natural, and the others keep silent.

GLAUCON: You are introducing an odd image there, and odd prisoners.

SOCRATES: They are human beings like us. For is it your opinion that such creatures would see anything of themselves or others than the shadows that the firelight behind them casts upon the cave wall facing them?

GLAUCON: How else, if they are compelled lifelong to hold their heads immobile?

SOCRATES: But what about the equipment being carried by? Don't they see the very same thing, namely, its shadows?

GLAUCON: What else?

SOCRATES: If they were in a position to discuss with one another what they have seen, don't you believe that they would consider what they see to be actual beings?

GLAUCON: Necessarily!

SOCRATES: But what if the dungeon had a echo from the facing wall? Do you believe that whenever one of those passing behind them spoke, they would take anything but the passing shadows to be what was speaking?

GLAUCON: No, by Zeus!

SOCRATES: Therefore such people {these prisoners in the cave} would consider nothing else to be the unconcealed than the shadows of fabricated things.

GLAUCON: Absolutely!

The *first section* depicts the condition of human beings in the underground cave, which has its way out above, toward the daylight that nevertheless does not shine in. In the cave there are human beings chained by the legs and neck; they are forced to look straight ahead at the wall of the cave that faces them. Behind them burns a fire that casts a light. Between the fire and the prisoners there is a passageway behind a little wall; objects—implements and equipment—are carried back and forth along this passageway. Sometimes the carriers keep silent, sometimes they talk.

If there were an echo in the cave, then the prisoners would attribute the sounds of the words to the human beings they saw on the wall. This is the question: how does the presentation of this first stage end? With an explicit indication that what is at stake here is ἀλήθεια in the sense of the unconcealed. Socrates says that these prisoners would take nothing other than *shadows* of things to be the *unconcealed*. So the question is how these human beings relate and behave toward the ἀληθές, the unconcealed.

As strange as the condition of these human beings is, and as odd as the setting is, these human beings are nevertheless related to τὸ ἀληθές, to the unconcealed itself: human beings from childhood on, by their nature, are set forth into the unconcealed, no matter how strange their condition may be. Human beings are set forth in advance into the unconcealed, that is, into a connection to the things πρὸς τὸ πρόσθεν [facing what is in front of them]. *To be human* means to stand in the unconcealed and relate to it.

But precisely because of this, the question will arise: *what* is unconcealed to human beings in this condition? It is simply what they immediately encounter, what faces them. These are the shadows that the people behind them cast against the wall in the glow of the fire.

§12. What is unconcealed in the cave

This presentation is ambiguous and calls for more precision. The prisoners see the shadows, to be sure, but they do not see them *as* shadows. What *they* see, *we* call mere shadows. They themselves are not in a position to call what shows up on the wall in front of them shadows. For this, they would have to know about the fire and about the light that it casts. Yet the prisoners cannot know anything about all this.

Although *we* can ask what is unconcealed, this is a question that the prisoners have no occasion to ask. They have to take the shadows as beings themselves. They have not noticed that the light is behind them and comes from behind their backs. Here we must distinguish between *fire* and *light, lux* and *lumen,* the source of light and brightness (like door and doorjamb). We use the expression "light" in a double sense (source of light and brightness).

The people there have no relation to the fire and the light, so they are unable to tell bright from dark. What they see is not a *semblance of something else,* but *beings themselves,* τὰ ὄντα = that which is. Automatically, so to speak, the prisoners take what is played out in front of them as that which is.

If they could discuss among themselves, διαλέγεσθαι, what is given to them and encountered by them, that is, if they could talk about a thing among themselves . . . (It would be misguided to want to think here about dialectic and dialogue. *Plato's dialectic* has its roots here, insofar as beings are not communicated, but instead, what one encounters is first addressed as a being.—Connection between the *Being* of things and the *discourse* of language.) So if they could express themselves, they would address it without further ado as *what is.* Man is such that he *relates* to the *unconcealed* as something that is. We designate this relation of man to something that is as the *comportment* on the basis of which, and within which, man comports himself toward beings and stands in relation to them, as *Being* toward something that is. Beings as revealed.

We want to clarify the concept of *relationship.* An *animal* that comports itself thus and so. The animal cannot *comport* itself toward something that is, otherwise it would have to be able to speak. (Dog in relation to the bone!) We will encounter the fundamental relationship between animal and man again as we proceed.

These people really do not even have an experience of themselves and of the others. They see, at most, their own shadows, without recognizing them as such; they are completely given over to what is given. They have no relationship to themselves.

The unconcealed is not given to them as unconcealed. They are not familiar with the difference between the concealed and the unconcealed. They are completely gone, they are all eyes and all ears for what they are encountering.

This is quite a remarkable situation these people are in. Glaucon calls it ἄτοπον, a situation I don't know how to place anywhere, I have no *place* for it within what I am familiar with.

This situation is the everyday situation of man; it is not an exception but the situation of man in everydayness, insofar as he is given over to idle talk, to the customary, what lies closest at hand, the everyday, business as usual. Man in everydayness loses himself, forgets himself in the press of things.

Now, what is listed in this first characterization? The situation: *shadows; people in chains; fire and light,* a light that burns behind them; *people* who have no *relationship* to this; people who do not understand the *unconcealed.*

All these moments seem at first to be accidental elements in the depiction of this remarkable situation; but they are all connected. It is precisely this inner connection that constitutes what we will exhibit as the essence of truth.

If we restrict ourselves completely to the first stage, we must participate in all of this, completely caught up in what is playing itself out on the wall in front of us. Even there, and already there, what we know as ἀλήθεια, unconcealment, reigns. So we are not talking about truth as correctness, but as unconcealment.

B. The second stage (515c–515e5)
§13. A "liberation" of the human being within the cave

In our previous lecture,[5] we attempted to interpret more precisely the first stage of the people in the cave by bringing out the individual moments more precisely. We closed with a reference to the last sentence, which makes it clear that what is at stake is the ἀληθές, the unconcealed.

The unconcealed here is definitely and positively stated: it is not *some arbitrary* unconcealed but rather *the* unconcealed, such that human beings in *every circumstance* are *related* to the unconcealed and in the broadest sense stand in truth (and in untruth). To be human and to exist as human means, in the end: to stand in truth.

So then what is, in this circumstance, the unconcealed, the true? What is the unconcealed to *them,* then? The shadows! But they do not experience them *as* shadows. A precondition for that would be telling the difference between light and dark. That is impossible for them. The light and the source of light are at their backs. But they cannot turn themselves around. Accordingly, this arrangement of the illumination in the cave as a whole is essential to the status of the human beings, and so is their being chained.

The people address the unconcealed as *beings.* The unconcealed *is* what is. The people are not just in the unconcealed, they are in it through διαλέγεσθαι—first, in the sense of talking things through

---

5. {In the session of 5 December 1933. The recapitulation from the beginning of the session of 7 December 1933 has been inserted by the editor here.}

with one another. Second, this means the manner of talking and asserting in which beings are grasped in their Being: dialectic.

This is only a crude outline. We saw in the explication of the condition of the people in the cave that they are not in a position to experience themselves and others as beings; instead, they can experience only the shadows that they themselves cast. Therefore, they have in no way *reached* the distinction of light and dark and are entirely caught up in what the senses have to offer. Their condition is ἄτοπον, entirely exceptional, impossible to place. But precisely this condition is the *everyday* condition of human beings.

As we said before, we should not simply line the stages up one after another; instead, we must always carry forward with us what has been said about the previous stage. The first stage described the situation. The second stage must begin with a story, because it is about a story (a happening). *What* happens?

SOCRATES: Now envision what it would mean for someone to be released {λύσις} from the chains and have his lack of discernment healed, and consider what must necessarily and essentially occur as a consequence {οἵα τις ἂν εἴη φύσει},[6] if the following should happen: one of them is unchained and compelled suddenly to stand up, to turn his neck around, to go and to gaze upon the light. But he could do all this only in pain, and, owing to the blaze of the fire, he would be unable to look at those things whose shadows he saw previously. Assuming that all of this were to happen to the prisoner, what do you believe he would say if someone were to claim that previously he had seen empty nothings, but now he was nearer to beings and turned toward what is *more* a being so that he saw more correctly? And if someone were to show him each of the things being carried past {which he would now see directly} and compelled him to say what each one was, don't you believe that he wouldn't know how to begin, and would hold that what he had seen before was more unconcealed than what was now being shown to him?

GLAUCON: Absolutely!

SOCRATES: And surely if someone required him to look, not just at the things but now at the *light itself,* then wouldn't his eyes hurt, and wouldn't he turn away and flee back to what he had the capacity to see; and wouldn't he be of the opinion that these {namely, the shad-

---

6. [A conventional translation would be: "what would naturally be."] {Textual variant adopted by Heidegger from Schleiermacher's edition of Plato, 3rd edition (Berlin, 1855-1862). Cf. the lecture course of the same name from Winter Semester 1931-1932 (GA 34), p. 30 n. 1: "thus I read 515c5 with Schleiermacher."}

ows} were in fact clearer, more visible, than what one had just now
wanted to show him?
GLAUCON: That's how it is!

We see that in the second stage a story begins. History begins.[7] Something happens. The interpretation must now clarify what is happening
here and what, through the happening, is being said to us about the essence of truth.

The chains by which these prisoners are bound by leg and neck are
taken off. The question needs to be asked: What does this happening
bring with it (οἵα τις ἂν εἴη φύσει)? What must now happen by an essential necessity? Not some arbitrary event, but a happening that
touches the *essence of human beings*.

This is the question: what is the aim of the removal of the chains as
a happening? The happening makes it evident, {. . .}[8] ἡγεῖσθαι τὰ τότε
[he would hold that what (he had seen) before . . .]. Someone unchained in this way would have to hold that the ἀληθές he had previously seen was more unconcealed than what he was looking at now,
namely the things that he formerly had behind him and which he
now would see in front of him.

What is at issue again is the ἀληθές, but now in an entirely different sense: ἀληθέστερα (the comparative) = truer, more unconcealed.
Something is happening now with unconcealment. Unconcealment
starts to *move*, so to speak.

In the first stage, the following are connected with unconcealment:
chains, light, Being. But now that this unconcealment starts to move,
we get a first sense of *what* the relationship is between being enchained
and light, and between light and unconcealment.[9]

§14. Expanded conception of unconcealment in the failure of the first attempt at liberation

What is most striking is the talk of unconcealment in the comparative.
Unconcealment can be unconcealment to a greater or lesser degree.
This does not mean a numerical difference in unconcealment—not
shadows anymore, but *something else that is unconcealed*. The mode of
unconcealment has clearly changed. What the prisoner saw before

7. [*Geschichte* means either "story" or "history." Throughout his interpretation
of the allegory of the cave, Heidegger seems to trade on this ambiguity.]
8. {One word illegible here.}
9. {W. Hallwachs's note: "The inner relation of the enchained and the fact
that they are also interwoven??"}

and what he is looking at now—that is, the shadows and the things that used to be behind him—now move apart. Each has the fundamental property of being accessible, each is unconcealed.

Now they move apart; and in fact, now each is judged differently, as it is established that what is shown now *is* more, μᾶλλον ὄντα. Not only the true and unconcealed has degrees and levels, but so do beings. Something can be *in Being* to a greater or lesser degree; even man can be in Being to a greater or lesser degree.

The *increase* of unconcealment itself is perhaps just a consequence of a quite definite *nearness* of man to beings, a nearness that depends on the human way of Being in each case.

One point is now clear: truth and Being-true are not some indifferent, universal thing, not something immutable that remains the same for everyone. And not everyone has the same right to every truth, nor the same strength for it. Every truth has its time. Particular truths, particular human beings find their own time at particular times. It won't do to talk to everyone about everything. Truth has its degree, its rank, and its nobility—in each case according to the way in which man himself is worthy of standing near or distant from beings.

The nearness or distance changes the unconcealed, in a certain sense. The second point is an initial insight into the relation between the two forms of truth, *unconcealment* and *correctness*. In Plato, these two forms collided.

The one who is turned toward what *is more of a being,* toward what *is* more than something else, sees *more correctly,* ὀρθότερον. Correctness comes up in connection with unconcealment. The *correctness* of seeing and looking is based on the *bestowal* and *nearness* of Being in each case, on the way in which beings are revealed and unconcealed. *Truth as correctness is impossible without truth as unconcealment.*

When one has grasped this, one can only wonder how it was possible to attach the concept of truth exclusively to correctness or validity. In order for all discourse and defining to *direct* themselves toward something, beings must be unconcealed *in advance.* The concept of correctness already brings unconcealment with it.

The question of rank order is thereby already decided. The more originary and higher concept is truth as unconcealment. Truth as correctness is *grounded* upon it. Yet there are differences of opinion about what has more truth or Being.

We must ask: how does the unchained prisoner determine what he prefers if he turns back toward the shadows, and if he looks upon the shadows as the unconcealed—if, turned toward the shadows, he has calmly accustomed himself to that place, so that his eyes are no longer in pain from the blazing glow of the fire? He goes along with what he *likes,* what makes no *trouble* for him, what takes care of itself; he goes along with what demands no effort, with business as usual. The standard for his preference is the preservation of untroubled immunity to every demand, to every necessity. But now, what would provoke him to turn to the things themselves? After all, he is making quite an amazing effort to chase after the shadows.

So it is not enough just to take away the chains; he has to be turned around. The liberated man *resists,* because this liberation—that is, this removal of the chains—is supposed to happen *suddenly.* He is not cured when the chains are suddenly removed. He is not yet able to recognize what he used to see as shadows.

Instead of shadowy images, he is now placed before the light (the blazing glow) of things. He has no other possibility for comparison. On the one side he has the comfortable view of the shadows, on the other, the painful blaze. He will make an effort to escape his confusion and return to his peaceful condition.

Taking away the chains is *not an actual liberation,* it is only an external liberation. It does not take hold of the man in his *own Being.* It does not change his inner condition, his will. His will is a not-willing. He shrinks back and shrinks away from every demand. So he is also far from understanding that in each case, man *is* only as much as he has the strength to demand of himself.

The second stage, which looks like a liberation, remains a failure. We experience what is being said about the essence of truth by means of the second stage—over and above the first: now it is clear that human liberation, and the turn toward beings and the Being of things, cannot be carried out as long as the man does not know about the unconcealed *as* unconcealed. He is unable to make the *distinction,* for he has no insight into unconcealment: shadows, things, self, light, Being and beings.

How must we think the essential connection between *the Being-free of humans* and their *relationship to light, concealment, and unconcealment* if we want to grasp the *inner essential structure of truth* as such?

C. The third stage (515e5-516e2)
§15. The authentic liberation of the human being to the originary light[10]

In the last session we interpreted the second stage and by doing so we experienced that through the attempt at a liberation, two things were distinguished for the first time: what was previously seen, what we call the shadows, and what is now shown. At the same time, this distinction opens up a *difference* in kind whereby the things themselves

10. For the second stage was already a liberation to the light—but not really.

and the fire in the cave are addressed as the *truer*, as the *more revealed*, as what *is* more.

In turning toward what *is* more, looking and asserting must also be formed *more correctly*. This is the first passage where we encounter the *doubling of the concept of truth*. At the same time, this passage shows us that *truth as correctness is grounded upon truth as unconcealment.*

It might now be assumed that the liberated prisoner willingly turns toward the truer Being; however, this is absolutely not the case. On the contrary, we experience that the man who has been rid of his chains wants to go *back* to the shadows, because he takes them for what is truer. We saw that the absence of all compulsion, of all pain, was decisive for him; what he saw previously (the shadows) is considered more comfortable.

Why does it come to this? The liberation happens suddenly. It brings confusion with it because of the brightness and the glare of the light. It is obvious that such a *turning around* requires a slow *rehabituation* and that before the latter is embarked upon, one cannot speak of an *authentic* liberation. This attempt at liberation as merely removing the chains will not be taken up again in the third stage.

SOCRATES: But if someone were now to drag him {the one rid of his chains} by force along the rough, steep ascent from the cave and not let go of him until he had pulled him out into the light of the sun, wouldn't the one who was dragged feel pain and resist, and as soon as he came into the brightness, his eyes full of the glare, wouldn't he also be unable to see even one of the things that he was now being told were the unconcealed?

GLAUCON: No, at least not immediately.

SOCRATES: In my opinion, it would require a habituation for him to see what is above. And surely at first he would most easily be able to look at shadows, and next, in water, the mirrored reflections of human beings and other things, and only later {the things} themselves. And among these {the things themselves and no longer the shadows and reflections}, he will more easily observe at night those found in the heavens and firmament itself, looking into the brightness of the stars and moon. He will be able to look at them more easily than he would look by day at the sun and its light.

GLAUCON: Certainly!

SOCRATES: So, finally, in my opinion, he will be able to gaze not just at the reflection of the sun in water and elsewhere but at the sun itself as itself, in its proper place, and observe how it is.

GLAUCON: Necessarily.

SOCRATES: And next he will come to the conclusion about it {the sun} that it is what bestows the seasons and governs the years and every-

thing that has a visible place and that it is also the ground for everything that they {in the cave} saw in a certain way {and so is also the
ground for the possibility of the shadows in the cave}.

GLAUCON: Obviously, he would arrive at this conclusion after the other
{one after the other}. {At the same time, this rehabituation distinguishes the different regions.}

SOCRATES: What then, if he were to remember the first dwelling, and
the wisdom of that place, and those who were prisoners with him
back then? Don't you believe that he would count himself lucky for
the reversal that happened to him, but pity those others?

GLAUCON: Very much so!

SOCRATES: And what if back then {in the cave} they had among themselves agreed on honors, praise, and awards for the one who sees
the things passing by the most sharply and best keeps in mind what
tends to pass by before and after and at the same time, and who
thus is most ready to predict what will come within this realm of
shadows? Do you believe that he would long for such {honors} and
that he would envy those who stand in renown and power among
the people down there? Or wouldn't he much prefer to endure what
Homer speaks of, namely "to serve some other impoverished man
for hire,"[11] and wouldn't he prefer to take anything upon himself
rather than to take these {the shadows} as the true, the unconcealed, and to live like that {like the prisoners}?

GLAUCON: In my opinion, yes. He would rather suffer anything else
than live in this way.

You can already see roughly that the third stage brings about an
authentic liberation.

In the third stage, a *second* attempt at liberation occurs in which the
one rid of his chains is *dragged* out, *hauled* out of the cave into the *daylight,* where it becomes possible to experience particular appearances,
shadows, mirror images in water, and so forth, and finally daylight and
the *sun.*

In the third stage we see the *core* of the whole story, because we
grasp the connections: the connection between shadow and light,
concealment in shadow and unconcealment in light; all of this, in
turn, in connection with the opposition between *enchained* and *liberated.* The question in the third stage is how, in this story, the essence
of truth gets clarified.

11. {*Odyssey* XI, ll. 489-90.}

§16. Liberation and unconcealment.
Four questions about their connection

We already saw from the rudimentary content of this stage that this liberation no longer consists in the *negative*, but in climbing up to the light of day, and thus also in *passing beyond* artificial light, the fire in the cave. But here, too, the aim is truth: τὰ νῦν λεγόμενα ἀληθῆ,[12] what is addressed *now* in this liberation as unconcealment.

We were observing the *situation of the human being*, whether in chains or freed. Each situation, each stage, has its *own* kind of unconcealment and truth. *The kind and manner of truth depends on the kind and manner of the human being.* This is not to say that truth is *subjective*, that it depends on arbitrary human preference. That is not the case at all.

1. The transition to what is now unconcealed happens βίᾳ [by force]. The one found in the cave must be dragged out. The *liberation is violent.* It involves acts of violence, and thus a *resistance* on the part of the man; he does not want to leave his old situation at all. The climb is onerous, along a rough path. Liberation demands effort. Here, what is distinctive about *Greek* Dasein comes to light.

    The Dasein of the Greeks is not as most prep-school teachers present it—not lying on one's back in the sun, not golden blessedness and cheer, but a great, immense *struggle* with the most immense and darkest powers, a struggle that is apparent in Aeschylus' tragedies. The rough path is the last remembrance of this struggle. Liberation is no walk in the park.

2. Neither undoing the chains nor merely coming out of the cave is enough for the liberation to reach its goal and succeed. The *authentic* happening of the liberation first begins *outside* the cave by way of the man's *rehabituation*, συνήδεια—a slow, steady rehabituating, in which he slowly grows familiar with what is out there; this means with the *brightness* out there, with the light, not so much with the particular things.

    The reeducation takes this direction first: the man's gaze (i.e. his comportment) is at first guided toward what, outside the cave, has a certain kinship with what was in the cave. So at first he does not understand the light and the sun, but his eyes are drawn to the shadows, to the reflections. This is why he also sees best at night, by the stars and moon. At first he gets used to dim light.

3. Only once his gaze has slowly been rehabituated do his eyes get used to the daylight and to *what* is in the daylight, and *finally* to

---

12. [Reading ἀληθῆ for ἀλήθεια. See German p. 167, below, and *Republic* 516a3.]

the *source* of light, the *sun*, which is not only *light* but also rules over *time*, as the cause of time. Then as now, time was measured by the sun. The sun says what time it is; time is bound to it.

Time and all that shows itself depends on the sun and its light. The sun is the ground of Being and of all that man encounters there, even of every worn-out {?}[13] and manmade fire, and thus even the fire in the cave. All this first becomes intelligible by virtue of the sun. The sun itself is *the ground of all Being.*

4. The *authentic* liberation demands not only violence but *endurance*, a long *courage* that is sufficient to run through the stages in all their heights, a courage that can endure setbacks. Only this intimate acquaintance with the stages in their necessary order can ensure success.

When we get clear on the whole situation and the whole happening, according to this interpretation, everything seems to be transparent and clear. Only one difficulty remains: what is this whole happening supposed to mean? After all, the whole thing is an allegory.

The starting point is precisely a sensory image of the life of human beings as they live *outside* the cave. But what does the life of human beings outside the cave signify?

An interpretation can be found in Plato himself (517b ff.): the cave is the picture of human beings as living on earth under the vault of heaven. We are, in a way, in a cave. The fire in this cave is the sun. The shadows are the things we deal with. But what does the stage *outside* the cave depict? This "outside" means the sojourn of man in the place *above* the vault of heaven (ὑπερουράνιος τόπος) [*Phaedrus* 247c], that is, the place of the *idea*. The sun is nothing other than the *highest* of the ideas, the *idea of the good.*

Now, we do not yet know *what an idea is.* The fire in the cave is the sun, its shining is the light of the sun, the shadows are what we see every day. We are, in a way, prisoners, inasmuch as we are bound to the self-evident, to business as usual.

What do we encounter if we exit the cave? Can we still get out of the cave? What does that mean?

We saw that what is being discussed in the third stage is rehabituation to the light. That is the authentic process of liberation, whereby the things outside become visible in the right way. Here too, a connection between light and freedom, unconcealment and Being is apparent—an obscure connection, to begin with.

---

13. [*Abgängig:* the editor has marked this reading as uncertain. It is possibly a misreading of *abhängig*, "dependent."]

A new world emerges: the world of the ideas, which is represented by the heaven above heaven. We are faced with *four questions:*

1. What is the connection between idea and light?
2. What is the connection between light and freedom?
3. What is the connection between freedom and beings?
4. What is the essence of truth as unconcealment that now comes to light from these three connections?

For the moment I will leave aside the idea of the good. Plato already treated it in detail earlier, in book VI. We will come back to the question of the connection between the good and the idea only at the end of the story, in the context of the whole. Only on that basis will we be able to enter into the confrontation with the Platonic conception that determined the next two millennia.

---

§17. On the concept of the idea

a) Preliminary remark on the significance of the doctrine of the ideas in the history of spirit[14]

What is the connection between idea and light? What does idea mean?

With this question, we touch upon a fundamental element—indeed, upon the *fundamental constitution*—of our Western historical Dasein. With the help of what Plato's doctrine of the ideas prepared, the Christian concept of God was conceived. This became the standard for the next millennia, for what is genuinely real and unreal. The doctrine of the ideas became the standard for the conception of the Being of things in general.

Secondly, at the beginning of modernity, Plato's doctrine of the ideas developed and helped to form the modern concept of reason and of rational natural science. Even Romanticism depends on the reign of the idea.

Rationalism and the idea of God come together in the highest completion of Western thinking, in Hegelian philosophy. It is no accident that *Hegel* himself identified himself as the one who had completed Western philosophy, to the extent that it is the Greek world reconstructed in a Christian way.

From here, there developed in the nineteenth century: 1. *Marxism's* doctrine of ideologies, which can be understood only on the basis of Hegel; 2. the new interpretation of Christianity through *Kierkegaard.*

---

14. {On this point, cf. the lecture of the same name of Winter Semester 1931-1932 (GA 34), appendices 3 and 4, pp. 324-25.}

These ideas, blended and made innocuous, produced the characteristic picture of cultural philistinism that finally drove *Nietzsche* to despair.

Nietzsche saw the coming struggle in advance. Nietzsche struggles on three fronts: a) with *humanism;* b) with a *baseless Christianity;* c) with the *Enlightenment.* In keeping with the urgency of the circumstances, he drew his weapons from these three armories themselves.

Since then, there has been no further clear, originary, spiritual-historical position or attitude left for human beings. Only mishmash! Human beings today are no longer able to see and to experience their own position on the earth. They will once again be able to do so from the moment that they experience the fundamental condition for doing so, namely, the necessity of coming to a *decision* in the face of the essential powers of humanity in general, Dasein itself, in so far as the powers of humanity press upon them and compel them to a choice.

This tremendous moment into which National Socialism is being driven today is the coming to be of a *new spirit of the entire earth.* In this perspective, it must become plain what it means to get clear about this and about much else.

The doctrine of the ideas contains living powers that still dominate us even today, even if they are entirely flat and unrecognizable. We are asking ourselves systematically about the connections from which something like the idea of the doctrine of the ideas grew.

b) The fundamental orientation of knowledge toward "seeing" and what is seen

When we look at our circumstances with an eye to this history, we might say: inasmuch as our everyday circumstances are depicted by the condition of the human beings in the cave, we human beings are given over to the everyday—by that which offers itself to us, by the shadows on the wall. What all this means is that, in carrying on in this way, we are not with genuine beings and not in genuine truth.

There is out beyond this something else, which is depicted by the daylight—or to speak without images: *the idea.* The word "idea" comes from ἰδέα (εἰδεῖν), with the root *vid-*, in Latin *videre*, to see. ἰδέα means: what *is seen in seeing.*

The question is simply this: what is it that is seen in seeing, what is it that we see in seeing? In other words, what does "seeing" mean?

If we proceed from the natural concept of seeing, seeing means a *behavior*, the fact that we *perceive* something with the *eyes:* benches, book, door.—But with what do we see, really? If we look more closely into whether we in fact see the book with our eyes, do we see it with our eyes? What do we see with them?

This becomes plain if we contrast it to what we *hear* with our *ears*. We perceive something, hear noises. We see colors, brightness, illumination, bright-dark. But we don't just see colors, but rather the whole shape, the spatial form. But things already get difficult here, for the spatial shape is not given in seeing alone. I can also feel it. Movement is not just given through seeing. I can also hear it: for example, a car.

The perception of spatial shape is no longer limited to *one* sense organ. With the eyes, we perceive only color and illumination. We call perception with the eyes or with the senses in general *sensation*. Seeing colors as sensation! But if we see this book, are we sensing it? No! We sense only the particular coloration. There is no sensation of the book cover. We do not see the book at all; at most we see a specific color, but never the book.

And nevertheless we say: I see the book! I see and I do not see. Thus the expression and term "seeing" is *ambiguous*.

The question is whether seeing with the eye is the originary seeing or whether seeing with the eye is a specific mode of seeing, whether something like the eye is integrated into the process of seeing. Why should the organ for seeing be the eye in particular?

The organic composition of the sense organs is, taken purely *metaphysically, accidental.* Any other apparatus would alter nothing in seeing. The organ as *organ* is not essential; rather, what is essential is the behavior into which the organ is integrated. The eye does not see at all. It is just a *passageway,* not an endpoint; it is not the seer's own seeing. The eye can never see a book.

From this we see that the expression "seeing" has a remarkable breadth that, we must now suspect, is attached to words in the Greek world—to the meaning and the concept of ἰδέα.

Our designation for cognition in general and for *theoretical* scientific cognition is also drawn from this connection to what is seen. "Theoretical" comes from θεωρεῖν, which means nothing other than looking, seeing. *Knowing is oriented to the fundamental phenomenon of the idea and of what is seen.*

The connection between *idea* and *light* is no accidental one; rather, light is a condition for the possibility of experiencing what is visible, whether living or not. On what paths and in what phases did the natural concept of seeing achieve this expansion, such that what is seen means that which, as *idea,* constitutes *genuine Being* and *reality?*

§18. Idea and light

a) On the idea in the context of Platonic thought.
The priority of seeing and its broader concept[15]

We attempted to decide how to ground the determination of the essence of truth through a confrontation with Platonic philosophy, to begin with, because it is in this philosophy that the concepts of truth, having come to life, are set forth in such a way that the one—the concept of correctness—gains the upper hand, while the other—the concept of unconcealment—moves into the background.

We have interpreted what really happens *inside* the cave and the liberation of the man *from* the cave. We attempted to extract the core content. In this attempt, we ran up against the need to interpret the whole allegory *in advance*. Plato shows what this allegory exhibits as a *sensory image of human Dasein*.

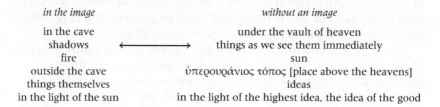

in the image	*without an image*
in the cave	under the vault of heaven
shadows ⟷	things as we see them immediately
fire	sun
outside the cave	ὑπερουράνιος τόπος [place above the heavens]
things themselves	ideas
in the light of the sun	in the light of the highest idea, the idea of the good

Now, what does Plato mean by the ὑπερουράνιος τόπος [place above the heavens]? What does the "idea" mean, and what does the idea of the good mean? What we call ideas develop for the first time in the context of Platonic thought. The discovery of the idea is to be made understandable on the basis of the inner context of Plato's way of posing questions.

The entire spiritual Dasein of the West is determined to this day by this doctrine of ideas. Even the concept of God arises from the idea, even natural science is oriented toward it. Christian and rationalist thought are combined in *Hegel*. Hegel, in turn, is the foundation for currents of thought and worldviews, above all for *Marxism*. If there had been no doctrine of ideas, there would be no Marxism. So Marxism cannot be defeated once and for all unless we first confront the doctrine of ideas and its two-millennia-long history.

For the moment, we want to restrict ourselves to the allegory of the cave. What does the word "idea" mean for Plato—and thus for the entire history of the spirit? What connection is there between the idea

15. {Recapitulation at the beginning of the session of 19 December 1933.}

and what is presented in the image as the sun, fire, and light? What does light mean? What is the connection between idea and light?

Ἰδέα (ἰδεῖν, to see) = what is seen, what is perceived in seeing. Now, what does "seeing" mean here? Seeing as perceiving with the help of the eyes. We see the book, so we say. But if we look more precisely at what we actually see with the eyes, distinguishing it from what we hear from the ears, we reach the conclusion that with the eyes, we see things such as color, brightness, and something shiny.

But we also say: we see that something is moving. But we hear this too. For example, we hear that a car is getting closer or farther away. But the perception of things in motion is not restricted to the senses of hearing and seeing. I can also feel it. The proper domain for visual perception is color, brightness, clarity. So we really cannot say: we see the book. And the dog does not "see" the book either, nor can it ever see it; it sees something colored.

If we now say, despite all this, that we see the book, then we are using a concept that is *broader* than seeing as sensory perception. This broader concept becomes definitive for ἰδεῖν and ἰδέα. So, in the strict sense, I cannot see the book.

b) The seeing of what-Being. Idea and Being: presencing—self-presence in the view

But we can say: I see *in* this given, tangible, audible, visible, graspable thing that it is a book. I see this *in* it. What is given offers me *in*sight, a *look at* a book. So that *as which* something offers itself (as chalk, as book, as lamp) is that within which the relevant thing presents itself, that is, exhibits its *self-presence*.

The Greeks call the presentness of a thing *Presence*. Presentness is equivalent to *Being* for them. οὐσία = presence, that as which a thing is presencing; that which is its essence, or in short, its Being; that as which a thing offers itself, what a thing looks like = εἶδος. ἰδέα is just another form of the word εἶδος. ἰδεῖν: the seeing of a thing. ἰδέα: the appearance, the look that it offers; that in which something shows itself *as it is;* what something looks like, the appearance of something.

For the Greeks, the *idea* is nothing other than *Being,* what something is: the Being that pertains to it.

If we look more closely, supposing that our comprehension were limited to the realm of what the things give us—color, brightness, and the like—if we had only all these as givens, then we would have no *world* at all.

I can identify this thing in front of me as a book only insofar as I know and understand in advance what a book is. If we did not have the *understanding,* the possibility of seeing this book *as* a book could never come up. But instead there is a distinctive *advance knowledge of things* on the basis of which the particular, factual things in each case are given to us in their Being-such-and-such, and can become accessible.

In the first stage, the prisoners see only shadows, because they are in chains and are incapable of knowing anything about fire and light, because they are given over only to the shadows, which are the only things they accept as the given. We, in everyday Dasein, are given over to the *things*, we comport ourselves toward them in the opinion that we see a thing and just need to open our eyes. In this we know nothing about the fact that at bottom, in experiencing a thing we must already know about the essence of things *in advance*.

c) The essence of light and brightness:
transparency that is perceived and seen in advance

The prisoner in the cave must be freed and led out, he must reach a realm in which he sees the *light* (the idea as daylight). The *light* is the *sensory image* of the *idea*.

What fundamental function do the idea and light have in common? What is the *essence of light*?

We already indicated earlier [German p. 132] that we must distinguish linguistically between

> φῶς: light, brightness, *lumen* and
> πῦρ: fire, *source* of light, *lux*.

Our word "light" has the double meaning of φῶς and πῦρ. φωσφόρος (phosphorus) is a thing that carries a *source of light* with it, an illuminator, a *bearer* of brightness.

What does light mean? What is the essence of light? On what basis can the essence of the *idea* be depicted in a sensory image as *light*?

Our concept of *cognition* is oriented to *seeing* and *light*. Theoretical cognition, theory (θεωρία), is looking, perceiving in the broadest sense. It is no accident that later, in Christian speculative thought (already in Augustine), *God* is conceived as the *lumen*. In distinction from God we have the *natural* light of *reason* (*lumen naturale*).

So in what does the essence of light consist? Color is the sort of thing that belongs in the domain of sight; but obviously brightness is not something thinglike. We cannot grasp brightness as if it were some thing. Brightness is, as it were, ungraspable—like the nothing, like emptiness.

Nevertheless, for centuries already there have been theories of light (Newton; the particle theory, the wave theory, the electromagnetic theory, etc.). All these theories may be correct as physical theories, and yet they can be untrue and miss the *phenomenon*. They cannot illuminate the *essence* of light. The issue here is not periodic changes of condition, it is not a question of comprehending the process as one of movement; the issue is *the* clarity and *the* light in which we *human beings* move—the essence of light itself. We can grasp light only if we hold firmly to the phenomenon, tying it to our *natural seeing and looking.*

Even *looking* is not explained either in physiology or in psychology, because looking, in its highest, proper sense, is a *phenomenon* that is not reached at all by any natural science—for example, when one human being looks another in the eye.

Let us see how things stand with brightness and darkness. We see something colored, sparkling, glittering. If we say in addition that we *also* see bright and dark, we do not get at the sense of the matter. We always see bright and dark to begin with. When we wake up from sleep, we never see things, to begin with, but bright and dark. However, bright and dark are not just *also* seen, but are the *condition* for the fact that I see or do not see *things in general.*

Brightness and darkness have a certain *priority,* consisting in the fact that brightness and darkness *make it possible* for something to be seen or not to be seen. From this we can gather that brightness and darkness are always what we already see *in advance;* we gather that we always see things and light together, and in the darkness we no longer see. Light, brightness, darkness are what is seen in advance in all perceiving. Things must first stand in the light in order to be visible.

Now, what does brightness mean? What does the bright really bring about in the human seeing and grasping of things? The [German] word *Helle* [brightness, clarity] comes from *Hallen* [resounding], so originally it does not belong in the domain of the visible, but in the domain of tone, of sound. A tone can be clear or muted. Clarity is not originally a special characteristic of the *visible,* but it was first transferred to the visible in *language.* We speak of a clear, bright day. But this transference is not accidental; it emerged from many insights. Here again, the deep truth of language reveals itself.

If a transference has taken place here, we must ask: what do *clarity* (as a fundamental property of tone) and *light* have in common? The clear tone, that is, the resounding tone, can be intensified into a *shrill* [gellenden] tone. The nightin*gale* is what *shrills* through the night. The muted tone is left behind.

The clear and the shrill have the character of the *piercing.* This is the moment that links light and tone: light, too, spreads and penetrates; it *enables the piercing quality of sight.* Light and the clear are the transparent, what one can see through. The *essence of clarity and light* consists in *enabling one to see through,* in being transparent. Chalk is not transparent. Glass and water are transparent.

But clarity, brightness, is transparent in a different sense than glass is. To be transparent, a glass requires light—it still needs light and its "transparency." Light and brightness are a *more originary* form of the transparent; they are what *makes it possible* for us to see-through.

Darkness is only a limit case of brightness, that which no longer lets our gaze pass through. A wooden wall is also impenetrable, because it does not have the possibility of letting the gaze pass through. But darkness has the possibility of being penetrated by the gaze.

The character of light is what lets through, the character of darkness is what blocks the way of the gaze. To sum up the character of each: a) light is what is perceived and seen in advance, and b) as such, light is also what lets the gaze and seeing pass through.

On the basis of this *double* characterization it is not hard to clarify how *light* can emerge as the sensory image of the *idea*. ἰδέα = εἶδος, appearance of something, what a thing is, its what-Being, in short: its *Being*. I must already understand (see) *in advance* what a thing is—book, door, window. This understood *essence* (book, door, window) is what lets the gaze pass through in order to see it as a *thing* (book, etc.)—that which must be known in advance in order to let a being be encountered as *this* being.

Accordingly, the *seeing of ideas* does not signify anything fantastic, but rather something *originary*. For to grasp what is simplest and press it into words, to understand the Being and essence of things in advance = *understanding of Being*.

If man did not have this understanding of Being in the ground of his essence, then he could not even relate to beings; he could not say "I" to himself and "you" to another. He could not speak. The essence of language and the sight of the ideas are the same as existing as a human being.

This perceiving of shadows, coming into the light, and perceiving of things, are connected to undoing the chains, to the liberation from the cave. The next question is: what connection is there between *light* and *freedom*, between *idea* and *freedom*?

What is the entire contexture of what we call the essence of truth?

---

§19. Light and freedom

a) On the determination of man on the basis of seeing, hearing, and speaking

The elements that constitute the inner connection in Plato's story are the following:

1. idea and light;
2. light and freedom;
3. freedom and beings;

4. the question about the connection between all these factors and truth.

We have previously attempted to clarify *idea* according to its essence. The word ἰδέα is related to a fundamental fact about the conception of human beings in Greek Dasein (and therefore in the entire spiritual life of the West, too). In this conception of human beings, visual comprehension, θεωρεῖν (from which "theory" derives) takes on a predominant role—the eye, seeing. Accordingly, *the seen* becomes especially preeminent in the comprehensive conception of the world.

But alongside this, another fact also emerges, even if late—that is, first with *Aristotle*—a fact that rules over Greek Dasein as essentially as ideas and seeing. This is *hearing*. Indeed, Aristotle asks whether hearing might not somehow be the higher sense and, accordingly, whether it might condition the higher comportment of human beings.

In this context, hearing and seeing are not conceived of as confined to mere sense perception; rather, they are taken more broadly, as listening to what has been spoken, hearing the word of the other. *Language* is the fundamental element of the being-with-one-another of human beings. For the Greeks, *discourse* is a defining moment for the essence of human beings. The human being is a ζῷον λόγον ἔχον, that is, the sort of living being that has the capacity for talk, the sort that, insofar as it exists, *speaks out* to others.

This hearing the other, and at the same time, one another, is therefore no merely acoustic phenomenon; rather, it means hearing a summons, lending an ear to a wish, listening to an order, assignment, and so on.

In the same context [*Politics* 1.2], Aristotle also says that the human being is a ζῷον πολιτικόν [usually translated "political animal"]. This phrase was later much abused, as when one translated it as, "The human being is a *social* being." But this is not what is meant here; rather, the human being is the sort of living being that belongs from the start to a *with-one-another in the state*. This with-one-another cannot be understood as based on the fact that there are many human beings whom one must keep in order; instead, we belong with one another to the state, we exist on the basis of the state. And this existence fulfills itself and takes shape through discourse, λόγος. The science that is concerned with the ability to talk, *rhetoric*, is the fundamental science of human beings, the *political* science.

In this connection we understand by what right, even in the face of the overpowering definition of the human being as *seeing ideas*, Aristotle nevertheless arrived at the question of whether *hearing* does not have preeminence. But the issue did not reach a complete decision. Therefore, both definitions were later misinterpreted and reinter-

preted: λόγος was taken as reason. The idea itself was also misinterpreted. (We will come back to this later.)

So, what is the meaning of idea? It is the look of things that we already have in view in advance when we see individual things, when
we want to grasp this and that. ἰδέα = *Being that is viewed in advance.*

Now, about *light.*

1. Light, if we are to take this phenomenon as we immediately
   experience it, gives itself to us as that which we always view in
   advance in the sense of bright and dark, even if we do not grasp
   it objectively.
2. We have shown that brightness is the *transparent,* the *penetrating,*
   that which seeks and creates a way through, what *allows a way
   through.*

From this, we will now arrive at the common feature of *idea and
light,* which will enable us to see how the idea is depicted by the sensory image of light. Idea and light enable us to grasp beings, to provide us with a connection and pathway to individual things, to what
they are.

b) Freedom as binding oneself to the illuminating

We must provisionally outline what *freedom* means, not arbitrarily according to some random concept, but rather by holding to what the
story in the allegory itself shows us.

The *second stage* resulted in *one* mode of liberation, the third in *another.* The liberation in the second stage is nothing other than the removal of the chains on the neck and legs. Liberation here is therefore
a mere taking-away of something, becoming free from something, no
longer being bound by something. Hence, the second stage means *lack
of restraint,* therefore something *negative.* Someone liberated in this
way consequently falls into confusion; he is helpless as soon as he
gazes into the fire and wants to go back to the chains. What he really
seeks is *support, certainty,* and *stability:* these are what he finds lacking
in the supposed liberation at the first stage.

The *third stage* does not merely take away the chains, but leads the
human being up and out of the cave into the light. Now, *to be free* is not
to be released from something but to be led forth to something. Not to
be free from, but to become free *for something*—for the light.

In this, a step-by-step habituation to the light takes place. Habituation is nothing but becoming increasingly accustomed and binding
oneself to the light and the source of light; habituation is *binding oneself
to the self-binding and becoming accustomed to the light,* putting oneself
under the *binding obligation* of what the things in the light demand,
and willing this.

We therefore see *two different modes of liberation* (or of freedom). The latter stands in connection with the light, *freedom in the positive sense.* We see that to become free in the authentic sense means to bind oneself to the light, to habituate oneself to it.

How are looking into the light and habituating oneself to the light an *increase in freedom?* Light and brightness as what illuminates. But light has yet another characteristic that is also expressed in language. Compare Schiller: "Bright as day the night is lit."[16] The night is permeable, something like a forest clearing free of trees, so that it allows a view through it. Light liberates, it sets free a passage, an opening, an overview; it clears. The dark is cleared, goes over into the light.

Binding oneself to the light is what liberates. Binding oneself in this way is the highest relation to freedom, is being-free itself.

§20. Freedom and beings (Being)

a) Freedom as binding oneself to the essential law of Dasein and of things

Freedom, to be free, means to bind oneself to what makes one free, what lets one through, the penetrable, or to speak without images: the *ideas,* which are depicted in a sensory image as light.

The ideas give the appearance of beings, that is, their *Being.* Becoming free for the light means making the effort to authentically understand what things are, *binding oneself to the essential law of things* on the basis of which we first grasp things in their Being-such-and-such.

The freer we become and the more originally we bind ourselves to the essential laws of things, the nearer we come to beings and the more we *come to be.* In each case, the degree and the extent of human *actuality* depends on the degree and the greatness of human *freedom.* This freedom is not lack of restraint; rather, it is all the greater the more originary and broad the *binding* of man is, the more that in his comportment, man sets his Being back into the *roots* of his Dasein, into the fundamental domains into which he is thrown as a historical being.

These are theses and things that man today finds difficult to understand. All scientific cognition secures *nearness* to beings only if it grows from a *historical* binding of man to Dasein.

16. "Das Lied von der Glocke," v. 192. [In Friedrich Schiller, *Sämtliche Werke in 5 Bänden,* vol. 1: *Gedichte* (Munich: Hanser, 2004), pp. 429–42; and see "The Song of the Bell" in *The Poems of Schiller,* trans. E. P. Arnold-Foster (New York: Henry Holt, 1902), pp. 246–59.]

(This is not being said for purposes of the "Alignment."[17] Nor is it necessary for me to defend myself. . . .[18] If one now demands of scholars that they subscribe to a proclamation that all science is grounded. . . . This all indicates that today, our Dasein is confused. A transformation of our entire Dasein is necessary, a transformation that can come about only step by step, and cannot be dealt with by knowledge alone.)

b) The view of essence that reaches ahead as a projection of Being (with examples from nature, history, art, and poetry)

The point is that *freedom means binding to the essential law of humanity. Originary* binding means a binding that must *take place in advance;* we do not first grasp essence on the basis of the greatest possible investigation of facts, but instead, we can determine facts only once we have comprehended the essence of things.

This is the *fundamental condition for all sciences.* I will give some examples here to show that all comportment, even the knowing comportment toward beings, even scientific comportment, is grounded on an *originary view of essence* that must develop in each case according to the depth of human beings.

Let us think of particular great discoveries about nature (by Kepler, Newton, Galileo). What is the basis for the great achievements of these much-admired natural scientists from the beginning of modernity? What is the difference between modern natural science and that of antiquity? One may say that modern science introduced the *experiment.* But that is an error. Neither does the meaning of modern science lie in the fact that, in contrast to the earlier, qualitative form of observation, quantitative observation gained ground—"mathematization"!

Both things already existed among the Greeks, and both fail to characterize modernity, because both have the decisive point as their *condition of possibility:* namely, that Galileo, with the means of ancient physics, established a *new fundamental position toward actuality;* that, *before* all experiments and all mathematics, *before* all questions and determinations, he first laid down what *should belong to the essence of a nature,* in that he approached it as the *spatiotemporal totality of the motion of mass-points.* By *reaching ahead* into actuality, he laid down what a nature should be. Only on the basis of this approach did it become possible to experiment, to question nature, to listen in on it, as it were,

17. [*Gleichschaltung:* the Nazi party's systematic program of eliminating all rival organizations and ideologies, bringing all political and civic institutions into line with the will of the Führer.]

18. {This and the following ellipses are omissions in the transcript by Wilhelm Hallwachs.}

and then to measure it. So here is a quite *definite advance understanding* of what nature as a being should be.

It is a completely different question whether, regardless of this approach and despite it, nature was held directly close to man and kept within his power, or whether quite different domains inserted themselves between nature and man, so that this hollowing out of man could come about—so that man no longer has a relation to nature. *Technology* has blocked this relation.

How great the distance has become, natural science itself is quite incapable of deciding. That is philosophy's prerogative. "The world-view of the natural sciences" is nonsense from the start.

Another area of knowledge is that of the *science of history* and its knowledge of human work and fate. *Burckhardt* is not a great historian simply because he read sources and promulgated them, or because he discovered manuscripts, but because on the basis of the greater depth of his existence, he had a view of the essence of human action that reached ahead, a view of what human greatness, human limitation, and human fate are. He *actually understood the Being* of this domain, he had an *understanding* of it *in advance.* Only thereby did he manage to research the facts in a new way.

Now, one says that since then, science has made powerful progress, that so much new material has been discovered that an individual would no longer be in a position to achieve a synthesis. The very fact that one speaks of a synthesis proves that one does not know what one is talking about. *In advance* of all synthesis, there must be the *fundamental understanding* of what history is. This first makes it possible to experience and comprehend facts.

Only the weakness of today's humanity has brought us to the point where we are now just piling up facts. It is as if this infinitely increasing material were the reason why we do not see any history anymore. Humanity remains in submission to the hopelessness of its inner impoverishment and inner baselessness.

The fact that every essential, fundamental relationship to actuality is conditioned by this view of essence applies to *art* as well, and above all to *poetry.* Art and its essence have been misinterpreted, just like history. One sees art and artworks as that in which the artist expresses his psychic life! The essence of art does not consist, either, in picturing reality. Nor is its purpose that we should take pleasure in it, should enjoy it, but rather, the innermost sense of all artistic formation is to reveal the *possible,* that is, the *free, creative projection* of what is *possible for the Being of humanity.*

Through art, we first attain the basis and directive for seeing reality, for comprehending each individual reality as what it is, in the light of the possibilities. This is why poetry signifies far more than all science.

The great poets *Dante, Shakespeare, Goethe, Homer* have achieved far more than any scientist.

This binding oneself to what things are in their essence, this *projection that reaches ahead*, is what makes the individual being in everyday reality visible in the first place. *Freedom, that is, the binding to the essential lawfulness of things, is a fundamental precondition for beings*, a precondition for *beings to announce themselves as such*.

This binding is to be achieved by the *individual* human being. But the achievement is not up to the arbitrary will of the individual, but depends on the historical Dasein of humanity.

If idea, light, and freedom go together in this way, this will clarify what Plato wants to say in the allegory about the *essence of truth as unconcealment*.

Next time we will attempt to bring the essence of freedom and the essence of light and beings into close connection with the essence of truth.

§21. On the question of the essence of truth as unconcealment

a) The doctrine of ideas and the question of truth[19]

We were asking about the essence of truth. In this question, we were not seeking a detached, abstract concept, which, the more general it is, the more empty and unrestrained it becomes. Rather, we were seeking the essence of truth as that which rules our Dasein through and through as a historical Dasein and thereby defines it. This essence cannot be conceived in the moment on the basis of some accidental circumstance; rather, it must be drawn from the decision for the future through historical confrontation.

In this confrontation, we have encountered two fundamental orientations of the essence of truth: truth as unconcealment and truth as correctness, as they were experienced and grasped conceptually among the Greeks.

We have seen that, with the Greeks in the sixth century, the concept of truth as unconcealment was driven back and the concept of correctness became predominant. In Plato, the two fundamental orientations collided once more, although Plato neither knew this nor intended it. Instead, this collision happened on its own under the compulsion of the questions raised.

19. {Recapitulation at the beginning of the session of 8 January 1934.}

We have focused on Plato's philosophy, not because it deserves our particular esteem, but because it is the crux of Greek philosophy. It is no accident that one characterizes Plato's philosophy as the *doctrine of ideas*. It is not accidental, although it is not necessary either, that this doctrine has been grasped only from this point of view.

For us, the issue is whether we can arrive at an essential understanding of the essence of truth through the doctrine of ideas. If we talk of the doctrine of ideas, then we are displacing the fundamental question into the framework of ideas. If one interprets ideas as representations and thoughts that contain a value, a norm, a law, a rule, such that ideas then become conceived of as norms, then the one subject to these norms is the human being—not the historical human being, but rather the human being in general, the human being in itself, or humanity. Here, the conception of the human being is one of a *rational being in general*. In the Enlightenment and in liberalism, this conception achieves a definite form. Here all of the powers against which we must struggle today have their root.

Opposed to this conception are the *finitude, temporality*, and *historicity* of human beings. The confrontation in the direction of the future is not accidental either; rather, to the extent that our philosophical questioning has not just now, but for decades. . .[20]

On the basis of this new starting point, as it has been developed in our thinking, the whole concept {of beings and of Being}[21] is entirely new. *On this basis* we will ask about the essence of truth and *here* we will complete the confrontation with antiquity.

The *inception* is decisive. Only the *inception* of things is *great, powerful*, and *fruitful* in itself. Plato sets down this inception in a myth (*not* in a definition), in the story of the prisoners in the cave. This story develops in four stages. Up to this point, we have presented the first three stages.

The third stage encompasses the authentic liberation of the human being from the cave into the light of the sun. This gives us various elements: idea, light, freedom, beings, truth. We were to observe the connection between *idea and light, light and freedom, freedom and Being*, and finally *the connection of all of these with truth*.

b) Degrees of unconcealment.
The ideas as what is originally unconcealed (ἀληθινόν)
and what *is* in the proper sense (ὄντως ὄν)

We will attempt a coherent presentation of what we presented in the previous lectures, as it is set down in the Platonic approach. Every interpretation of a poetic work goes beyond what is to be interpreted;

20. {Gap in Hallwachs's transcript.}
21. {Conjecture; gap in Hallwachs's transcript.}

it must understand the author better than he understood himself, so that in this way we can create something positive for ourselves, given that we ourselves did not create the work in question. Our interpretation maintains itself in the orientation to Greek philosophy, but it goes beyond Plato.

Now, in the third stage, what is said *directly* about truth? [The liberated prisoner would be unable to see even one of] τὰ νῦν λεγόμενα ἀληθῆ (516a3)—even one of the things that are now claimed as unconcealed in this state of liberation from the cave. ἀληθῆ ["unconcealed," plural]—it is not *one* Being that is spoken of, but rather a *multiplicity* (multiplicity of the ideas), τὰ νῦν [the things now].

Unconcealment is also spoken of in the second stage, in the comparative: that what is seen in the second stage is *more unconcealed* (ἀληθέστερα, 515d6-7) than what was seen in the first stage. There is, therefore, an *increase in unconcealment.* So presumably an increase will also take place in the third stage—in fact, in the third stage the *highest level* will be reached, which is followed by no further levels, so that we stand beside what is *unconcealed in the proper sense and in the first rank.*

What is now unconcealed in the third stage is *the most unconcealed of all* that is given within the domain of truth. Granted, Plato does not use the expression ἀληθέστατα [most unconcealed], but instead, as he does in other places, when he speaks of the *genuinely* unconcealed, he uses the word ἀληθινόν. This is a very particular construction that can be made clear through examples. τὸ ξύλον = wood; ξύλινον = wooden. Hence, ἀληθινόν = what is unconcealed through and through, what constitutes pure unconcealment.

The question is now whether Plato in fact addresses the *ideas* as what is most unconcealed and whether he calls what is most unconcealed ἀληθινόν, *true* and *in Being.* True in the sense of unconcealment means the unconcealment of *Being,* the revelation of *Being;* beings are the revealed. Accordingly, the increase in the revealed corresponds to an increase of Being, μᾶλλον ὄν, what is *to a greater degree.*

In the second stage, what is seen is what *is* to a greater degree, a being in the more genuine sense. The first stage describes how the prisoners take what has been assigned to them, the shadows, as what is. Here in the third stage, which describes *the genuinely revealed,* the genuine *beings* also come to light.

Where Plato now speaks of these, he expresses a characteristic in the following way: τὸ ὄντως ὄν, the being that *is* in such a way that only something that *is* can be. The being that is a being through and through is the highest intensification of the unconcealed. The ὄντως ὄν is the highest intensification on the part of the ὄν [what is], just as the ἀληθινόν is the highest intensification on the part of the ἀληθές [the unconcealed]. (Both are the idea.)

We need to show that the idea is in fact addressed as the revealed. We will take up two characteristic passages as evidence in order to make clear the inner connection between the ideas and the designation ὄντως ὄν, what genuinely is.

Republic, book VI, 490a8ff.: The question here concerns the kind of human being whom the Greeks call a φιλομαθής, one who has the drive to learn. What kind of human being is this, the one who authentically wills to know?

> ... ὅτι πρὸς τὸ ὂν πεφυκὼς εἴη ἁμιλλᾶσθαι ὅ γε ὄντως φιλομαθής, καὶ οὐκ ἐπιμένοι ἐπὶ τοῖς δοξαζομένοις εἶναι πολλοῖς ἑκάστοις, ἀλλ' ἴοι καὶ οὐκ ἀμβλύνοιτο οὐδ' ἀπολήγοι τοῦ ἔρωτος, πρὶν αὐτοῦ ὃ ἐστιν²² ἑκάστου τῆς φύσεως ἅψασθαι ᾧ προσήκει ψυχῆς ἐφάπτεσθαι τοῦ τοιούτου— προσήκει δὲ συγγενεῖ—ᾧ πλησιάσας καὶ μιγεὶς τῷ ὄντι ὄντως, γεννήσας νοῦν καὶ ἀλήθειαν, γνοίη τε καὶ ἀληθῶς ζῴη καὶ τρέφοιτο καὶ οὕτω λήγοι ὠδῖνος, πρὶν δ' οὔ;

This one, the one who authentically wills to know, is one who, in his very essence, feels a fervor for what *is* as such, who cannot stand idle among the assortment of individual things, which one so commonly takes for what *is* {first and second stages of the cave}. In contrast, he sets out on the path, he is constantly under way and does not allow himself to be dazzled by what is right in front of him, he does not relinquish ἔρως [eros, passion] until he has grasped what constitutes the *what-Being,* the *essence* of things within the whole of what is, and has done so by using the capacity suited to grasping this what-Being: eros. With this capacity, he brings himself together with the ὂν ὄντως, with what *is* in the genuine sense. By engendering understanding and unconcealment, he will truly know and live and nourish himself, and thereby rid himself of pain.

The one who, in the drive to know, reaches out to grasp the ideas, is inspired by the drive to bring himself together with what genuinely is. The *idea* is grasped here as what is *genuinely.*

Our next question is: does Plato also refer to this *Being that most is* as *the most unconcealed?*

Second passage: Sophist, 240a7ff. The issue here is, what is an εἴδωλον? In the first three stages, we have seen that human beings are not in a position to look right away into the light and at the sun. Instead, their blind eyes must slowly become accustomed {to the glare and the brightness of the light and the sun}.²³

---

22. {Heidegger's variant reading of the text; Oxford edition: ὃ ἔστιν.}
23. {Conjecture; gap in Hallwachs's transcript.}

This difference between εἴδωλον and ἰδέα, or εἶδος, plays an important role in the philosophy of Plato. εἶδος (ἰδέα) means the look of something itself, what, for example, makes a house what it is. εἴδωλον is an image, a likeness; it too is a kind of look. For example, a photograph also gives us a look, but it does not give us the house itself. εἶδος is applied to the things themselves. The essence of the house is τὸ κοινόν [the common], what pertains to each individual house. Individual houses, tables, and the like are likenesses, εἴδωλα, to the extent that each looks like the essence. εἴδωλον is the name for the individual being. This chair is a quite specific image of chairs in general.

—Τί δῆτα, ὦ ξένε, εἴδωλον ἂν φαῖμεν εἶναι πλήν γε τὸ πρὸς τἀληθινὸν
    ἀφωμοιωμένον ἕτερον τοιοῦτον;
—Ἕτερον δὲ λέγεις τοιοῦτον ἀληθινόν, ἢ ἐπὶ τίνι τὸ τοιοῦτον εἶπες;
—Οὐδαμῶς ἀληθινόν γε, ἀλλ᾽ ἐοικὸς μέν.
—Ἆρα τὸ ἀληθινὸν ὄντως ὂν λέγων;
—Οὕτως.

—What should we understand by εἴδωλον? What should we understand by likeness or copy other than that which is likened to the genuinely unconcealed and consequently is secondary and heterogeneous? {Here, an image of something is given, an image that in a certain sense is likened to the thing itself. In this sense, it is a second thing just like the prototype. This is correct in a certain sense, but it is also a distortion.}
—Another thing like this, that is, another *genuinely* unconcealed thing, do you mean? {If the copy is designated as a second thing just like what it copies, then it *too* is an ἀληθινόν.}
—No, I mean that the image is like the being itself. {The copy is indeed like the genuine object in a certain sense, but *as* the copy it is never the authentic object itself (ἀληθινόν).}
—So do you understand by ἀληθινόν the ὄντως ὄν, the unconcealed in the genuine sense, what *is* in the genuine sense {the *idea*}?
—Yes, that's it.

In Plato, then, the *idea* is *what is in the genuine sense.* The third stage, which treats the unconcealed in the sense of the idea, also treats what is *unconcealed* in the *highest* sense and therefore what *is* in the *highest* sense.

c) The ideas as what is seen in a
pre-figuring (projective) viewing

How can the ideas be called what is unconcealed in the first rank? They are, so to speak, the vanguard for the genuinely true, they prepare the way for experiencing and pre-figuring a specific idea, a form;

they carry out a projection. This first makes it possible to show how individual things look and how individual things are to be grasped.

They (the ideas) achieve what comes first of all; they open the entryway to, the experience of, individual beings. They are *what is true*, because they first achieve all this. They give access to Being, just as light is the condition for our seeing individual things. They open up the understanding of what a thing is, as a *pre-understanding*. This gives access, it gives light, it is the condition of the possibility for us to see individual things. (The openness of beings and their belonging-together arise from Being and from the idea.)

The ideas, then, let the openness of beings arise *with* them. Hence, they themselves are genuinely *what is true*. Arise *with*! They themselves, by themselves alone, cannot achieve this, because we cannot speak of the ideas *by themselves*. It lies in the essence of the idea that it is always related to a *seeing*. The relation to a seeing belongs to the idea. This characteristic of what Plato calls the idea is no mere supplement; to be *seen* always belongs to the idea. (What is seen is always in relation to a seeing. Idea is always seen.)

This is a special kind of *seeing*, which is different from experiencing things. We encounter things, things come counter to us, are given to us. *Grasping the ideas* has nothing to do with tracking down some present-at-hand thing somewhere. The ideas *are* at all only *in* and *through* a *beholding* that first creates what can be beheld, a special sort of *creative* seeing. This sighting is not gaping at something; rather, it is *catching* sight, *creating*. *Kant* says that the human being, taken in this sense, is *creative*.

d) On the question of the character of the Being of the ideas

With this determination of the essence of the idea, we have achieved an essential insight, namely, that the ideas are not values present at hand somewhere, not a set of rules posted somewhere; instead, they *are*, and are encountered, in the comportment of human beings as they catch sight of things.

But neither are they just something subjective, an invention, a fantasy of human beings. They are neither objects nor subjects. This distinction between subject and object is by no means suitable and is unable to express the relationship between beholding and the idea itself.

What the ideas are, how they are, and whether they can be addressed as *Being* could not be answered up to this point—not because the question, as question, has not been adequately examined, but rather because it has not yet been posed at all.

Against the many attempts to pass off the idea as something subjective or, alternatively, to ground it objectively—this is still the most

philosophically valuable and genuine conception: *Augustine's* conception of the idea as *correlate of divine thought*—not the idea in itself, float-
ing about freely, but rather in *relation* to an absolute subject, God. This
is simply a *deflection of the question,* but nevertheless, it endured until
Hegel. Since then: decline. It was not so long ago that one wanted to
tell us that there are something like ideas in empty space, values in
themselves, on the basis of which culture might then be formed.

Now, what follows for the conception of the essence of truth as it is
in the third stage? With respect to what genuinely is, there are no
truth and openness *in themselves* any more than there are ideas in
themselves; rather, openness *becomes,* and it becomes only in the innermost essential relationship with *human beings.* Only insofar as the
human being *exists* in a definite *history* are beings given, is truth given.
There is no truth given in itself; rather, truth is *decision* and *fate* for
human beings; it is something *human.*

But where can we find a human being who can definitively say
what the truth is? This objection seems correct—when as we are doing
here, truth is conceived as something human. One says that such a
conception leads to *relativism* and then to *skepticism.*

We pose an opposing question! If it is said that this concept de-
grades the truth, then I ask in advance: does one know what *human
being* means here and what is *human?* Or is the question of *who* man is
perhaps a *fundamental question,* and even one that stands in an innermost connection with the question that we are asking, namely, the
question of truth?

We are asking *what* the human being is and *what* is human. A problem arises: What is the inner connection between the essence of truth
and the essence of the human being? Does the essence of truth determine the essence of the human being—or the other way around?

§22. The happening of truth and the human essence

a) The allegory of the cave as history (happening) of man

In our previous session[24] we tried to grasp the whole content of what
is presented in the third stage, with the intention of experiencing how
the essence of truth is to be determined on the basis of this stage. We
have done so in a quite preliminary way. What is being directly said
here about the true, the unconcealed?

What is under discussion is what is unconcealed *now,* in the third
stage. We can gather from the entire content that a certain intensifica-

24. {Recapitulation at the beginning of the session of 11 January 1934.}

tion of the unconcealed is at work. (Even in the second stage an intensification already took place.) The third stage deals with the *most unconcealed,* the ἀληθινόν, what is unconcealed through and through, what has no remnant left of concealment: the *idea* as what most *is,* that which *genuinely* constitutes what is.

This authentic being is in turn the most unconcealed. We proved this on the basis of two passages in the *Republic* and the *Sophist.* The φιλομαθής [lover of learning] is the one who endeavors to experience what *is* most of all, what authentically is; the one who is driven to strive for what *is* most of all.

The ἀληθινόν is what is unconcealed in the highest sense. What does it signify that the *idea* is the truest, the most unconcealed? We said that the idea is what always *precedes* in all unconcealment. So the understanding and experience of the idea is the precedent that must be comprehended in order to understand the particular. The view of the idea *opens up* the view to the Being of the particular.

The idea *clears,* it sheds light on the particular. Because the ideas are originally involved in providing access to the particular being, they constitute the *origin* of the unconcealed. They are essentially *implicated,* because the idea as what is seen *gives sight.* They are *implicated,* yet are never *in themselves* truth and validity.

But *what is seen* is given only as long as there is a *seeing*—seeing not as mere staring, but projecting, creative seeing, catching sight in the sense of creative viewing; taking into one's gaze and thereby first bringing about what one catches sight of.

Ideas are neither objectively present at hand, nor a matter of subjective opinion. Both orientations (as two poles) are equally askew and miss what was initiated in Plato, but not developed.

Nevertheless, truth in the genuine sense (unconcealment) is not the idea, but the seeing of the idea, the catching-sight of the idea or the creative *projection* of the essence of things.

Therefore truth is not an incident but a *happening* (the creative projecting of things). This happening, which up to now we have exhibited in its essential moments—which we posed to ourselves as questions about light and freedom, freedom and beings, truth and beings (Being)— is now resolved into a *happening of the creative catching sight of things.*

This catching sight is a self-binding. This binding of oneself is the authentic essence of liberation. This liberation is an access to beings.

b) Unconcealing as a fundamental characteristic of human ex-sistence

We can now indicate this happening in language on the basis of an opposition. We speak of ἀλήθεια (unconcealment); the contrary concept is *concealment.* Accordingly, we can say: the contrary happening is *unconcealing.* This unconcealing happens through the creative projection of essence and of the essential law. This is a happening that *happens with humanity itself.* Revealing things in *human history* is something *human.*

This was the source of the objection that with this, the essence of truth is degraded to the preference and prerogative of the individual human being. Truth is humanized. This objection seems justified at first. In response to it we demand that the objector inform us what human means, give us a definition of the essence of humanity. What is man? This cannot be answered arbitrarily.

If up to now we have been considering the allegory of the cave {as the happening of the liberation of man for what is genuinely unconcealed},[25] we must experience what man is on the basis of this story, because on its basis we experience what truth and unconcealment are.

We are not humanizing the essence of truth: to the contrary, we are *determining the essence of human beings on the basis of truth.* Man is transposed into the various gradations of truth. Truth is not above or in man, but *man is in truth.* Man is in truth inasmuch as truth is this happening of the unconcealment of things on the basis of creative projection. Each individual does not consciously carry out this creative projection; instead, he is already born into a *community;* he already grows up within a quite *definite* truth, which he confronts to a greater or lesser degree.

Man is the one whose *history* displays the *happening of truth.*

There is one more thing that we can experience here. By way of the allegory of the cave we gain access to the essence of man insofar as *he* is that essence, in relation to himself, as himself. In this context we experience what man is, and we recognize that this question of who man is simply cannot be answered, say, by picking some random person on the face of the earth, listening in on him and interrogating him. This question can be answered only if it is *correctly posed.* One must always ask first: *Who are we?*

c) On the essential determination of man.
Truth as a fundamental happening in the human essence

We could not yet decide what man is (as viewed now from the allegory of the cave). This we can decide only if we participate in the entire *"story"* of the liberation. The liberation does not happen without violence (βία). So if man wants to know who he is, he *himself* must engage in the *movement* of these questions and become unsettled. The question is posed only where a decision is posed for man—a decision about himself and his relation to the powers that afflict him.

25. {Conjecture; gap in Hallwachs's transcript.}

Thus the question of who man is, is a question with its very own character and cannot be compared to other questions, such as "What is a table?" or "What is a house?"

For the time being, we will simply have to stick to the answer that the allegory of the cave gives us. We must say: man is the one who, insofar as he *is*, *comports himself toward beings as revealed,* and who *in this Being,* becomes *revealed to himself.*

Man is this being who comports himself to beings as revealed because the *fundamental happening* is precisely that *creative* catching sight of the essence of things by *reaching forward.* Terminologically, we say: the human way *to be* is *existence.*

Only human beings *exist.* That is, in this manner of speaking we are taking the words "existence" and "exist" in a sense that is supposed to express solely the *Being of man. Ex-sistence:* man is ex-sistent, something that *steps out* of itself. In and during his Being, he is also always outside it. He is always with other beings, and it is only on this basis that he has his essential relation to himself, exposed to *beings as a whole.*

This fundamental mode of man as existing, as stepping outside himself, having stepped out into the confrontation of Being—we can get clearer about this mode of man by contrasting it to the Being of a *plant,* say, which has in common with man the fact that it is alive. But the plant, in its living Being, is completely confined within itself, dull, without relation to anything else that we call "revealed."

The *animal* is also, to a certain extent, confined within itself, has no consciousness "of itself," but has a different relation to its environment, so that it is *benumbed* by the environment, to which the animal relates on the basis of its drives. But the environment is something essential that belongs to the animal. The animal is confined within itself and at the same time benumbed. The essence of the organism is precisely to be connected to a environment, but to be benumbed in this connectedness.

With *man,* this connection to the environment is *cleared.* Man understands the environment *as* environment; he is thereby able to *master* it and *form* it.

Things are different with the *stone,* which is not confined within itself, because it is not opened up in the manner of living things. It simply occurs.

The *fundamental act* in *the human way of Being* is this, that man understands the Being and essence of things in advance, that is, the *fundamental happening of truth.* If man were not put into this happening, then he would be unable to exist, to be as man.

From this point on, we must free ourselves from a centuries-old error, the error of saying that man is an animal with *reason* as a supplement. We must rather define man from *above,* and *then* his character as a living thing is to be determined. Reason should not be a super-structure added to the human body; instead, *embodiment* must be transposed *into the existence* of man.

This is why even an infant is not some sort of animal, but is *immediately* human. None of the utterances of a young human being may be grasped on the basis of animal biology; race and lineage, too, are to be understood on this [higher] basis, and are not to be represented by an antiquated biology based on liberalism.

The essence of truth opens itself to us not in just any cognition, in just any property, but as the *fundamental happening in the human essence*. With this, the question has been posed; but by no means has an answer been reached. We must say that all statements such as "man exists," "truth is the fundamental happening of existence," "the ideas have the character of truth"—these are all *philosophical* statements.

Philosophical truth is of a different sort from everyday truth. *Scientific truths* can and must be *proved* in a twofold sense. It must be possible to *support* what scientific propositions say with facts, or to *derive* them using formal logic.

In both regards, philosophical statements cannot be proved. But this is *no flaw*, for what is *essential* in all things in general is *unprovable*, and the advantage is precisely that every access to philosophy entails a fundamental disposition and a fundamental decision on the part of human beings. There can be no *philosophy that is standpoint-free*, with whose aid we find the truth. That is an error and a fraud.

We *initially* took the essence of truth as unconcealment; *now* we see that it is a happening, in the sense that a thing is taken out of concealment through *unconcealing*. This happening is the *fundamental happening of man*. It is subject to quite definite *conditions* and *forms of its occurrence*.

D. The fourth stage (516e3–517a6)
§23. The return of the liberated man into the cave

With this answer, we seem to have reached the goal of our question concerning how *Plato* defined ἀλήθεια. (Ascent and liberation would bind one to the idea.) But obviously Plato's allegory still has a fourth stage. The ascent into liberation, which began inside the cave and led out up into the light, goes no further now in the fourth stage. Instead, the story goes back. The fourth stage presents *the descent of the liberated prisoner back into the cave*.

Let us resume narrating the full story.

SOCRATES: And now consider this: if the one who had become free in this manner were to descend back down {into the cave} again and sit back down in the same place, wouldn't he suddenly find his eyes full of darkness there, having come out of the sun?

GLAUCON: Very much so.

SOCRATES: And if now, while his eyes were still defective, he had to compete again in asserting opinions about the shadows with those continually enchained, before he had adjusted his eyes again to the dark—which requires no insignificant period of time—wouldn't he be exposed to ridicule there, and wouldn't they say of him that he had made the ascent only to come back with his eyes corrupted and that going up is a complete waste of time? And the one who *now* wanted to lay hands on them to release them from the chains and to lead them up and out: if they {the enchained prisoners} could get hold of him to kill him, wouldn't they actually kill him, too?

GLAUCON: Certainly.

What happens here in the fourth stage? On the surface, we turn back to where we already were at the beginning, to what we already know. Taken this way, the fourth stage brings nothing new.

In this section, there is no more talk of what we have always asked about: the ἀληθές [the unconcealed]. For all the gradations of uncon-cealment have already been displayed. There is no more talk of light, freedom, what *is*, and ideas.

If we consider this, we might at first doubt whether this last seg-ment should be taken as a last stage, whether Plato is not just provid-ing a particular conclusion without essential content. That is how it looks on the surface, if we forget that the story as a whole is dealing with *human history*.

But if we do pay attention to this, then we really begin to wonder. The story ends with the prospect of *death*, which has not been dealt with up to this point. This glimpse of the possibility of the fate of death is not an accidental feature of animal life. Death is everyone's concern, as the ultimate *exit;* therefore, this is an essential section that deter-mines the whole. We must attempt to draw out the essential strands, as we did in the other stages.

The whole story ends with the prospect of the fate of being killed, of the most radical expulsion of a human being from human commu-nity. *Whose* death is at issue here? The death of the one who makes it his task to will the liberation of the prisoners in the cave.

This liberator has not been dealt with up to this point. Now we hear explicitly about the liberator as part of this story. Earlier we heard that the liberator will commit acts of violence, and accordingly he gets paid back with an overpowering counter-violence.

The decisive question is, *who* is this liberator? And how is his exis-tence to be grasped? What does a more precise characterization of the liberator tell us about liberation—and therefore about the entire fate of the revelation of Being?

----

§24. The philosopher as liberator. His fate in the happening of revealing and concealing

The person of whom Plato speaks in the fourth section, who descends again, who perhaps seizes hold of some person or other to lead him out, is none other than the *philosopher*.

We know that in other passages, Plato defines the philosopher as follows: "The philosopher is the one whose innermost desire is to take into view what is, as such. It lies in the essence of the brightness of the place where the philosopher stands that he is never easy to see; for the view of the masses is incapable of seeing when it gazes toward what exceeds the everyday."[26]

We can already gather what is being said here from the Greek word "philosophy." The σοφός is not the "wise man," but one who understands how to do something, who knows a matter from the bottom up and thus can carry out the decision that sets standards. (The expression σοφός did not arise immediately with Greek philosophy, but later.) φίλος: the friend, the one who has the drive, the one in whom the innermost "must" is decisive.

Philosophy has nothing to do with science. All science is only research into things in a limited domain, with a limited way of posing questions. One cannot determine philosophy definitively on the basis of a science, such as philology, mathematics, biology, and so on. Instead, philosophizing is a *fundamental way of being human* that precedes all science.

Such a philosopher is the one who has climbed out of the cave, gotten used to the light, and then climbs back down as the liberator of the prisoners. *This* philosopher exposes himself to the fate of death, death in the cave at the hands of the powerful cave dwellers who set the standards in the cave.

Plato wants to remind us of the death of *Socrates* here. One will say that this case is unique, that in general the philosopher's fate does not include drinking the cup of hemlock. On the whole, philosophers have had a pretty good time of it, superficially speaking. "They sit in their studies and occupy themselves with their thoughts." But this would be a superficial way of thinking.

----

26. {Plato, *Sophist* 254a8–b1. Cf. Heidegger's more literal translation in the lecture course of the same name from Winter Semester 1931–1932 (GA 34), p. 82: ". . . for the view of the soul of the masses is incapable of sustaining the gaze at the divine."}

We are dealing here with an allegory. Killing does not have to consist exactly in offering the poison cup. Bodily death is not what is meant. And besides, this death is not the most difficult; it can take place biologically in sleep, in an unconscious state. What is really difficult about dying is rather that death in its full relentlessness stands before the eyes of man during his whole Being. Inner life becomes null and powerless.

This fate is one that no philosopher has yet avoided. This fate would still be ineluctable even today—if there were any philosophers. The *killing* consists in the fact that the philosopher and his questioning are suddenly transferred into the language of the cave dwellers, that he makes himself ridiculous before them, that he falls prey to public ridicule.

Therefore it belongs to the essence of the philosopher that he is *solitary;* it lies in his way to be, in the position he has in the world. He is all the more solitary because in the cave he cannot retreat. Speaking out from solitude, he speaks at the decisive moment. He speaks with the danger that what he says may suddenly turn into its opposite.

Nevertheless, the philosopher *must* climb down into the cave, but not in order to get into debates with the cave dwellers there, but only in order to seize this or that person whom he thinks he has recognized and lead him up the steep path, not through a one-time act but through the happening of history itself.

When we try to grasp the final section, we see that the *end* cannot be a matter of indifference. But we have not yet decided the question of the inner connection of this end with the whole history of the liberation of the man from the cave that has been carried out up to now.

We saw that what characterizes the individual stages of the story is the way in which, from stage to stage, truth and unconcealment change and intensify. In the fourth stage, we had no further experience of truth. But can we conclude from the fact that in the fourth stage, the topic is not explicitly ἀλήθεια, light, what *is*—can we conclude from this that ἀλήθεια is no longer central to what is happening here?

What happens in the fourth stage? The liberated man turns back into the cave, he himself is supposed to be in the cave, if only in order to liberate *one* other person. The one who has been filled with the sight of light is now supposed to go back to the cave dwellers and get into a conversation with them. He can do this only if he remains himself. On the basis of this attitude, he will say what he sees with his new eyes.

What he catches sight of, is from the start something different from what the cave dwellers see. He knows and sees what is light and what is shadow, what is true reality and what is semblance. He can decide from the start what sort of reality it is that the cave dwellers take as what *is*.

He is in a different situation from the cave dwellers, who are incapable of recognizing the shadows *as* shadows. He thus recognizes that there are people to whom something is revealed, something like what he recognizes as the shadows. But he also recognizes that what is revealed to them does not constitute true reality. Instead, he recognizes that although a certain unconcealment does subsist within the cave, the people cling to the shadows, so what is unconcealed for the prisoners—the shadows as such—at the same time *covers up* (genuine) unconcealment for them.

The ἀλήθεια (in the cave) is also real, to be sure, but as such it conceals the reality outside. The unconcealment out there takes place in unison with the reality of the shadows. With the return of the liberated prisoner into the cave, he realizes above all that in unison with unconcealment, *concealment, semblance,* and *deception* happen and must happen. Accordingly, only *now* does he gain insight into the necessity of liberation; he realizes that this liberation cannot lead to some tranquil enjoyment and possession outside the cave, but that unconcealment happens in history, in the constant confrontation with the false and with semblance.

This leads to the fundamental insight that there is no *truth in itself* at all, but instead, truth *happens* in the innermost confrontation with *concealment* in the sense of *disguise* and *covering up*.

Thus we say that man, insofar as he exists, is thrust into relations on the basis of which beings and the world are revealed to him. Man, insofar as he exists, *is* in the truth. But it is evident that man exists as a historical people in community.

Man exists in the truth and in the untruth, in concealment and unconcealment *together*. These are not two separate spheres; instead, standing in the truth is always confrontation, an act of struggle. To persist in untruth is to slacken in the struggle. The more intensely man as historical man is afflicted and overwhelmed, the more intensely a people is afflicted and overwhelmed, the more necessary is the struggle for truth, that is, the confrontation with untruth.

The precondition for this is that the human being engaged in struggle must first of all decide for reality in *such a way* that the truly determinative forces of Dasein will *illuminate* the history and reality of a people and bring Dasein into them. Reality cannot provide the people with a place to stand; instead, spirit and the spiritual world of a people develop within history. History is not fulfilled in a time frame that ends in 1934 or 1935—maybe not until 1960.

Chapter Two
The Idea of the
Good and Unconcealment

§25. Being free: acting together in
the historical con-frontation of truth and untruth

a) The philosopher's freedom:
being a liberator in the transition[1]

In the previous session, we attempted to get clear about the *fourth stage*. What does it involve? What is its position within the whole? We discovered that the fourth stage is no mere appendix, nor a recapitulation: instead, the person under discussion here is fundamentally different from the other inhabitants of the cave. He has been transformed and he now has a different fate.

Plato designates him as the *philosopher*. Through this story, he intends to show what the philosopher is. The philosopher is a liberator, and he *is* only as such a liberator. Authentic freedom does not consist in dragging an inhabitant of the cave out into the light and leaving him there to laze about in the sun. Authentic freedom does not consist in tranquil enjoyment: to be free means to be a *liberator*.

The philosopher is not secure; as a liberator, he acts with others in the history of those who belong with him in a community according to their Being. Given what we have said, all human beings would have to become philosophers if they wanted to exist *authentically*. This is true inasmuch as being a philosopher, among the many possibilities for existing, means the fundamental way in which man takes a stance with respect to the *whole* of beings and toward the *history* of human beings.

We derive the fundamental character of philosophical Being from the allegory. We see that what makes one human *is not* to be bound in the cave, to feel at ease and to chatter away; *nor* is it to be in the opposite

---

1. {Recapitulation at the beginning of the session of 18 January 1934.}

condition outside of the cave. Instead, the human *is the transition* out of the cave into the light and back into the cave. This *transition* is the authentic history of man, a fate that one cannot shake off by declaring that one is not interested in philosophy. A fate can only be surmounted—or one can founder on that fate without knowing it.

b) Truth and untruth. Modes of untruth as concealment

This story is supposed to tell us what *truth* is. Our interpretation of the fourth stage allows us a remarkable expansion of this question: we concluded that only the one who turns back is in a position to comprehend what those down below are seeing, namely, the shadows. On the basis of the return, the *difference between Being and seeming* only now becomes possible. Only now does the difference between *unconcealment and idea* as opposed to *the concealed* open up.

But if this transition belongs to human history, if human beings cannot get away from it, then this means that there is no pure unconcealment. Instead, to this unconcealment there also belong semblance, disguise, and the covering-up of things, or, as we also say: *untruth*.

This is the decisive answer: *untruth belongs to the essence of truth*. Untruth is not simply truth's opposite; rather, only as confrontation is truth as unconcealment cast into untruth and embedded there.

From this there follows a double concept of untruth. In Greek, truth is a negative, a privative in the expression "unconcealment." Now we understand why the Greeks do not express truth positively. From the very first, what *is* must be torn out of concealment into history, must be wrested from concealment. Truth is not a possession.

The initial counter-concept to unconcealment in the sense of truth is, in a formal linguistic sense, *concealment;* but now we see that for us this would be untruth. But if something is concealed, that does not yet mean that we therefore know something false; it is simply *not knowing*. The concealed has a double sense: 1) something with which we are unfamiliar; 2) something to which we have no possible connection.

Concealment is a characteristic of what we call a *secret*. But concealment is not untruth in the sense of *falsehood*. Rather, concealment is the concealed in the sense that something is covered up, disguised to us. Mere *seeming*.

It belongs to the essence of *seeming* that it appears to us, that it shows itself. What a thing is, is its εἶδος, its look. Seeming means that something only seems (looks) *as if;* for example, a stage set of a house.

From this we arrive at the view that what we routinely call untruth is integral to entirely essential relations. *First, concealment* is the *secret* of the not-yet-experienced, of what cannot be experienced; *second*, it means covering-up, disguise, seeming. Accordingly, if *philosophy* is this *primor-*

dial history of man, in which he is in his historical Being . . .² This philosophizing is not some arbitrary, detached speculation about arbitrary
things; rather, philosophy and philosophizing are the *genuine process* in
the history of a human being and a people.

Accordingly, the *philosopher* is the one who creates the preview and
purview into which this happening presses and drives. The philosopher is not the one who retrospectively applies philosophical concepts
to his time; instead, he is the one who is cast out in advance of his time
and anticipates its fate.³ For the philosopher, this cannot be a pretext
to withdraw as a superior being; instead, he must suffer this fate in the
highest degree, in the sense that one bears one's fate.

§26. The idea of the good as highest idea: the empowerment of Being and unconcealment

When we look over the whole in this way, we recall that we have not
completed our interpretation of this story as regards a major point, for
we asked: what does the fate of man as liberator look like?

It has come to light that he has the ability to catch sight of the highest of the ideas, ἡ τοῦ ἀγαθοῦ ἰδέα, the *idea of the good*. We have said
that we wanted to leave the elucidation of what Plato understood by
the highest idea until the end. We now want to ask, considering the
whole story: what does this *highest idea of the good* mean? With this, we
will also gain some insight into Platonic philosophy.

The ideas are in a place above the heavens (ὑπερουράνιος τόπος),
out beyond the heavens (in the allegory: outside the cave). This ascent
out of the cave, to speak without any allegory, is the progress to a place,
the upward path that the soul traverses to reach a place that Plato calls
the τόπος νοητός. νοητός = the apprehensible; νοεῖν = to apprehend;
νοῦς = the faculty of apprehending, reason; τὰ νοητά = the ideas.

Plato says: in the field of what can be apprehended by man in general, what is caught sight of *last* is the idea of the good; and it can barely
be brought into view, only with trouble, with effort. The ascent, and
thus the history of liberation, comes to an end only when man's apprehension has reached *what can be apprehended only last,* τελευταῖα ἰδέα.
The idea of the good is what stands, in a certain sense, at the end.

τέλος (τελευταῖος), end, does not mean goal. Neither is it a negative concept. It means end in the sense of limit, limitation—the form
that stamps and thus really determines everything, the limit that really embraces and determines all.

2. {Gap in Hallwachs's transcript.}
3. [Alternate translation: "anticipates his own fate."]

a) The idea of the idea. On grasping the highest idea
on the basis of the general essence of idea

Plato speaks of the idea of the good in two major passages: at the beginning of book VII of the *Republic* and in book VI, 506–511. Now we
want to get clear about what the idea of the good really means here.

To begin with, as regards *grasping* the idea: it can be glimpsed only
with effort, so it is even harder to speak of it, much less conceive of it.
In both passages, Plato speaks of this idea only indirectly, in the *sensory image* with which we are already familiar: the sun as the sensory
image of the highest idea.

If this is how matters stand with the highest idea—that one can
barely catch sight of it—then we must get clear that everything depends on bringing our questioning in the right direction, that we cannot just run out and snap it up, in a readymade formula as it were, an
answer that's handy for everyday use. We may not apply standards
from our everyday life and opinions as we try to grasp what Plato
means here.

On the other hand, we have to get clear that Plato is not thinking
about something mysterious, some sort of remote thing that you can
get to only with tricks, or with an extraordinary vision based on an
enigmatic faculty; instead, Plato insists quite soberly that one has to
attain what is at work in the idea through serious, step-by-step philosophizing, by asking one's way through. Only philosophizing labor,
not a so-called intuition, leads to what Plato intends.

Even then, what we are to grasp cannot be said, at least not in the
way that everything else that we can learn and know can be said.
What is to be known philosophically must be known and said, or not
said, in a different form from that of all scientific cognition.

But then again, the unsayable in the strict sense is what I run up
against if I exert myself and have exerted myself to reach what is sayable in the highest sense. Not what any dunderhead can say, but the
sayable that assails us more and more as we work our way through
things with the greatest rigor.

Two ways to Plato's views are possible: 1. A thorough interpretation
of book VI. But with this, we would pass beyond the frame and context of our work so far. 2. We will try to discover what *"highest* idea"
means here by a process of intensification, on the basis of the characteristics of the essence of the idea that we clarified earlier. We then
want to see whether what we have attained in this way is what Plato
says elsewhere about the highest idea.

  1. The extrapolation of the *highest* idea from the general essence of
     idea,
  2. Investigation of whether the result accords with what Plato says.

So we must try once again to characterize the essence of the idea; we must see what the ideas are. The ideas are what is most unconcealed and what most *is*. They are the most unconcealed, inasmuch as they make possible the unconcealment of particular beings in their Being-such-and-such. They are what most of all *is*, in that by virtue of {them, *Being* becomes understandable, "in the light of which," as we still say today, that which individually is, is first of all a *being,* and is *the* being *that* it is.}[4] So it is apparent that the characterization of the essence of the idea already involves a highest intensification. The *idea as such* is something that has been intensified to the highest degree: the *most unconcealed* and what *most of all is.*

Now we should ask: is a still higher intensification possible? For there is still supposed to be a *highest idea* over and above this, what genuinely lets unconcealment and Being *arise* and makes them possible.

We also saw that the idea has the function of letting beings become *visible* in that which they are, and thus letting *truth* arise. The *highest* idea has the task of making unconcealment *in general* possible, of empowering beings to be what they properly *are as* beings. This amounts to the *formal* extrapolation of the *idea of the idea.*

If we ask for the *content* of what the highest idea is and what the *good* means, we must free ourselves from every sentimental notion, but also from conceptions that have become run-of-the-mill through Christian morality and then in secularized ethics. ἀγαθός, good, originally has no moral meaning.

The good, for the Greeks, is not the opposite of the evil, much less of the "sinful." There is sin only where there is Christian faith. But neither is the good to be understood in the feeble sense of "he's a good person" (but a bad musician)—in an innocuous, ladylike sense.

ἀγαθός is when we say, as after a confrontation or discussion: good, the matter is settled (after a decision). The good is what succeeds, stands fast, holds up, what is fit for something. A pair of good skis, boards that hold something up. What demands the highest decision and the highest seriousness and intensity of Dasein.

It is hopeless to want to comprehend the essence of the good on the basis of the Christian concept—this concept will not take us one step closer to understanding what the good actually means.

The idea of the good has a completely different sense. We now want to look at Plato himself and ask how he, for his part, expresses himself regarding the good as the highest idea. In our next session we want to get into the closing section of book VI, in order then to make it clear in what sense the essence of truth coincides with the highest idea, and thus with the essence of the good.

---

4. {Gap in Hallwachs's transcript. Editor's conjecture based on the lecture course of the same name from Winter Semester 1931–1932 (GA 34), p. 99.}

b) Approach to the complete determination of
the idea of the good as the highest idea

We ask: what do we understand by the idea of the good? Furthermore, what does the essential determination of the highest idea yield us for the determination of the essence of truth?

We have cited two major passages from Plato's *Republic* (VI, 506–511; VII, 517a–e). Plato does not clarify the essence of the highest idea directly; this already tells us that the highest idea is hard to grasp and even harder to say. The *sensory image of the sun* is the *path* to clarifying what Plato understands as the highest idea.

We now want to pursue *this* path of clarification: on the basis of the essence of the idea that we explained earlier, we will set out *in advance* what the highest idea is, using a procedure of intensification. Then we want to examine to what extent Plato's own interpretation corresponds to what we ourselves have set out in advance as the essence of the highest idea.

The idea was the ὄντως ὄν and the ἀληθινόν, that which most *is* and is most revealed. The ἀληθινόν is what in the first place, that is, before all things, must be revealed to us in order for us to grasp a being as such. We must understand in advance what it means to be a book. In every thing, the idea is the *most genuine* Being and the *most unconcealed*.

This elucidation of the idea shows that a characteristic of the idea is intensification. This characteristic of intensification means that *this*, as what is highest, is, insofar as it *rules, also* the *origin* for what stands beneath it, that is, for what is revealed to us as something that is. The idea as such has the general function of *making possible* this characteristic of ruling, making beings as beings possible in their openness. It is the *essence of the idea* to *make beings possible*.

The *highest* idea is the *good*. ἀγαθός means for the Greeks what prevails, what stands firm. Being good means to prevail, to stand firm, and thus to take a stand, to provide a place to stand. The essence of the idea corresponds to this: what makes possible that which is and is revealed. The idea as the enabling must be what truly prevails and makes things stand ready. Hence the *highest* idea is the *good*. So much for the *formal* explanation, so to speak.

We now ask how Plato, for his part, develops the essence of the highest idea of the good on the basis of the sensory image.

As regards the essence of matters of state in general—the state, πόλις—Plato accepts the principle that the *rule* of human being-with-one-another in the state must essentially be determined by a definite kind of ruling human beings, and a definite form of ruling.

Taken in the usual sense, one who rules in the state must be a *philosopher*. This naturally does not mean that professors of philosophy should become Reich-chancellors—that would be a disaster from the start. But it means that the people who are endowed with the rule of the state must be philosophizing human beings. Philosophers, as philosophizing human beings, have the task and function of φύλακες, guardians. They have to be on guard to make sure that rulership and the state's ruling structure are thoroughly under the sway of philosophy—not as some system, but as a knowing that is the deepest and broadest knowledge of man and man's Being.

On the basis of this knowing, standards and rules are to be established within which every authentic decision and setting of standards takes place. In a state, says Plato, there can be only *a few* such guardians.

Now, Plato's whole work {the *Republic*} is concerned with the question: in what way, by what means, and in what form can a state educate its own guardians of this sort? In this context Plato asks (in the allegory of the cave as well) what knowing is.

Plato did not pose the question of the essence of knowing because it belongs to the academic concept of epistemology, but because *knowing* constitutes the innermost content of the *Being of the state* itself, inasmuch as the state is a *free*, which also means *binding* power of a people. *This is why* the question of the essence of knowing is *the fundamental question*.

§27. The idea of the good and light as the yoke between seeing and the visible—truth and Being

Plato says that those who know in the highest sense must be united in knowing—in a knowing that is acquired every time by beginning with verbal knowledge, that is, with what is common chatter, but that ascends upward along the steep path from the cave to understand and grasp the ideas.

a) Seeing (ὁρᾶν) and understanding that apprehends (νοεῖν)

To explain this knowing and grasping of the ideas adequately, Plato distinguishes between two fundamental modes of cognition:

1. seeing with the eyes, ὁρᾶν,
2. νοεῖν, the apprehending understanding of the ideas.

This latter knowing, in the sense of knowing the true essence of things, is to be explained through the *sensory image* of *natural* apprehending and understanding. Here Plato presents the essence of genuine comprehension through the ideas, explaining this essence as a schematic counterpart to natural seeing and what pertains to it. Thereby Plato also displays what pertains to genuine comprehension.

In this context Plato presents the idea of the *good* anew. In the following schema, there stands on one side the phenomenon that we take as our point of departure: seeing, ὁρᾶν, seeing with the eyes; on the other side stands that which is to be symbolized by this seeing: νοεῖν as the seeing and grasping of the idea.

To all seeing there belongs the following:

1. the performance of the act, the activity of seeing, ὁρᾶν,
2. something that is seen in this activity of seeing, what is caught sight of (the thing seen), ὁρώμενα.

Correspondingly, we understand knowing as:

1. the seeing of the essence of things, νοεῖν,
2. what is understood and grasped in this, νοούμενα.

Schema

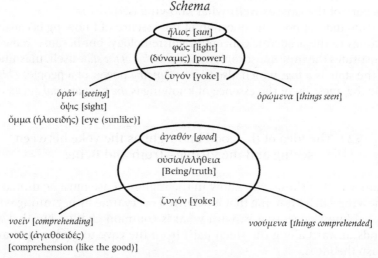

Proceeding from ordinary seeing, Plato says: for the act of seeing to be performed, there must be a possibility and a capacity for it. There must be something that makes the performance of this act possible. Similarly, there must be something that puts a being in the position to become *something visible,* that enables the being to happen.

An enabling power, δύναμις, is required for the fact of seeing and being seen in each instance. These powers, δυνάμεις, which enable the performance of *seeing and* the fact of *being seen,* must be one and the same. Both of these, seeing as act and being seen, must be joined in the yoke (ζυγόν) of the same power.

If we now focus on these facts and *formally* transpose them to the *higher* seeing of things, we can say, on the basis of natural experience, that in order for things to become *visible,* it must be *bright.* To visibility there belongs the enabling power, brightness, light, and therefore the *sun.*

Therefore the *yoke* just mentioned, the one that joins both (ὁρᾶν and ὁρώμενα), is in some sense the *light,* and correspondingly the source of light = the sun (φῶς, ἥλιος). As we said, in keeping with this fundamental thought that these powers of seeing and being seen go hand in hand, the light, the sun, must be the enabling power for seeing itself. (It is impossible that different powers underlie seeing and being seen.)

We know from our earlier discussions that, among all the forms of sensory perception, the Greeks gave preeminence to *sight* and *seeing.* The most preeminent sense is ὄψις [sight] because, in their experience, from their very Dasein, ὄψις makes things in their unmediated presence accessible in their form and in their interrelation. For the Greeks, to have an unmediated stamp means to be.

The sense that makes *beings* accessible is ὄψις. Therefore, light and the sun must also be the enabling power for *seeing.* (This is taken as the starting point for constructing a higher seeing.)

To say it in Greek: sight or the eye must be ἡλιοειδής. Goethe says: sun-like.[5] The eye must be defined by light. The act of seeing is *lit.* We also say, when something comes over us, when we grasp something in a really new and creative way: I see the light, I've had a flash of inspiration. What this points to is that we grasp seeing itself as standing under the power of light and the sun.

This seeing, ὄψις, ὁρᾶν, is that mode of unmediated perception that is the most complete (πολυτελεστάτη αἴσθησις). It becomes the way to explain how we comprehend the essence of the idea.

For the idea as νοούμενον to be comprehensible, there must be a *yoke* here *too,* a *light,* as it were. This light must have a *light source.*

The light is what enables us to comprehend what *is;* it is Being, οὐσία, and at the same time, ἀλήθεια, openness. Plato, in a genuinely Greek fashion (in contrast to our conception today), says: truth is not something like the condition for the possibility of thinking and comprehension, but rather it is the condition for the possibility that *something comprehended* is given, the condition for *beings* themselves (openness corresponds to comprehensibility).

---

5. ["Wär nicht das Auge sonnenhaft, / Die Sonne könnt' es nie erblicken; / Läg' nicht in uns des Gottes eigne Kraft, / Wie könnt uns Göttliches entzücken?" J. W. von Goethe, *Goethes Werke,* vol. 1: *Gedichte und Epen,* ed. Erich Trunz (Munich: C. H. Beck, 1996), p. 367. "If the eye were not sun-like it could not see the sun; if we did not carry within us the very power of the god, how could anything god-like delight us?" Translation by David Luke in Goethe, *Selected Verse* (Harmondsworth: Penguin, 1982), p. 282. Goethe's poem is based on Plotinus's *Enneads* 1.6.9, and indirectly reflects *Republic* 508b. Goethe published a slightly different version of the verses in the preface to his 1810 *Theory of Colors:* see *Werke,* vol. 1, p. 730.]

Just as the eye must obviously be ἡλιοειδής, so must the comprehension of the idea (νοεῖν) have a character that corresponds to what determines and enables *this yoke as yoke* (the ἀγαθόν). It must be ἀγαθοειδής [like the good]. As the eye is sun-like, so must the comprehension of the idea be ἀγαθοειδές.

b) The good as the higher empowering power
for Being and truth in their linked essence

This is only a preliminary explication of sensory seeing and the non-sensory comprehension of the idea. We perceive that what extends the span of the yoke, so to speak—light and Being and truth—is determined by something higher. "And so this, what grants unconcealment to the knowable beings and lends to the knower the capacity to know, is the idea of the good" (book VI, 508e1ff).

It should be noted that one and the same ground enables knowledge of the idea and the openness of the idea: the *good*—that although *Being* and *unconcealment* or *truth* do essentially *co-participate* in enabling essential knowledge, something still *higher* is given. "There is still something higher to esteem, beyond Being and truth, something that surpasses the power of these, and only by virtue of this, which surpasses truth, is knowledge really possible" (book VI, 509a3–4). Final passage (509a9–10): "But fix your eye once more, as we have been doing, on the image for the highest idea, namely, the sun! The sun may be plumbed still more deeply and more thoroughly to draw forth yet more correlations."

A further characteristic of the sun as sensory image of the good is developed:

SOCRATES: In my opinion, you might say that the sun bestows upon the visible things not just the quality of being seen, but also their emergence, growth, and nourishment, while the sun itself is not becoming.

GLAUCON: How could it be!

SOCRATES: And so we must now also say that not only does being known {ἀλήθεια} belong to the knowable things on the basis of the good, but even this {namely, that these things are always something composed in this and that way; in short, Being}, and that therefore Being, too, belongs to them only on the basis of the good, while the good itself is not a type of Being, but is beyond Being and towers over it in power and worth. (Book VI, 509b2ff)

This, in the whole of the Platonic corpus, is surely where Plato expresses his decisive thought about the good.

The good is *beyond* Being, ἐπέκεινα τῆς οὐσίας (book IV, 509b9), and therefore = nothing (to put it *formally*). This means that if we ask about the good as we would ask about a good thing, then we will not find it, we will always run up against *the nothing*. The good can never be found at all among beings or Being. It requires that we ask in a different way.

The ἀγαθόν is not simply beyond Being; *in its beyondness,* it is precisely *related to Being and truth* (ἀλήθεια), namely, as that which *empowers* both of them as what they are. With respect to worth and δύναμις and power, the good is superior to everything else; the good is itself also power, the power of empowering. The good is the highest power, in that it empowers what is already the most powerful, raising it to the level of the ὄντως ὄν and the ἀληθινόν. The good is the most powerful, which deploys itself and stands fast before everything else and for everything else.

In the treatment of the essence of the good, what is at issue is not *content,* nor is it values; rather, what is at issue is a *how,* the *manner* of the deployment of power. It (the idea of the good) becomes perceptible not when I take it as a thing, but when I submit myself to the *power,* thereby orienting and opening up my comportment so that I adjust myself to the power and so that power as power addresses me. What is at issue here will never be grasped by "sound common sense."

Exactly the same characterization is found at the close of the allegory of the cave (book VII, 517c3). Plato says: in the field of νοεῖν, of the really knowable, the good itself (αὐτόν) is mistress. And this mastery is explained in this way: it bestows, it gives. παρέχειν is not simply to bestow; it is both a *bestowing* and a *holding*—giving (and letting go), and in giving, holding. In other words, *the good gives and it binds.*

With this we discover how the sun corresponds to the good. The good binds (a) ἀλήθεια, that which pertains to the *seen,* openness, together with (b) νοῦς, the capacity for conceiving and understanding, for the *understanding of Being.*

The good is the empowerment of Being and of unconcealment to their essences, which intrinsically belong together. (But this says nothing if it is only a definition and is not conceived on the basis of how we *hold* ourselves.)

In the image, the good is what emanates the *yoke* from itself, as it were, and yokes together Being and truth so that something is possible that fulfills itself among human beings in historically *free* human beings.

§28. The development of the essence of truth as history of humanity

a) Review: the inner order of the question of the essence of truth[6]

We are approaching the conclusion of an essential line of thought. So now we should once again lay out and follow the inner order of our inquiry.

---

6. {Recapitulation at the beginning of the session of 25 January 1934.}

We asked ourselves: what is *truth*? We had two answers: (1) truth as *unconcealment*, ἀλήθεια; (2) truth as *correctness, adaequatio*. Each has a particular relation to the other. To begin with externals: truth as unconcealment is the older, truth as correctness the more recent. Today "correctness" dominates exclusively.

We asked whether this initial conception (unconcealment) was there at the inception only chronologically, or whether this inception is at the same time meant substantively, in the sense of the *origin*, so that correctness arises from unconcealment, and arises in such a way that it gains a superior power and becomes exclusively dominant.

These are not questions of some "history of philosophy," but questions of essence, questions whose *Being* is based on the moment of *our Dasein* itself. These two answers, correctness and unconcealment, do not merely offer a content, two definitions. They are only the law-like summations of two interpretations found in Dasein's comportment among beings as a whole and toward itself. Why did the universally accepted definition become dominant?

These two conceptions are grounded in turn on *fundamental orientations*. The issue is not the difference between two definitions, but the opposition between two fundamental positions in the history of man. The question of truth does not hang in the air; it is *historical*. The issue is not the conceptual differences between various human epochs, but differences in the *innermost Being* of man.

These two differentiated concepts are in juxtaposition, even if the juxtaposition goes unspoken. We have tried to grasp this *juxtaposition of the two concepts of truth* in a passage where both determinations are found in an *originary* way, in Plato.

Plato answers the question, "What is truth?" by means of the allegory of the cave, in four stages. The third stage provides the culmination. Only the fourth presents and defines the authentic liberation; it is not, so to speak, a mere appendix.

In characterizing the third stage, we passed over the closer determination, the peak, as it were, of the whole happening, from which the whole can be surveyed—namely, the determination of the *highest idea of the good.*

We illuminated the highest idea of the good in two steps.

1. We attempted to discover what the highest idea might be with a free construction, as it were. The highest idea is what makes possible *Being* as well as *unconcealment*. The good, ἀγαθόν, is a word from everyday language that means nothing other than this: what *makes possible*, what *prevails* before everything else and *determines* it. ἀγαθόν never signifies a content, but a "how," a distinctive mode of Being.

2. We tried to exhibit how Plato himself delimits the highest idea. He works with a presentation in sensory images. The sensory image of the highest idea is the sun, and in relation to the sun, the comprehension of the highest idea is sensory perception with the eyes.

By means of correlation we will now show how the *good* is like the sun in its own domain. This fundamental state of affairs is, as it were, the basis for showing how the ἀγαθόν, the good, in its domain—the idea—is like the sun, in order to clarify which question is the decisive one in determining the ἀγαθόν.

In the state of perceiving with the eyes, there stands on one side the act of seeing, on the other being seen. There is an inner connection between seeing and the visibility of things. Both require a δύναμις, a making-possible. This is the same for both. The bridge, as it were, is light. The eye must be sun-like, and so must the visible being.

To the sun-likeness of seeing—both that of the eye and that of the visible being—there corresponds the goodness of the idea and of the comprehension of the idea. Both must have arisen from a common origin in order for the bridge to be possible.

b) The good as the empowerment of truth and Being in their belonging together

Now it is important for us to see what features of the highest idea Plato gains by characterizing it through sensory images. To put it in brief slogans, it becomes apparent from the passage in book VI that the highest idea, the ἀγαθόν, is ἐπέκεινα τῆς οὐσίας, beyond Being, over and above Being, towering over it; towering not in an indefinite sense or in a spatial sense (a higher stratum), but towering over Being in two quite definite respects: πρεσβείᾳ καὶ δυνάμει (book VI, 509b9); (1) *age*, older origin and thus a higher *rank*; (2) *power*.

The good towers over Being in *rank* and in *power*. We should gather from this that in general the ἀγαθόν is seen only in these two respects, that it has rank and that it is powerful.

This is the first feature, from book VI. Book VII is immediately connected to it (allegory of the cave). The idea of the good here is κυρία παρασχομένη ἀλήθειαν καὶ νοῦν (book VII, 517c4). From this (κυρία [sovereign]) we see the good's *character of mastery*. Furthermore, it is παρασχομένη, *granting*; to grant something and to *bind* by the granting. The good, as the sovereign mistress, grants (1) *truth*, makes truth possible, and (2) *Being* or the understanding of Being, νοῦς.

The *idea of the good*, as *highest idea*, is what *towers above, grants mastery*, and *binds*. We can sum up this description—what towers above, grants, and binds—in the fundamental act of *empowering* (that which empowers). This feature is nothing other than what we know as δύναμις, what *makes possible*.

The first conception was formal. The second conception pointed us to mastery, power, rank. We must leave it at that. If we ask what Plato understood by the idea of the good, we must stick to this fundamental characteristic, in order not to fall into the mistake that nearly everyone makes, the mistake of taking some individual thing for the good. *The good is empowerment.*

In interpreting Platonic philosophy, one has said rather often that Plato gave up the idea of the good in his late period. This way of thinking is typical of philosophy professors, who change their view every year and think that with this, they are developing.

What is essential in a philosophy is that it is the same from its inception to its end. It never occurred to Plato to give up his doctrine. This we can gather without further ado from the Seventh Letter. Here we encounter the undiminished dominance of the good.

What do we gather from this treatment of what the whole story offers in the way of a response to our question of what *truth* is? What do we gather from the characterization of the *highest idea* as regards the essence of truth?

1. The first result is that truth, ἀλήθεια, is itself nothing ultimate, but stands under a higher *empowerment*. In this there lies already the methodological indication that the illumination of the question of truth must get clear about the fundamental fact that truth is nothing ultimate.

2. The second result is the *fundamental context* within which something like truth belongs. We should not poke around in other concepts to find out what truth is; instead, we must be directed toward finding the space and horizon through which and in which truth is surpassed, is empowered in its essence, and *is* under a more powerful form.

3. This applies not only to truth and its essence, but also to *Being*. Being too is nothing ultimate, but over Being there still stands something else. The question is what.

4. The fourth result is that not only are both—truth and Being itself in general—subordinate to something higher from which they receive their origin, but both are also interconnected in this subordination. *Truth* as the openness of beings, *Being* as the possibility of grasping beings, both stand under a *yoke* (ζυγόν), inasmuch as the yoke extends over both and thus first makes possible their essential connection. The ἀγαθόν has the character of a yoke, it forms the span that joins the experience of the openness of things to the experience of their Being.

5. What we gather from the essence of the good—that it is what empowers truth and Being to their inner connection and to their own proper essence—this for its own part stands in an essential relationship to *man,* as that which liberates man and precisely thereby binds him, and in this *binding,* brings authentic *necessity* into human Dasein as the presupposition of *freedom.*

6. This fundamental relation of man to what authentically liberates him is his *liberation* itself, and at the same time his *history.* Human history is a history that Plato has presented through images, a story that tells us that liberation takes place as working one's way up into the unconcealment of things. This means that the transformation of the essence of man in his Dasein is not a change in man's external situation, but an *innermost change in the Being of man.*

c) Philosophy as παιδεία of humanity for
the innermost change in its Being.

The development of the essence of truth through human history

Plato himself has a very clear concept of this. He says after the presentation in book VII (521c5) that this whole story—what goes on with the people there and plays itself out in the course of the ascent, the happening of this whole transformation—is not, as it might seem to be, a mere turning of a potsherd in the hand, but a *leading of the essence of humanity around and out* (ψυχῆς περιαγωγή). The whole human essence is transfigured by being led out from a certain night-like day to a true day. Plato calls the Dasein in the cave a night-like day; it is not absolute darkness; even here, humanity stands in a certain openness.

This leading around and out (περιαγωγή) of humanity from one situation into the other is the ascent to what is, as such; we say of this happening that it is really *philosophizing.* The ascent to what is, as such, is really philosophizing. To sum up: the question of the essence of truth is thus the question of the first essential history and the essential transformation of man through and in philosophy.

With this, the question of the essence of truth, and truth itself, gain a fundamental place within the essential vocation of man—a fundamental place of which Plato also knew; he expressed it in *Phaedrus* (249b5): "For how could the soul (the essence of man) come into the figure of man if it had not seen what is unconcealed in things?"

Man as he is, insofar as he exists, is determined by the fact that he has already seen the unconcealed, as it were, and thus brings with him the luminous glimmer of the essence of things—and he is this way only insofar as he *develops* this glimmer. The question of the essence of truth is the dominant question for man.

This is said in the introduction of the story at the beginning of book VII (514a1ff.): Μετὰ ταῦτα . . . "After this, make yourself an image of our essence and understand this (direct your gaze) not in terms of just any features, but according to how its παιδεία is, as well as its ἀπαιδευσία." This is an indication that in listening to the story, we should direct our gaze to our own nature, to our innermost essence and Being in regards to παιδεία and ἀπαιδευσία, and not only as regards both individually, but looking at both together.

In German we have no word to express what the Greeks mean here. παιδεία is usually translated as "education" [*Erziehung*] or "cultivation" [*Bildung*], or more recently (Jaeger) as "formation of Greek humanity."[7] But this is an academic notion; this is not what is at stake, it is humanistic. παιδεία means, to paraphrase: the *inner binding-fast of human Dasein on the basis of the steadfastness that holds fast* to what fate demands. In contrast, ἀπαιδευσία means failure, powerlessness, not standing fast.

In the later, post-Platonic period, however, the meaning did develop in the direction of cultivation and education.

In our context, this means that what is at stake in this story is precisely the *essence and Being of man*—in regards to how he is *in his ground*. This grounding, fundamental happening in which the *essence of truth develops through human history*—and in this history, man acquires this inner steadfastness—this fundamental happening is *philosophy*.

But one will not comprehend even this fundamental thought of Plato, that the fundamental happening of history is philosophy, if one moves within ordinary conceptions. So first it is necessary to muffle, so to speak, all the points of view from which one is used to talking about philosophy.

1. Philosophy is *not* a *cultural phenomenon*, some domain of so-called spiritual creation within which works are produced that posterity admires. One can take philosophy this way, but then one does not understand it.
2. *Nor* is philosophy an opportunity and form in which individual *personalities develop* their talents by developing philosophy, and put themselves on display through their work.
3. *Nor* is philosophy an *area of scholarship* where research is carried out as in *science* and where there might be progress. In philosophy there is no progress. It is not an area of teaching and learning that can be systematized.
4. *Nor* is philosophy a *worldview* in the sense of the conclusion and

7. {Cf. Werner Jaeger, *Paideia: Die Formung des griechischen Menschen* (Berlin: de Gruyter, 1933).} [English translation: *Paideia: The Ideals of Greek Culture*, trans. Gilbert Highet (New York: Oxford University Press, 1939-1944).]

rounding out of a conception of things, a summation, as it were, of the individual results of the sciences and of human experience.

5. *Nor* is philosophy a particular form in which an individual human being, who perhaps is detached from traditional religion, creates a *standpoint* for himself.

Instead, *philosophy* is a *fundamental happening in the history of humanity itself* (not of some arbitrary human being), which has the character of a quite *distinctive questioning*, a questioning *in which and through which the essence of humanity transforms itself.* This fundamental happening is not up to the arbitrary choice of an age and a people, but is older than we are and extends beyond us. For us, the question is whether we comprehend this necessity or whether we believe that we can break away from it.

On 30 January 1933:[8,9] Kolbenheyer[10]

Every age and every people has its cave, and the cave dwellers to go with it. So do we today. And the prime example of a contemporary cave dweller and of the gossipy entourage that goes along with him is the popular philosopher and cultural politician Kolbenheyer, who made an appearance here yesterday. Here I do not mean Kolbenheyer as a poet, whose *Paracelsus* we admire.[11]

8. {Heidegger's notation on the cover page: "In the lecture course 30.I.34." On page 1 of the manuscript, next to the title, Heidegger wrote, "Kolbenheyer: In the lecture course on the day after the speech." On 29 January 1934, Kolbenheyer had given a speech in Freiburg on "The Value for Life and Effect on Life of Poetic Art in a People." The speech was written in 1932 and was delivered repeatedly in larger German cities during 1933; it was published in E. G. Kolbenheyer, *Gesammelte Werke* (Munich: Langen & Müller, 1941), vol. 8, pp. 63–86.}

9. {Wilhelm Hallwachs did not record Heidegger's remarks. His speech is reproduced here from his surviving handwritten notes and is printed in italics to distinguish it from the text of Wilhelm Hallwachs's transcript. [In the translators' judgment, this typographical device is not necessary for the English-language reader. The Hallwachs transcript resumes with section d, German p. 214.] Hallwachs mentions the speech in his transcript simply in the following form: "After a delay of nearly an hour, Heidegger appears and first delivers a speech on the occasion of the anniversary of the National Socialist revolution, in which he concludes by indicating the tasks of the university, which he sees in awakening the future and preparing for it spiritually. He then returns to his theme."}

10. {Erwin Guido Kolbenheyer, born 1878 in Budapest as the son of a Carpathian German, died 1962 in Munich. In the Third Reich, Kolbenheyer was a widely read writer and spokesman for the National Socialist regime. Cultural functionary since 1933 in the Prussian Academy of Arts; joined the National Socialist party in 1940.}

11. {Kolbenheyer's trilogy of novels: *Die Kindheit des Paracelsus* (1917), *Das Gestirn des Paracelsus* (1921), *Das dritte Reich des Paracelsus* (1926). His further works include *Karlsbader Novellen 1786* (1935) and *Das gottgelobte Herz* (1938).}

He is bound to the shadows and takes these as the only definitive reality and world; that is, he thinks and speaks in the schema of a biology that he got to know more than thirty years ago—at a time when it was the fashion to fabricate biological world views (cf. Bölsche[12] and the Kosmos books).

Kolbenheyer does not see, he cannot and does not want to see:

1. that this biology of 1900 is based on the fundamental approach of Darwinism and that this Darwinian doctrine of life is not something absolute, not even something *biological,* but is historically and *spiritually* determined by the liberal conception of humanity and human society that was dominant in the English positivism of the nineteenth century.

2 Kolbenheyer does not see and cannot see that his biology of plasma and cellular structure and organism has been fundamentally surpassed, and that today a completely new way of posing the problem of "life" is taking shape, an approach that is deeper in principle.—Destruction of the concept of the organism, which is only an offshoot of "idealism," isolated subject, "I," and biological subject. Fundamental constitution: relation to the environment, and this not a consequence of adaptation but, to the contrary, the condition of possibility for adaptation.

3. Kolbenheyer does not see and does not want to see that, even when the essential determination of life is more originary and appropriate than that of the nineteenth century, even then *life* (the way of Being of plant and animal) does *not* constitute *the dominant whole* of reality.

4. Kolbenheyer does not see and cannot see that, even if bodily life is in a certain way the *supporting ground* of human Being and of the ethnic sequence of its generations, this still does not yet prove that the *supporting* ground also has to be the *determining ground,* or even that it can be.

5. Kolbenheyer does not see and cannot see that man as people is a *historical* entity, that to historical Being there belongs the decision for a particular *will to be* and *fate*—engagement of action, responsibility in endurance and persistence, courage, confidence, faith, the strength for sacrifice.

All these fundamental modes of conduct of historical man are possible only on the basis of *freedom.*

12. {Wilhelm Bölsche (1861–1939), writer on nationalities and nature.} [Several of Bölsche's books were published by Kosmos, a "society of the friends of nature."]

But it is not enough to recognize, perhaps, these manifestations of human Being (after all, they are hard to deny), merely in order then to distort them into biological functional *capacities.* One thereby *perverts* decision—engagement—freedom—the courage for sacrifice into a process that is encumbered *from the outside* and fit into the biological reality which has been presupposed as the only definitive reality, without seeing and grasping that in engaging oneself and enduring and sacrificing, a *way of Being that is different in principle* becomes powerful—different in principle from, say, the functioning of gastric juices and sexual cells and tending to the brood. One fails to grasp that this way of Being does not arise from bodily Being simply because it is bound to the body; that this Being does not, among other things, "also" play itself out in the bodily organism, but rather it is precisely *bodily engagement* and struggle that are dominated and gripped by authentically, historically responsible Being (nobility!). The Prussian nobility—merely grown like an apple on a tree, or grown from historical experience in the spiritual-political reality of the world of Frederick the Great?

In principle this way of thinking is no different from the psychoanalysis of Freud and his ilk. And in principle it is also no different from Marxism, which takes the spiritual as a function of the economic production process; whether I take the biological or something else instead of this is all the same for the decisive question regarding the way of Being of the historical people.

6. Due to the blindness of this biologism to the historical, existentiell, fundamental reality of man or of a people, Kolbenheyer is incapable of truly seeing and grasping today's *historical-political German* reality; and this reality was not there at all in his speech—to the contrary: the revolution was falsified into a mere *organizational operation.*

7. What is on exhibit here is the typical attitude of a reactionary, nationalistic, and folkish bourgeois. According to this attitude, the "political" is an unspiritual, disagreeable sphere which one leaves to certain people who then, for example, make a revolution. The bourgeois then waits until this process is at an end before he gets his turn; *now* he is ready for the task of *belatedly providing* the revolution with *spirit.*

For this tactic, one naturally appeals to a saying of the Führer: the revolution is at an end, the evolution is beginning. Yes—but we don't want to deal in counterfeit money. Evolution—certainly, but only where the revolution is at an end. But where the revolution has not yet come to an end but rather has not even begun—as in spiritual matters and, for example, in the educational system—how do things stand there?

We are grateful for the role that spiritual workers of this sort play in life, *for they are doing nothing but bringing to light a perhaps unintended justification of the most trite reactionary position*. The facts demonstrate it: *the weightiest objection* to the speech and the clearest sign of how questionable it is, is the deafening applause that I do not begrudge Herr Kolbenheyer.

8. Whoever has experienced and grasped even the slightest part of the new German reality that stands before us must already know after Kolbenheyer's first sentences how things stand with his attitude. He takes "vocation" as a purely *economic* phenomenon, which it has become in the bourgeois age. He does not see that it is precisely vocation that is being experienced and grasped anew in its essence from the ground up (not on the basis of so-called spirit), namely, in its fundamental political character and on the basis of the essence of *labor*.

9. Kolbenheyer is a folkish kind of man, a nationalist; he talks of estates and rejects the delusion of class—and yet he does not stand in the new political reality, but somewhere above it. Instead, he thinks and speaks within a spiritual world that was modern thirty years ago among intellectuals; he takes this world for the only true one and takes himself to be authorized to impart the impeccable answer without delay to every question set before him—like the advice columnist in a newspaper.

10. All honor and admiration to Kolbenheyer the poet, but yesterday's speech was a political, and that means a spiritual fiasco that could not have been conducted more perfectly.

If the poet Kolbenheyer had told us how art grows in a transformed way from the new reality and by shaping it in advance, builds a world, then—yes; but what we have here is just a bad popular philosophy.

The man of the cave sits in his dwelling and knows nothing of the history of the violent liberation and highest obligation. He measures everything with his standards and believes: in 1933, the revolution; in '34 and after, spirit as a supplement.

Evolution—certainly! Development, solidification, and radically questioning obligation = clarification of the revolutionary reality.— But not: revolution as something over and done with, and afterwards the development of what the so-called spiritual people believe about it. That is completely superfluous. But what remains decisive is helping to shape the *historical-political reality* so radically in all domains of Dasein that the *new necessities of Being come to have effect and take shape without falsification*.

d) On the proper approach to the
question of the human essence

Quite schematically, we can say that we are asking about *man*. This is the guiding question that we must pose in all our reflections, the question of *historical* man. In asking this question, we must ask in the correct way. This—asking in the correct way—is the task of the philosophy of the future. This asking *is* the fundamental happening, *philosophizing.*

Now, if we ask about man, we see that this question has, up to now, always been posed in the form: *what* is man? In this *form of the question* there already lies a quite definite *advance decision.* For in this, it has already been decided that man is *something* constituted in such and such a way, to which this and that component belongs. One takes man as an entity that is put together out of body, soul, and spirit. Each of these components can then be considered individually in definite forms of questioning. Biology asks about the body of man, plants, and animals; psychology asks about the soul; ethics asks about the human spirit. Everything can be summed up in an anthropology.

All these disciplines have accumulated a tremendous amount of information about man. Nevertheless, they are not in a position to answer the question of man, because they *do not even ask this question anymore.*

The authentic revolution in the question must be that the question as a *question* must already be posed in a different way. We do not ask, "*What* is man?" but "*Who* is man?"

With this question, we establish a *direction of questioning* that is different in principle. With this, it is posited that man is a *self,* a being that is not indifferent to its own mode and possibility of Being; instead, its *Being is that which is an issue* for this being *in its own Being.*

Man is a self, and not a living thing with some spiritual endowments, but a being that in advance *decides about its own Being,* in this or that way. This is a quite different fundamental position, based on man's possibility and necessity of Being.

Only because man is a *self* can he be an *I* and a *you* and a *we.* Being a self is not a consequence of being an I. This self-character of man is at the same time the ground for the fact that he has his *history.*

I say that the question of man must be *revolutionized. Historicity* is a fundamental moment of his Being. This demands a completely new relationship of man to his history and to the question of his Being.

Terminologically, I have designated this distinctive characteristic of man with the word "care"—not as the anxious fussing of some neurotic, but this *fundamentally human way of Being,* on the basis of which there are such things as resoluteness, readiness for service, struggle, mastery, action as an essential possibility. Only as long as man decides for or against his distinctiveness . . .[13] There is mastery only where there is also readiness for service.

On the basis of this question concerning the essence of man, his *Being* is revolutionized, the way he stands in relation to his historical tradition and historical mission is revolutionized.

13. {Gap in Hallwachs's transcript.}

Chapter Three
The Question of
the Essence of Untruth

§29. The disappearance of the fundamental experience of ἀλήθεια and the necessity of a transformed retrieval of the question of truth

a) The question of the essence of truth as the question of the history of the human essence[1]

We want to present a brief summary of the thoughts in our foregoing lectures. By clarifying the highest idea of the good, we want to grasp something about the essence of truth, to grasp which characteristics pertain to the essence of truth as a whole.

1. Truth is not something ultimate, but stands under something still higher, the idea of the good.
2. This also applies to Being.
3. Truth as unconcealment (a characteristic of objects) and Being as subject (what is seen) both stand under a yoke. And this yoke that holds Being and truth as object and subject together is the good.

Yet this good stands in an inner connection to the essence of man, as our last session explained. This liberation of man to the highest idea is the authentic essential history of man, whose Dasein is governed by philosophy.

This essential history of man in the allegory of the cave tells us that the transformation in the individual stages is not the mere turning of a potsherd in the hand, but an exit from night-like day into the real day; it is philosophizing.

---

1. {Recapitulation at the beginning of the session of 1 February 1934.}

The entire presentation of the allegory of the cave at the beginning of book VII is also introduced accordingly. The topic of this story is the history of man, our φύσις [nature, Being] in regards to παιδεία and ἀπαιδευσία. παιδεία does not mean education or cultivation; instead, παιδεία is the binding-fast of man in Dasein, insofar as he holds steadfastly to what is demanded of him; the topic is existence as a determination of man, and indeed the highest. This fundamental happening of man is philosophy.

The question is what philosophy is. This question and the question of truth depend on the fundamental question: what is man?

Today we are used to getting the answer to this fundamental question from sciences such as biology, psychology, anthropology, sociology, typology, and so on. These sciences, all together, provide diverse information about man and yet no answer, because none of them *asks* about man anymore, because they are already grounded on a quite definite answer, namely: man is something that is given among other things, something that consists of body, soul, spirit, personality . . . This is disseminated and expounded. All of this is correct, and yet, in the deepest sense, untrue.

A definite mode of questioning is already pre-delineated in these disciplines. Through this mode of *questioning*, the answer is already given in advance, that is, a definite range of possible answers is already demarcated. And no matter how far these disciplines may be developed, they will never get beyond what they have already decided about man in advance.

The way of questioning that lies at the foundation of these sciences can only be: *what* is man? The decision has already been taken in the question: man is something constituted in such and such a way. One might believe that the question cannot be posed in any other way.

Yet this *is* possible. We do not ask, *"What* is man?" but *"Who* is man?" In this way of posing the question, a decision has also been taken, namely, that man is a *self*, not a present-at-hand being but a being that is *delivered over* to itself in its Being. The self is not to be fit into the realm of present-at-hand things, but is delivered over to the constant choice and decision that it has to bear.

What is decisive is not that the self knows about itself, but that this knowing, in the sense of self-conscious knowing, is only a consequence of the fact that its own Being is an issue for this being.

This fundamental characteristic, that its own Being is an issue for it, itself belongs to the Being of this being. We designate this Being as *care*. This care has nothing to do with some sort of irritable surliness, but designates the fundamental characteristic of the self, that its Being is an issue for it. How—this is left to the choice and mission of man.

Only insofar as Being is care does a way of Being become possible such as resoluteness, labor, heroism, and so on. But because man has these possibilities, he also has, on the other side, the possibilities of innocuousness, busy-ness, cowardice, slavery, money-grubbing, and so on. These are not, as it were, regrettable additions. Only where there is busy-ness is there labor. Only on the basis of this Being (as care) is man a *historical* entity. Care is the condition of possibility for man's ability to be a *political* entity.

b) The existential determination of human Being
and the question of the truth of humanity

We designate this way of Being as *care,* insofar as we distinguish it as *existence* from other ways of Being (such as rock, animal). Although the tradition uses the expression "existence" simply for Being as actuality, we want to understand by *existence* a *way of Being in the sense of care,* and thus the relationship of Being in care, the fact that Being itself is an issue.

Thus, we cannot say "the animal exists" or "the stone exists." We make a distinction that fundamentally separates us from the way of Being of other domains. Every being that does not have the character of existence, everything that is in such a way that its own Being is closed off to it, all these beings that meet our eyes in any form whatsoever, beings that we encounter and experience only insofar as we address ourselves to them—this kind of being and its Being we call the *categorial.*

κατηγορεύειν = to speak out, to address something as what it is. A category is a determination I assign to beings insofar as I encounter them as something other. Organism, procreation, propagation are *categorial determinations.*

In contrast, tradition, decision, struggle, insight, are determinations that pertain to existence: *existential* concepts.

Because *care* characterizes *the self as self,* and in this we see the fundamental trait of man, we must say that man as we encounter him and as we experience him—as the you, I, we—is grounded in the fact that man is a self. The characteristic of *Being a self* is the condition for the fact that man is an I, and not vice versa. The self is the originary source that makes I and you possible. Only on the ground of the self is there the struggle for priority between I, you, and we.

Who man is, can be said only in philosophizing. We must beware of slipping into a false claim by laying down some definition. We can get farther in the domain of the question of who man is only by experiencing more of the essence of *philosophy.*

Can man know and find out something about the essence of the self at all by beginning with himself? How do we know that we know, and can know, who we ourselves are?

This question flows into the next: where do we get the truth about man himself? Only with this question does philosophy enter what is ultimate for it.

If man is a distinctive being, due to his existence, then the *truth* about him will also have its own character. Of what sort is this truth? According to Plato, we get an experience of what truth is from the essential history of man (in the allegory of the cave).

c) The lack of questioning about the Being of the good as yoke and about unconcealment as such

Here we are back in the circle, in the realm in which it becomes clear that we are philosophizing, that is, that we are standing firm in the question of what truth is. We must proceed through the circle as a circle. Standing firm in the question means not flagging in the questioning.

Precisely the highest peak, the elaboration of the idea of the good, must now become questionable for us. The ἀγαθόν has no content of its own, but means a *way in which* something is—something that prevails, that holds firm, that stands firm, that is upright and fit.

This ἀγαθόν in human Dasein is characterized by Plato as a *yoke* that yokes together, on the one hand, Being in the sense of the understanding of Being as the seeing of the idea, and on the other hand, truth in the Greek sense as the unconcealment of beings. Expressed in the language of modern philosophy, on the one hand the *subject*, on the other the *object*. The ἀγαθόν is the ζυγόν that completes the span.

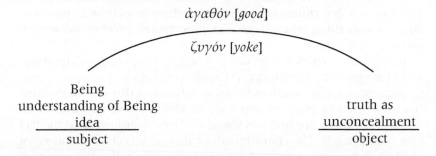

ἀγαθόν [*good*]

ζυγόν [*yoke*]

Being understanding of Being idea		truth as unconcealment
subject		object

With the question concerning this *yoke-like character* we encounter something questionable, inasmuch as Plato does not explain how matters really stand with this yoke. The explanation does not ensue because the question is no longer posed, because what stands under the yoke is posited in advance as two *juxtaposed things,* in order then to ask subsequently in what relationship they stand.

This rigid approach was incapable of inquiring into the specific character of the yoke in its Being; instead, what stands beneath the yoke is reinterpreted into subject and object, present-at-hand things. The question concerning the yoke is no longer posed.

Plato then determines the essence of Being, the essence and kind of Being as idea, in this characterization: that what is, is what is seen, what

I see about a thing in advance. This characteristic is *ambiguous*. On the one hand, the idea is what is seen, and thus is always linked to a seeing. But on the other hand, what is seen is always such-and-such, so it can be taken in two ways: as *what* it is, and also as something that is seen, as such.

The character of the idea falls back behind the content of what in each case comes forward as an individual thing that is seen. The ideas retain only this content (such as table, house, mountain), so that this being, seen in this way, is taken as a present-at-hand being; we see the individual things on the one hand and the ideas on the other hand, the individual perceptible mountain and the idea of the mountain. Between them is a χωρισμός [gap].

On this basis, the whole nexus of the ideas is taken as an objective stratum with various domains. With this, Plato's starting point is given up—his attempt to see the span between seeing and what is seen.

This is the occasion for diverting the question of the subject, and of subjectivity and objectivity, from its true path; the determination of truth as unconcealment is not developed, that is, what is seen in this originary issue is not exhausted.

ἀλήθεια as truth (unconcealment) is not a feature of the assertion, the proposition, but a characteristic of the things themselves that are; it happens to and with a being, without altering itself. Beings are to show themselves as they are.

Now, here unconcealment and openness move into the background. *Unconcealment itself is not really questioned anymore,* but reflection focuses on what stands in unconcealment in each case. Unconcealment becomes the term for that which is unconcealed.

The philosophy of *Aristotle* seeks and asks about ἀλήθεια. (Aristotle says that it asks about truth.) Philosophy asks about the unconcealed as such, that is, about beings in their Being. ἀλήθεια = ὄν, οὐσία, εἶναι [what is, beingness, to be]. This means, for the Greeks: whether or not they experienced it (?), they did not succeed in putting it (?) in the place where it can be interrogated.[2]

Connected to this is the fact that the essences themselves are posited as something present at hand, and are established as prototypes. Things are then images of the prototypes. But with this, one arrived at ὁμοίωσις, *adaequatio* [conformity]. Individual things to which human thinking assimilates itself.

The Greeks accordingly had two interpretations of truth. Truth as openness prevailed first, but for essential reasons, truth as the assimilation of thinking and seeing took over.

---

2. {The sentence in Hallwachs's transcript includes the two question marks.}

In Plato, we experience the two kinds of truth flaring up once again. From Plato on, the determination of truth as a property of the proposition gains the upper hand. Today it is so self-evident that no one would allow himself to fall into believing otherwise, on pain of penalty.

d) The necessity of a transformed retrieval

Now, why don't we want to just leave things as they are with this concept? Such self-evidence in a conception is usually already an embarrassment, and is a sign that the question has slipped into the self-evident. Why aren't we leaving it at that? I have already indicated the inner difficulty.

To begin with: "This chalk is white." This is the proposition. The sense of the proposition, the nexus of meaning, is something totally different from the chalk itself, with which the sense is supposed to correspond. The sense is questionable. The correspondence of our thinking to this thing is possible, then, only if the thing is revealed to me in advance as it is given to me. Supposing that the correspondence of the proposition (with the thing) were a characteristic of truth, then the thing would already have to have truth so that the assertion could be measured against it. So the assertion already presupposes the openness of things.

A still more essential problem is that this concept of truth cannot help us determine *human truth*. On this basis we cannot comprehend conviction, inner decision, or the truth of a work of art.

We cannot even raise a question about these authentic truths on the basis of the usual concept of truth. Hence the inner necessity of posing the question of truth anew, not in isolation from the tradition, but neither by reaching blindly back into the inception of philosophy.

Given these two fundamental possibilities of interpreting truth, unconcealment and correctness, *we* must take up the question of the essence of truth anew and pursue it further, in the context of the historical situation of our Dasein. Precisely that which came to light for the first time among the Greeks, but which the Greeks could not get in hand, is to be extended on the basis of our concepts.

If we now take a look at things formally, we gather two points:

1. *Truth* is a *happening* that happens with humanity itself, that is not possible without the *history of the human essence*. Truth is something that happens to beings, a happening based on the entirety of human being.
2. *Truth as unconcealment* is essentially related to *concealment*: pulling one out of the cave, assailing the concealed, tearing beings out of concealment.

If we move in the direction of Greek experience, we must ask: what is it, really, that unconcealment assails? What does concealment mean?

We ask historically: to what extent did the Greeks know in their philosophies about the concealment of things, about what must be overcome in the happening of truth? We will see how against truth as unconcealment there stands *untruth* or *nontruth*. But nontruth is ambiguous. For the concealed can be conceived in two ways.

1. What has not yet been taken from concealment,
2. the concealed that was once taken from concealment, but sank back into concealment.

The first is the concealed, pure and simple. The second, which has passed through a process of unconcealing, is the hidden, the covered up, the disguised. We will encounter still further distinctions within both senses. Only in this way will we discover the kind of philosophizing that represents the contrary concept to the Greek concept of truth.

§30. The lack of questioning about the essence of concealment from which the un-concealed can be wrested

a) The transformation of the question of the essence of truth into the question of untruth[3]

We have brought the question of the essence of truth to a relative conclusion, inasmuch as the allegory of the cave showed us to what extent truth is connected with the *Being of man*. Truth is unconcealment. *Unconcealment* does not exist somewhere in itself, but is only insofar as it *happens as the history of human beings.*

Insofar as human history happens, the things that are, as a whole, come into openness. Now, this human history is not the history of theoretical thinking and opinion, but the total history of a people, such as happens before us, to a certain extent, with the Greeks.

That history has as a driving force within it the *liberation of man to the essence of his Being.* This liberation begins with *Homer* and is fulfilled in the formation of the Greek states, in conjunction with worship, tragedy, architecture, and so on, together with the awakening of *philosophy.*

This total happening carries out a *projection* of the world within which the Greek people exists. This projection of the world is the presupposition for the fact that man moves within what we call today a worldview. The worldview is not a derivative superstructure, but the projection of a world that a people carries out.

If today the Führer speaks again and again of reeducation for the National Socialist worldview, this does not mean promulgating this or

---

3. {Recapitulation at the beginning of the session of 15 February 1934.}

that slogan, but bringing forth a *total transformation*, a *projection of a world*, on the ground of which he educates the entire people. National Socialism is not some doctrine, but the transformation from the bottom up of the German world—and, as we believe, of the European world too.

This beginning of a great history of a people, such as we see among the Greeks, extends to all the dimensions of human creativity. With this beginning, things come into openness and truth. But in the same moment, man also comes into *untruth*. Untruth begins only then.

Openness is always limited, definite. The limit of an openness is always what is not revealed, what is concealed. This is the genuine sense of *untruth*. The concept, taken in this sense, has nothing inferior or derogatory about it, but signifies untruth only as *what is not revealed*.

The expression "untruth" is ambiguous; it can mean: (a) non-openness = concealment, and (b) concealed and yet at the same time revealed in some way. This is the essence of seeming—something that looks like something else; insofar as it looks like something else, it conceals something. This last characteristic is what we designate as untruth in *our* sense. From the essence of the Greeks we see that their concept of truth belongs immediately and intimately together with the essence of untruth. Truth, for the Greeks, is nothing but the *assault on untruth*. This is already expressed with the construction of the word ἀ-λήθεια: a negative, privative expression, which brings to light the fact that truth is something that must be wrested away from untruth. With us, the word "truth" is a positive expression.

Now, along what lines can the essence of truth be exhibited *more primordially* as unconcealment, as the assault on untruth? The issue is the *inner essential connection between truth and untruth*.

b) Preliminary clarification of the fundamental concepts: ψεῦδος, λήθη, and ἀ-λήθεια

Here, to begin with, we again want to stick with the concept in the *word*. How do the Greeks designate what *we* call untruth? The Greek word for untruth in the narrower sense of falsehood is ψεῦδος. The Greeks do not express the concept contrary to truth with a contrary word formed from the same stem. We also see that with the Greeks, untruth is expressed positively, and truth negatively (ἀ-λήθεια).

If the word for untruth is taken positively by the Greeks and if it has a different stem, what experience lies at the basis of this word? If we want to get clear about this *primordial word*, we are not just doing linguistic history, but we are convinced that language is always the interpretation of a people's Dasein, that word coinages give expression to completely essential fundamental experiences.

What does ψεῦδος mean for the Greeks? We want to clarify this with our loan word "pseudonym." It is put together from ψεῦδος (false) and ὄνομα (name). But "pseudonym" does not mean "false name." What is the thing, what does it mean? If, say, we called the chalk a sponge, we would be applying a false designation to it. A pseudonym is not a false name, but a designation behind which the author hides, a covering name that hides him. It is not that the name does not correspond to the author. The work faces the reader under a label behind which there hides someone other than what the name on the book says. The facts about the author are covered up, distorted.

That is the fundamental meaning of the Greek ψεῦδος: to turn the thing around in such a way that it is not seen as it really is. ψεῦδος is what twists and distorts.

Now, the Greeks also have a contrary concept and contrary word for ψεῦδος. It appears, for instance, in Democritus: ἀτρεκής (from τρέπω, to turn); that which is unturned, untwisted. The contrary concept ψεῦδος does not simply mean the false, but rather the distorted. The decisive moment is the twisting.

This meaning of ψεῦδος underlies a further development in the history of the meaning. ψεῦδος means what is turned toward man and his perception not only in such a way that what hides behind it is covered up, but also in such a way that there is the illusion that something is hiding behind it, when at bottom there is nothing behind it at all.

This means not only what is twisted, but also what is null, that behind which there lies nothing. This is the meaning that also comes out in the middle-voice form (ψεύδεσθαι): making something into nothing, explaining it in a way that is null and void.

A type of λόγος, discourse, that is null, that contains nothing and even deludes us by passing something off on us that is different from what it means—that is the lie.

These, then, are the main directions taken by the linguistic expression ψεῦδος.

Now we ask whether the Greek word for truth, ἀλήθεια, also found a corresponding positive word form. This is, in fact, the case, although this word form does not coincide with the concept of truth. The reference to the positive contrary concept should make it clear that truth and unconcealment of things are not a property of a proposition, not a property of cognition, but an objective happening into which the things themselves enter.

This becomes clear from the concept contrary to ἀλήθεια: λήθη, λάθω, λανθάνω = I am concealed, I remain concealed. This characteristic of remaining concealed applies to reality, to the thing that is.

An example of the "I remain concealed," of a definite type that we tend to translate as "forgetting," is found in Thucydides, book II, the end of chapter 49. During the course of the Peloponnesian War a great plague broke out in Athens, and its course and consequences are depicted. "Many people lost the use of their limbs once the illness came over them; some lost their eyes, others were attacked {assailed} immediately, once they recovered, by the remaining-concealed of all beings alike. And thus it came about that they knew nothing either of themselves or of their kin."

The topic, then, is the remaining-concealed of all things alike—a happening that breaks in on human beings like a fate. This (falling away) has the consequence that human beings as individuals are unable to know anything about themselves or about others. ἄγνοια [ignorance] = consequence of λήθη [concealment, oblivion] {. . .}[4]

We say simply: they lost their memory. This is a purely subjective expression that does not do justice to Greek reality. ἔλαβε: seize them, befall them. λήθη is an objective power; it came over people like φόβος, ἄλγος, ὕπνος [fear, pain, sleep]. (A quite definite mode of openness.)

Only through a quite specific process of subjectivization does λήθη receive the subjective meaning of forgetting. The question is whether forgetting can be explained at all in a subjective way. For this word λανθάνω (I am concealed) also calls for a very definite construction in the Greek language, such as λανθάνω ἥκων = I remain and am concealed as one who is coming. Concealment is a characteristic of my Being itself, and not a property based on the other's failure to grasp what is going on.

Openness, as well as concealment, is for the Greeks an objective happening. This is why in the Greek way of thinking, the *true* can substitute for *Being*. For what is unconcealed is precisely what *is*. *Being true* and *Being* are generally synonymous in Platonic language. On the one hand, Being means for the Greeks being present, not absent, not concealed; on the other hand, truth means unconcealment.

This *equivalence* has persisted in Western thought, and is still taught today—but in a different sense. Today one says: what is, is what is posited in a proposition as being.

These remarks should suffice to prepare us for the substantive question.

---

4. {In Hallwachs's transcript there follow two fragmentary sentences marked with question marks, whose sense is unrecognizable and which are thus not open to conjecture.}

PART TWO

An Interpretation of Plato's *Theaetetus*
with Regard to the Question of the Essence of Untruth

Chapter One
Preliminary Considerations on the Greek Concept of Knowledge

§31. On the question of the essence of ἐπιστήμη

In order to clarify the essence of untruth in the sense of falsehood, we will follow similes that Plato employs, as he does in all essential areas of questioning—two similes from the *Theaetetus*. We do this to evaluate how the concept of untruth has been passed over and how this has led to a situation in which the whole question about the essence of untruth and falsehood counts as a secondary one.

We have no logic of *error*, no real clarification of its essence, because we always take error as *negative*. This is the fundamental error that dominates the entire history of the concept of truth.

Theaetetus is taken to be the most important dialogue in the so-called theory of knowledge. One refers to this dialogue to demonstrate that the Greeks, too, were already busy with theory of knowledge. Through this conception, the interpretation of the dialogue is dragged off onto a completely false path.

The Greek question is, τί ἐστιν ἐπιστήμη?—How should we translate it?[1] The way we conceive of the content of the dialogue depends upon this translation.

ἐπίσταμαι = I place myself in front of something, I step close to something, I engage myself with it in order to dominate it, to do right by it, to be a match for it. To understand how to deal with a thing—be it the preparation of a piece of equipment, be it the conduct of a military undertaking, or be it the performance of a task in teaching and

---

1. [A conventional translation would be: "What is knowledge?"]

learning—everything that in some sense requires that one know one's way around a thing: this is what the Greeks designated as ἐπίσταμαι.

So the word does not designate science. Science—for example, geometry, mathematics—is certainly *one* mode of this know-how, but it is not *the* mode of know-how pure and simple. In ἐπιστήμη is realized the whole multiplicity of all questions and levels of know-how in all regions of human Being.

Therefore, because the concept has this broad meaning, the question arises: what is the inner, common core here that is ἐπιστήμη for human beings? This question does not pertain to theory of knowledge; instead, what must be explained is what the genuine essence is in all these modes of comportment in know-how.

If one makes the orientation of the question clear from the start, one is then also assured of steering the dialogue away from the sphere of science. Science is only *one form* of knowing, even if from one perspective it is perhaps the highest.

The question seems to aim at presenting the features or properties that belong to every form of knowing. It is a question about the *essence of knowing.*

If we are asking about the *essence* of knowing here, then the question about the essence of knowing is a question about *human Being* (about the essence of human beings). But this question has a *completely different methodological character* from questions such as: what is a house? a table? a book? These are things that lie before me as objects, things I can interrogate as something present at hand. By contrast, the question "What is knowing?" is a question about the human being himself as a being who is, who acts, who is historical. With this, the question is oriented to an answer that cannot be found in some statement. Rather, this question about the human being is at the same time a question about the measure, law, or rule that the human being, as one who knows, sets for himself.

Behind the question "What is knowing?" is concealed another claim entirely, a quite definite attack by the person who questions on the very person questioned, that is, an attack on the human being inasmuch as he hunkers down in the familiarity of his views and opinions. This attack on the human being is nothing other than the essence of philosophy.

With this, it is presumed methodologically that the answer does not consist in an enumeration of moments, but rather that the answer exposes itself only in the course of a confrontation, a struggle within which quite definite fundamental positions for man come to light.

This is precisely why this dialogue has its particular *agonistic* character. That does not just mean testing oneself in the sense of proving that one is in the right. Instead, the agonistic character consists in the fact that the opponents question their way ever more reciprocally into the most *acute questioning* possible.

So in the end, the dialogue concludes without giving an answer. But the answer lies precisely in the *confrontation,* not in some flat proposition that gives the definition at the end. The answer is so *prodigious* that up to this very day, philosophers have not exhausted its essential content, have not even taken up the question.

This assumes, as all historical interpretations do, that the interpreters themselves have experienced and clarified within themselves the essence of the things they are questioning. Only then are one's eyes likely to open.

We now wish to attempt to elucidate the main features of this Platonic approach to the essence of untruth, for if we can manage to do this, we will have the problem as a whole in hand.

---

§32. Fundamental points concerning the Greek concept of knowledge

a) The basis for the detour through Greek philosophy[2]

In our previous session, we broadened the question of the essence of truth in principle by posing the question of the essence of untruth. This question is unavoidable if one has gotten clear about the originary concept in the Greek word (ἀ-λήθεια) —for unconcealment has within it the relation to concealment.

The Greek word ψεῦδος has the meaning of disguise, covering up, seeming, falsehood. So then, from the very start, the question of the essence of untruth arose together with the question of truth. Yet it took centuries until the question of the inner connection between truth and untruth was seen and posed.

We want to answer the question of untruth along the same lines as the question of truth; we want to examine the question by way of the *Greek* approach to it, and specifically Plato's approach. We have carried out our guiding question by way of Greek philosophy.

But why the detour through the Greeks? Why can't we simply answer the question on the basis of today's needs? We are taking this detour because the answer depends on the way of posing the question. The *answer* always corresponds to the scope and depth of the *questioning*. The scope depends on the originality and essentiality of a people that poses it.

Because the question is not posed today anymore as an *essential* question at all, because it has atrophied into a topic for scholars, it has lost its

---

2. {Recapitulation at the beginning of the session of 20 February 1934.}

greatness. Hence the fundamental significance of first restoring the question to its rightful greatness and intensity, in order to gain standards for what the question means. If we had these standards, then we would not be faced today with the question of the sciences in a way that relegates it to idle talk and idle scribbling, where every journalist is allowed to jump in—then such barbarism would not be possible.

We want to reeducate ourselves for real seriousness. This is why we are taking the *detour*. We want to consider the question of the essence of untruth exactly as we considered the question of the essence of truth.

The Greek term for untruth is ψεῦδος. We note (1) a completely different stem of the word, which corresponds to a different fundamental experience: the experience of hiding, of twisting (dislocation). (2) Our concept of truth has a positive character, whereas the Greek is negative (ἀ-λήθεια).

Nevertheless, with the Greeks the two words stand opposed to each other as *antonyms*. This is possible only because the meaning of both words deteriorated right away.

ψεῦδος (known to us in the loan word "pseudonym") means *falsehood*—not only as incorrectness, as we often understand it, but also as when we speak of a "false person." We do not mean an "incorrect person," a person whose comportment does not follow the rule; that need not be a false person. This twisting of the state of affairs, putting up a front behind which the actual state of affairs is otherwise—this is the essence of the ψεῦδος. This meaning is sharpened when the front that is turned toward us, the semblance, is such that behind it there stands nothing at all. Thus ψεῦδος gains the meaning of *null, vain*.

ψεύδεσθαι: (1) to be insufficient {?}, (2) to speak in such a way that although something is said, what is said covers up precisely what is meant.

This fundamental meaning was extended so far that in the end it gained dominance over ψεῦδος as the contrary concept to ἀλήθεια. The latter completely disappeared from the realm of experience of the West.

b) The breadth and the fundamental meaning of the Greek concept
of knowledge and the origin of the question of untruth

Transition to the topic at hand. We want to develop this question, too—what is untruth?—on the basis of a text by Plato, following the question as it is asked in the *Theaetetus*; not for the sake of congruence with our earlier discussions, but because Plato in fact poses the question of the essence of the ψεῦδος in a fundamental sense for the first time in the *Theaetetus*.

We should note, however, that this question was already essentially prepared in pre-Platonic times. The question of truth brings with it the question of untruth, but this coupling does not yet amount to any *es-*

sential insight. To the contrary, in the beginnings of Greek philosophy there persisted a *fundamental difficulty* in grasping the essence of seeming, of the null, of the false. This difficulty is based on the principle: what is, *is;* what is not, *is not.*

Now if error, as the false and null, is something negative, and if what is not, cannot be, then there can be no error and no falsehood. But on the contrary, falsehood and lies constitute a power in human Dasein. The *power of untruth* stands opposed to the *non-Being of the null,* which *is* not at all.

It was thus an essential step in philosophy to grasp this question in the first place and to develop how it is to be understood: how that which in itself is null, such as the false, the erroneous—how, nevertheless, this could be, and could be allowed to develop its power.

As a result of this question, the question of the essence of *Being* was subjected to an essential transformation. It was recognized that even what *is not,* the null, *is.* But we must also say *how* it is. This demands a transformation of the essence of Being, which, however, was carried out only in its first stages. And there matters have stood to this day.

The question of *untruth* is no arbitrary question. Neither is it simply about the contrary concept to truth. It inserts us into the *fundamental question of all philosophizing* and all knowledge. We want to see on what path the question is posed and developed by *Plato.*

We can also get closer to the question by saying: is there error because man gets into errancy and because this errancy subsists somewhere in itself, so to speak; or is there this errancy only because man errs, and does he err only because man, in the ground of his Being, is errant? Among the Greeks, however, the question does not reach this level.

To begin with, we ask along Plato's lines: where does the false as what is not and as the null belong, and how is this possible in general? For this it is necessary to get clear about the fundamental features of the dialogue in the course of which Plato comes to this question—that is, we must define the guiding question of this dialogue and then follow the course of its questioning and its development up to the point where, within the question of ἐπιστήμη, the question of the ψεῦδος comes up.

Next we must determine on what basis and in what space this question arises for the Greeks. First we will develop the guiding question up to the point where the question of the ψεῦδος comes up; then we have to get closer to the question of the ψεῦδος and the fundamental ways it is treated.

The guiding question is: τί ἐστιν ἐπιστήμη? What is knowing? This question does not mean: what is science? And it does not deal with the doctrine and theory of science, but with the question of the essence of knowing in a quite broad and originary sense (that is, in the Greek sense).

ἐπίστασθαι means: to oversee a thing, to stand over it, to stand before and understand it, to be fit for it, to know one's way around it. Simultaneously with ἐπιστήμη, the word τέχνη is used (the root of our "technique"), erroneously translated as "art." τέχνη is not a way of fabricating, but a cognitive concept, a concept of cognition, knowledge, know-how, being capable of forming, producing something.

For the Greeks, art too is a kind of knowing, an actualization of truth, a revelation of beings themselves, of beings that were not yet known before. Art was the fundamental way in which reality was discovered. Only through formation does humanity learn the greatness of Being.

Among the Greeks, the word "knowledge" had the very broad sense of every type of know-how, not only the knowledge that was later termed theoretical knowledge. Knowledge means gaining a foothold and standpoint in the openness of things and their happening.

Only with *Aristotle* did a separation between ἐπιστήμη and τέχνη come to pass, but in such a way that even here the fundamental meaning of knowledge is retained. ἐπιστήμη is knowledge of and familiarity with a particular field; τέχνη is knowledge that is directed to handmade and other products.

This is the knowledge (in the broad sense) that is the topic of the question, τί ἐστιν ἐπιστήμη? τί ἐστιν, what something is, we call the question of essence. In the question of essence, what something is, we intend to experience what belongs to an object *as such*. What is a house? What belongs to such a thing as a house? The answer is supposed to bring out what belongs to every thing, what pertains in general to some matter at hand, the universal concept that delimits what, in general, belongs to a thing.

But now, if I ask about the essence of Frederick the Great, this being that has been and will be given only once, this cannot be some universal concept. The essence of a thing cannot be found in what belongs to it in general; instead, universal characteristics are only characteristics derived from an essential content. I do not look for the universal characteristics that can be found in it, but for what *makes possible this* thing, the *inner possibility* of a thing.

I ask further about the *ground* of the inner possibility and thus about the *genuine* essence, I ask about the inner possibility of what we call knowing. This question—what is knowing?—is today one that everyone who pretends to join in the discussion of the question of the essence of science must have thought through to the very end.

The course of the question has the following character. A series of answers to this question are proposed, which are always rejected as inadequate. In the end, the dialogue concludes negatively: it has no result. But the result is not what stands at the end, but is the *course of the questioning itself.* This course is always also the path (the essence) of every philosophy.

The *act* of questioning and the persistence *in* questioning are what allow the essence of things to open up; every answer ruins the question. Only in the *question* is truth that is capable of becoming knowledge possible and given.

Therefore we must prepare ourselves for the fact that what is at stake here is a philosophy, and not storytelling. Behind the *rejections* of the answers, there in fact *hides* an *answer.*

Chapter Two
Theaetetus's Answers to the Question of the Essence of Knowledge and their Rejection

§33. The first answer: ἐπιστήμη is αἴσθησις.
Critical delimitation of the essence of perception

a) αἴσθησις as the fundamental form of apprehending things and allowing them to come upon us. The determinate, yet limited openness of αἴσθησις

Τί ἐστιν ἐπιστήμη? This is the guiding question of the dialogue *Theaetetus*. The *first answer* runs: ἐπιστήμη = αἴσθησις, to know is to perceive, is perception. This answer will be rejected later on, but initially we will ask why precisely this answer is given and why *this* answer is given as the *first*.

We may make the assumption that in the dialogues the interlocutors do not babble randomly back and forth. Rather, the sequence of the discussion unfolds on the grounds of an originary understanding and speaking with one another.

Why precisely *this* answer? One can of course recall something from psychology textbooks: perception (αἴσθησις) is the lower cognitive capacity as compared to a higher one. But this is not what the conversation is about, nor is it a question of Plato's wanting to refute *Protagoras* and perceptual relativism. His goal is not to refute but to exhibit the matter at hand.

The ground [for the first answer] in Plato's text is more essential and deeper: it lies in the relationship between what ἐπιστήμη is in fact and what αἴσθησις means for the Greeks. We can recognize that this answer is not arbitrary from the fact that Aristotle, when he wants to designate the highest kind of knowing, νοῦς, designates this apprehending as αἴσθησίς τις [a kind of perception]. By this, he does not mean that somehow the essential relations of mores or of all the historicity of Being can be smelled with the nose or heard with the ears. Instead, αἴσθησις in its proper meaning as perceiving is taken up first as the essence of knowing, spontaneously as it were, because for the Greeks, perceiving and being perceived mean the same thing as φαίνεται: to say that this shows itself, something shows itself, is the same as saying that something is perceived.

"Something shows itself": a Greek understands this in the sense of *presenting* itself; it gives itself in its *presence* and, in this presence, it becomes *revealed*. Being perceived—the fact that things enter the realm of experience—is the happening in which things come to manifestation, come into openness, show themselves, appear. We should not debase its meaning by thinking of it only in terms of ears, noses, and the like. Its meaning is a *self-showing* that openly comes forth.

φαντασία also has *this* meaning and not the later meaning of the fantastical, the merely imaginary; rather, it is the becoming-visible, the self-showing, of a being as it is. Plato says: φαντασία and perception are the same, the same happening as being perceived. When someone speaks from the perspective of a "theory of knowledge," it makes perfect sense that φαντασία would be a mere fancy, not the same happening as what is perceived.

In being perceived, the openness of things happens: immediate, everyday experience. In the question of what knowledge is, this has led to giving this answer: knowledge is perception.

How does this conform to the fundamental meaning of knowing: to understand one's way around a thing, to oversee it? To the extent that I am a match for the matter at hand, then it is in my grasp, it is at my disposal, it is open to me. Despite the fact that this answer is fundamentally justified, it is rejected, not because it is simply false and does not hit upon the facts of the matter, but because it is *insufficient*.

It does hit the mark that something like openness has to do with knowing, but knowing as standing in openness in the sense of truth is *more* than this. Truth is not simply openness; rather, it is the openness and unconcealment of *beings*.

We can clarify the distinction by way of an example. A stone that lies on the ground clearly stands in a spatial relationship with the ground, in that it lies upon it. But the ground upon which the stone lies is not given to the stone. The stone does not encounter the ground; it is not accessible to the stone. Things are different for the dog running on the ground. The dog can feel the ground in its paws. Something is given to the dog. But *what* is given to the dog is not accessible to it (as street, hot surface, and so on), it is not revealed to the dog. Something is revealed—the relationship between the dog and the ground—but not as a being that is so and so and is understood as such and such. There is an openness, but not an openness of *beings*.

Plato seeks to show that αἴσθησις belongs, in a certain way, to knowing and to the knowable, but that at the same time something essential is lacking.

b) The insufficiency of αἴσθησις for distinguishing the manifold domains of what is perceived and the characteristics of their Being

In the previous session,[1] we started out with the meaning of the word ψεῦδος and we moved on to the question of what this untruth really is. At what point in the *Theaetetus* does the question of ψεῦδος get introduced? By determining this place, we will determine in advance the horizon within which the question is posed.

The *guiding question* of the dialogue was: what is knowing? This is *knowing* in the widest sense, according to which knowing illuminates, raises up, carries, and leads each mode of human comportment. It is precisely the multiplicity in which knowing is experienced that has raised in advance the question of *unity*. At issue is not the specialized question of what science is; that question develops only incidentally.

Two fundamental concepts and words go together for the Greeks: ἐπιστήμη and τέχνη. That they go together testifies that knowing should not be taken as science but rather as know-how. Science is only a very specific mode of knowing, and it has very definite boundaries. With the blurring of this boundary between philosophy and science it came about that the *question of knowing* was deformed and today has been entirely lost.

This *guiding question* about what knowing is, is clarified through a variety of answers without any of these answers being taken as conclusive.

Why does this statement unfold as the first answer: knowing (ἐπιστήμη) = perception (αἴσθησις)? Knowing means planting one's feet (ἐπίστημι [I know, I stand on]), taking a stand within the openness of beings as what are to be unveiled first of all. To what extent does αἴσθησις correspond to this fundamental conception of ἐπιστήμη?

αἴσθησις = perceiving is an entry into a *definite* openness. The answer that ἐπιστήμη = αἴσθησις lies close at hand because αἴσθησις comes upon us *immediately*, because it is the fundamental form in which things are *there* for us. Given the originary experience and the fundamental character of Being, this had to be the first answer.

In being perceived, there lies a definite openness that Plato expresses with the term φαίνεται = shows itself, comes upon us. With this characterization of perceiving as openness, it is not yet established what knowing is: standing (ἐπίστασθαι) in the truth and untruth of beings.

---

1. {Recapitulation at the beginning of the session of 22 February 1934.}

We illustrated this by discussing how a stone, an animal, and a human being relate to the ground. For the stone, the ground is not revealed; for the animal, it is, inasmuch the ground pushes against the animal, but the animal is unable to experience the ground as ground. The human being, in contrast, is able to experience immediately where, how, and upon what we are standing; the human being has an experience of what is supporting us here and how it is constituted.

This first answer—knowing is perception and being perceived—is rejected because, while a *certain* openness surely takes place in perception, this openness is not yet in itself the openness of *beings as such*. In a certain sense, αἴσθησις is necessary, for *through it* something *comes upon* us, but perception and being-perceived are insufficient to make openness equal the truth of a *being* for us.

Plato now shows that, for us, the perception of things is *more* than the mere encounter with things. When I gaze out through the window and listen to the song of a bird while at the same time seeing the color of the foliage of the trees, I can take in both through immediate experience. I experience the coloration of the leaves and the song of the bird, and I can distinguish each immediately as *different.*

If I experience each (the song and the color of the foliage) as not the same, then this question follows: on what grounds is *such* an experience of this given domain possible? I can see the color, I can hear the song, but the *difference*—that the song is different from the color—I can neither see nor hear. I can neither see nor hear, and yet I immediately take in the *otherness* of both.

This emphasizes that, when we take in the multiplicity, a mode of experience enters into the Being that is given directly, a mode that is not encompassed by αἴσθησις. What is involved here that goes above and beyond *mere* apprehending, so that we can experience *being-different* all at once?

c) The soul as the relation to beings that unifies and holds open

One usually answers: thinking! But this is no answer, because what thinking is still stands in question. Plato does indeed speak of διάνοια (from νοῦς and διά), which we are accustomed to translate as "thinking." διάνοια = to run through something given in advance, to go through it and under it, in that I take it in thoroughly in all directions according to how it is and what it is.

This is, first of all, an assertion about what the given makes accessible to us, over and above αἴσθησις. Plato carefully and clearly says that beyond our merely allowing something to come upon us, it must somehow happen that we take in what we encounter *as a being,* and this must happen in such a way that we ourselves, *for our part,* comprehend the given.

The soul, the essence of the human being, must itself, for itself— from itself and for itself—get involved in the sphere of beings and in relation to them: ἡ ψυχή, ὅταν αὐτὴ καθ' αὑτὴν πραγματεύεται περὶ τὰ ὄντα (187a5ff). Not merely taking things in through the senses—the human being involves himself with what he encounters, with what he takes in.

There are two things going on: (a) taking in or perceiving; (b) involving oneself. From this it is clearly evident that both must be grasped, and in their unity, in order to offer an answer to the question about ἐπιστήμη, an answer in which beings *as* beings will be revealed.

The *first* answer (ἐπιστήμη = αἴσθησις) is not simply false; it provides the positively determined *condition* for the possibility of beings—but this answer is *insufficient*.

§34. The second answer: ἐπιστήμη is δόξα

a) The double sense of δόξα as view: look and belief

Keeping in view the development of the first answer, we once again pose the question, "What is knowing?" The *second* answer is that knowledge is δοξάζειν, δόξα. We can initially translate the word as "belief." But this translation is incomplete.

We pose the question: *why* is *this* answer given now? We can gather why by considering what the Greeks think of with the word δόξα, on the basis of its *original* content. δόξα—δοκέω = I show myself to others, I also show myself to myself; still better, as we say in German: I feel a certain way [*ich komme mir vor*: literally, "I come forth to myself"], so and so strikes me [*kommt mir vor*] as peculiar. I myself can strike myself in such and such a way, offer a definite look, appear such and such.

This fundamental meaning of the Greek word δόξα can be documented without further ado in as many passages as you like. We wish to cite a passage from our dialogue (143e4ff.). At the beginning of the conversation, Socrates challenges Theodorus to tell him of a very promising person among the Athenian youth, so that Socrates may engage him in philosophical conversation. Theodorus replies: I do know such a youth, and if he were beautiful I would hesitate to name him, lest I make it seem to anyone that I have (lest I strike anyone as having) a passion for him: μὴ καί τῳ δόξω ἐν ἐπιθυμίᾳ αὐτοῦ εἶναι (143e7). This coming forth, this striking people as being such and such or otherwise, was translated by Schleiermacher as, "so that no one may believe of me" (*Werke* II, 1, 3rd ed. 1836, p. 132).

Here we find the same fundamental relation between language and word-concept that we met in the contrary concept to truth, in λανθάνω.[2]

2. {See above, [German] pp. 229-30.}

The German speaker always grasps the situation beginning with the other ("one believes"), but the Greek begins with himself: δοκέω, λανθάνω [I seem, I escape notice].

An example from Homer, *Odyssey* VIII, 93, where Odysseus says that he remained concealed before all the others as one who was shedding tears.[3] A person, then, remains in a certain concealment. We do not say: he remained concealed to all the others. We say: he shed tears without any of the others noticing. We speak beginning with the other who is perceiving.

These are quite clear proofs of the tremendous power that ἀλήθεια had in the Greek experience of Dasein. Before we enter the confrontation with the Greeks, our fundamental task is to have a completely clear knowledge of how they stood in relation to beings.

The word δόξα also belongs among these fundamental meanings: I come forth; that which comes forth, that is, strikes others as such and such, that which shows itself; the look, the appearance of something, the *respect* in which something—an achievement, a person—stands; also fame. δόξα θεοῦ in the New Testament = the majesty of God. But what is decisive is this meaning of δόξα: *looking* a certain way, standing in *visibility and respectability.*

Now, this meaning goes together with a *second* meaning. The second we grasp in a certain sense with the words *believe, belief.* With this, a *double meaning* comes to light. We are familiar with this double meaning when we translate δόξα as *view.* A picture postcard or vista postcard, is a card that shows a picture, a vista—a view in the objective sense; it shows the look of a landscape as it strikes us. View in the objective sense of a multiplicity of objects. But we also use the word "view" in this sense: My view is . . . The postcard has no belief, it offers a look. So there is a double sense: (a) as a characteristic of the thing, look; (b) in the sense of believing, thinking such and such. This double character always resonates among the Greeks from the start; it is based on what the word means.

From this clarification of the fundamental meaning of δόξα and δοξάζειν we can already gather why the second answer must run as it does.

b) The apparent suitability of δόξα as ἐπιστήμη: its double character corresponds to αἴσθησις and διάνοια

Two things belong to the experience of a being (for the Greeks): (1) the being somehow comes upon us, but also (2) on *our* part there is a way of *grasping* it. Both seem to be fulfilled in δόξα. (1) Color of the leaf, song of the bird, given to me by sight and hearing. To this there

3. {. . . ἔνθ᾽ ἄλλους μὲν πάντας ἐλάνθανε δάκρυα λείβων.}

belongs (2) the grasping of both as different; thinking such and such about them, having a view about them.

This requirement of an experience in order for it to give us a being as a being is satisfied by the *twofold character* of δόξα. The first meaning of δόξα corresponds to αἴσθησις [perception] (φαίνεται [it shows itself]), the second to διάνοια [thought].

There are also other places in Plato where it is shown that the fundamental meaning of human cognition is δόξα, although Plato himself does not at all develop the special combination of meanings in δόξα; he does not even see it in this connection, but rather finds himself and moves within the turbulence of this whole ambiguity.

c) The multiple ambiguity of δόξα. The split between letting-appear and distorting: the arising of the ψεῦδος in the question of the essence of knowledge

As soon as the second answer has been given, a further problem intrudes. Something that presents a look, that appears in such and such a way, can immediately, insofar as it appears, create an *illusion*. In this (in the illusion) there lies the possibility that what *shows* itself may *conceal* what lies behind it.

Accordingly, δόξα as belief can have a view about something that corresponds to the object, but it can also, as a view, hide the object. Each of these *two-sided* meanings can either *fit* the object as it is or *disguise* it.

This ambiguity is found in the essential *duality* of the phenomenon in *our* word "view": it can be correct or incorrect, it can hit or miss. This involves some leeway, a distinctive sort of wavering, to which there nevertheless corresponds a firmness, inasmuch as I insist on the view without being able to prove that what I believe in this view is true.

This double character makes it the case that the wavering can be just as great as the resoluteness that stands behind it. This constitutes the sense of an authentic, genuine *faith*. The possibility: it could at bottom be so, it could also be otherwise; nevertheless, the insistence: it is so. This is characteristic of faith, quite independently of belief in the sense of a justified cognition.

With this we have reached the point where the ψεῦδος, the untrue, the distorting, the false, comes up; and because δόξα is *view* and has in it the possibility of creating an *illusion*, distortion belongs to it. A view is always in danger of being a mere view, mere seeming, of being unmasked as mere seeming. At the moment when the question of knowledge comes up against δόξα, it becomes necessary to get into ψεῦδος.

Now we must pursue ψεῦδος on its own, and thus deviate from the dialogue. We must point out only one notable fact, that in considering the second answer Plato, who at bottom is really aiming at the question,

"What is knowledge?" dwells on the question of the *distorted view* (ψευδὴς δόξα).

If a view (δόξα) has something to do with knowledge, it is the *true* belief—or so one would believe; then I know the thing. But we are faced with the remarkable fact that Plato deals with δόξα ἀληθής [true belief] only very fleetingly (200b-201c), while ψεῦδος is treated much more thoroughly (187c-200).

Interpreters have wondered over and over why Plato always deals with falsehood so extensively. There is no reason other than that Plato consciously ran up against a fundamental problem of philosophy in general.

This much is clear: the question of ψεῦδος is treated in the context of the question of δόξα. This whole investigation of the distorted view (δόξα ψευδής), of believing something distorted, is set forth in the preliminary investigation (187d-191) and the main investigation (192-200).

The preliminary investigation is a characteristic Platonic development of the problem. It does not get into this phenomenon of "false belief" directly, but rather tries to develop the whole difficulty and wondrousness that lies in the problem of a "false view." The aim is to unfold this entire wonder, the τέρας.[4] Only the main investigation tries to find the answer in a positive way.

We have been so thoroughly warped by the long development, so deformed as regards the simplicity and greatness of the original question, that we cannot at all re-experience how the Greeks ran up against the phenomenon of a false view. We cannot feel the strangeness of the phenomenon anymore.

The phenomenon of the false is so puzzling for the Greeks because it cannot initially be brought into the domain with which they are familiar.

Plato now attempts to show through three examples that this phenomenon of the false view is so wondrous that we have to say: this really cannot be. It is shown in three phases that there cannot be a false view.

This is opposed just as vigorously by the position that there is such a thing as the *power of error,* of distortion, of the false. Plato forces us to decide. Which is true? Must we hold to the *impossibility of the false,* or hold that we stand under the *power of the fact of the false?*

4. [Reading τέρας ("marvel," "monster," or "wonder") here for πέρας ("limit"); cf. *Theaetetus* 188c4.]

Chapter Three
The Question of the
Possibility of ψευδὴς δόξα

§35. Preliminary investigation:
the impossibility of the phenomenon of ψευδὴς δόξα

a) The arising of the ψεῦδος in the elucidation of δόξα as ἐπιστήμη[1]

The second answer to the question, "What is knowing?" runs as follows: knowing is δόξα, belief, view. We sought to display the word
δόξα in its fundamental meaning, and we ran up against a special
ambiguity.

We grasped this ambiguity in the word "view," which has the sense,
first, of the look that something offers, as in a postcard vista; second,
it also means "it is my view," "it is my belief." Both meanings lie in the
one word δόξα and resonate in one another.

A *further* division of meaning is made possible on the basis of *this*
ambiguity. A view can be a positive force; it can *hit the mark*. But the
appearance can also *miss* the mark. A view can give a thing as it is, but
it can also offer a mere appearance in the sense of semblance. It can be
a mere view, a mere belief.

It was important to elucidate this fundamental meaning of δόξα because in Plato, in the discussion of whether δόξα constitutes the essence
of knowing, the question arose concerning the ψευδὴς δόξα, the ψεῦδος,
the false, the untrue. The place where the ψεῦδος emerges in Plato is, as
it were, fixed. We will confine ourselves to considering the ψευδὴς δόξα.

Even though this investigation into false belief does not really come
under consideration immediately for the question about the essence of
knowing, it is remarkable that Plato has nevertheless treated false be-

1. {Recapitulation at the beginning of the session of 27 February 1934.}

192

lief in considerably more detail in comparison to the treatment of true belief. This suggests that behind this is hidden a *fundamental problem.*

b) The field of vision of the preliminary investigation as an advance decision about the impossibility of the phenomenon

According to the stage of philosophical questioning at this point, the *preliminary investigation* of the question about false belief should demonstrate the *impossibility* of something like *a false belief.* This impossibility is demonstrated on the basis of ancient propositions that were valid until then for Greek philosophy. We can trace this in short order.

We therefore want to establish the question in advance: is something like a false view possible *at all?* In order not to leave the discussion lying in abstraction, we wish to invoke an example mentioned in the dialogue (188b6ff.): if someone in Athens takes a man who is approaching him for Socrates (when in truth it is Theaetetus), then this false view that I have about a man I am encountering is not accidental (one might observe, as a matter of comparison, that Theaetetus, just like Socrates, has a snub nose and is popeyed). I therefore take Theaetetus for Socrates. I am laboring under a false view regarding the person I am encountering.

But on the basis of recognized philosophical principles of ancient philosophy, this cannot be possible. The proof unfolds in this way:

α) The alternatives of familiarity and unfamiliarity

Granted, if I should labor under a false view like this, then because of this I have, in a certain way, a familiarity with the person encountered: [he is] snub-nosed, popeyed—but at the same time, since I take Theaetetus for Socrates, I am not familiar with the person encountered. Therefore, one could insist that with respect to one and the same thing (the same man), I am both familiar and unfamiliar. But in relation to an object there is no possibility other than being either familiar or unfamiliar with it.

Therefore we would have to be familiar and unfamiliar with the same object at the same time. But this is impossible. This proves in principle that something like a false view cannot be. According to fundamental principles, it is not possible that someone, insofar as he is familiar with something, is unfamiliar with the very same thing, or that someone, insofar as he is unfamiliar with something, has familiarity with the same thing.

But while this is indeed correctly developed on the basis of fundamental principles, it still contradicts the facts of the matter. The *deduction from fundamental principles* stands *against the facts of the matter.*

The real meaning of this reflection is to indicate and explain what really belongs to this remarkable phenomenon, one that is called a marvel: namely, that I do not see *one* object, but rather two, and at the same time, that I operate in both familiarity and unfamiliarity—to explain that and why something like familiarity and unfamiliarity with one and the same object is possible.

β) The alternatives of Being and not-Being

The *second* proof of the impossibility of a false view or believing something false, ψευδῆ δοξάζειν, goes like this: the false is the *null*, but the *null* is the *nothing*. Therefore, to believe something false means to believe nothing.

It is asked whether there is such a thing in other contexts. My activity is a seeing because I see something. But if I see nothing, my activity is not a seeing; when I hear nothing, it is not a hearing.

If, correspondingly, I now believe nothing, then there is no believing whatsoever. Believing dissolves into itself. Something either *is,* or it *is not.*

It is not just the case that in a false view, I am familiar and unfamiliar with the same thing at the same time. Behind this is hidden the question of whether that which is *null* is necessarily a *nothing.* Plato finds the way for the first time.

γ) ψευδὴς δόξα as ἀλλοδοξία
(substitution instead of confusion)

The *third* proof proceeds in another manner. The false view is seen dogmatically as ἀλλοδοξία, a believing in which I *exchange* something that I believed at first for something else, such as when I encounter Theaetetus and *substitute* the person encountered for Socrates. I substitute Theaetetus for Socrates.

It is shown that this really never occurs. "It does not even occur in dreams that we take an ox for a horse" (cf. 190c2–3). There is no substitution. A false view in which such a thing would happen is impossible.

This also refers to a phenomenon that in fact lies concealed in the false view, in which I substitute something encountered for something else: I take something that looks this way, not as itself, but as something else.

All three of these arguments have reached the conclusion that, on the basis of prevalent principles, something like a false view is simply *impossible.* Against this stands the *actual matter of fact* of the existence of *error, illusion,* and *falsehood.* Which must now yield? The *matter of fact,* which is experienced on a daily basis, or the *principles* that have been valid for hundreds of years?

§36. The decision for the phenomenon of ψευδὴς δόξα

a) On the scope and character of the decision

The decision is made *for* the facts, *against* the principles (but only against these particular principles)—for the phenomenon, for the necessity of opening one's eyes now, before we engage in any deduction—in order to see what is going on in false belief.

The decision, in the sense of giving up a thing that at the time was self-evident for the Greeks, is the decision that carried and determined Platonic philosophizing. Plato expressed himself on this point in the *Sophist* [241d], saying that by giving up the proposition that something either is or is not, he had to become the murderer of his own father (Parmenides). With this saying Plato wants to announce the depths that this decision reaches. By way of this decision, the world is seen in a fundamentally new way.

We ourselves today have been standing—not just, as some might say, for the last year, but for quite a few years—before a *still greater decision* for philosophy, a decision that in its greatness, its breadth, and its depth extends far beyond even the decision of Plato's time. It finds expression in my book *Being and Time*. A transformation from the ground up.

The issue is whether the understanding of *Being* is transforming itself from the ground up. It will be a transformation that will first of all provide the *framework* for the spiritual history of our people. This cannot be proved, but it is a *faith* that must be borne out by history.

With this reflection Plato shows that it is necessary to retract the previous propositions altogether. He pursues the line of thought that leads him to what is positive about ψευδὴς δόξα, and thereby sees what the false is, given that the task at hand is now to disregard philosophical principles and stick to the *phenomenon*.

This cannot mean, as up to now one has always believed, that something like the facts of the matter in themselves could be grasped, purely on their own. Every fact is grasped or graspable by us only if we put it into a *particular perspective*, see it under particular principles. There is no such thing as being able to see things purely, without prejudice.

Everything that we experience or interrogate, we see and interrogate in a *particular perspective*. Because this is so, in the unprejudiced inspection of a factual situation we must not only open our eyes, but at the same time we have to know from which perspective I am seeing the object—whether the state of affairs is created by the perspective, whether the understanding corresponds to the object.

This does not mean that everything depends on one's standpoint. There is always a standpoint; but the question is whether a standpoint is genuine. It is not that I simply determine [the state of affairs], but the question is whether [I have adopted] a really appropriate standpoint. It must be decided whether the perspective in which I am questioning corresponds to the object itself.

Plato has defined the task—not methodically, but with immediate inspiration—through the preliminary investigation: we must be able to attain a point of view that makes it possible for there to be such a thing as being both familiar and unfamiliar with an object. A cognition in which an object that has been grasped is exchanged with another.

b) The new starting point for posing the question by way of the deepened question concerning the constitution of the soul

The posing of the question is directed into quite different dimensions. *Where* does something like a false view belong? A false view is, in any case, a condition of *ourselves,* a definite comportment. The human self is designated in Greek with ψυχή, soul. πάθος ψυχῆς is a condition of our soul, a definite comportment of *human Dasein.*

Accordingly, false views cannot adequately be clarified until *man* has *first* been clarified in this regard. So in illuminating falsehood, we run up against the question of what the *human soul* is.

Plato offers two similes for it; in these similes, just as in the procedure of the allegory of the cave, the question is led back to the question of humanity. Here too, the question of untruth emerges as a question about the *soul,* about the *constitution* of the soul, about the essence of human Dasein.

We want to pose three questions:

1. In what sort of contexts does Plato pose the problem of false views?
2. To what extent can the essence of δόξα be grasped in the light of these sorts of comportment?
3. What does this imply for the essence of ψεῦδος, of untruth?

Plato deals with the question of what the *domain of origin* for false views is by presenting two similes, in which the soul is presented first as

1. κήρινον ἐκμαγεῖον, a wax block, and then
2. as a περιστερεών, an aviary, taken as an ἀγγεῖον, box, container.

One should not insist on these images in every respect; they have been devised only for a very particular purpose. The images are supposed to help us understand a comportment of the soul. Historians have demonstrated that Plato took these images from somewhere else. That may be so. But what is decisive is what Plato makes of them.

---

§37. Determining the soul more deeply and broadly through two similes

a) The wax simile. Being mindful (making-present)

We ask, what is the first image (191c8ff.) meant to say? The soul as a wax block. This block is, given the various human types, now pure, now impure, now hard, now soft, receptive in different ways to the impressions that impinge upon the soul from the world.

Plato says that this feature of the soul is bequeathed to the soul by μνημοσύνη [memory], as the mother of the muses; it is an originary gift of the soul's essence; it belongs to the soul's *essential constitution*. This μνημονεύειν means: to be mindful of a thing, to have a connection to an object, to a thing, even when the object is not immediately present, as it is in αἴσθησις.

The capability of the soul to *make something present*, even when it is not there, is exhibited here in the image—to retain a connection to something absent, without leaving our location. We have an immediate relationship of Being to particular locales—Berlin, for example, or the Baltic Sea—without our being physically present there. This relationship is given by way of the image of the wax tablet.

Now, it has happened in the course of the development of the history of philosophy that one has mistaken this image and its way of illustrating the issue for the issue itself, that one takes the facts in such a way as to think that somewhere there are facts that somehow enter into the soul. Through this, the fundamental fact of the matter is not recognized from the start: that I can have and constantly do have an *immediate connection of Being to what is absent.*

The *corporeality of human beings* certainly plays a mediating role, but what role corporeality plays is a further question that can be posed only if the fundamental relationship is clarified.

We designate the relationship as a *making-present,* by virtue of which the domain of beings within which I am constantly moving extends out beyond what I see with my eyes and hear with my ears. This whole domain of what we, as it were, preserve, is what we call the *preserve.* This is what we live amidst—much more intensely and immediately than we live in what we immediately perceive and grasp when we act.

By virtue of this connection, *two* things happen:

1. The relation of making-present can slacken on our part and work itself loose, allowing the things in making-present to slip

away from us into *forgetting*. Forgetting is a specific mode of making-present.

2. Or, our relation to the content of the world is such that things become different without our involvement; things withdraw from us, so that we cast out into the void with our projects.

From us there arise certain connections—free forms in the sense of imagination and fantasy, and beyond these, creative formation (projection). Plato says that the soul has a characteristic *expansiveness, εὐρυχωρία* [194d], that towers out over the narrowness of what is merely grasped with the senses.

b) The aviary simile. Modes of containing

The symbolism of the second image, an aviary (197b8ff.), intrinsically belongs with the first image. According to the second image, the soul is an aviary into which particular doves fly from our earliest youth onwards. We become acquainted with beings of various sorts, we move according to specific representations that are distinguished by Plato in three ways. There are some that keep together in tight flocks, {those that break away from the flock = things in their particularity and uniqueness},[2] then those in looser groups = mutable things and relations, and finally those doves that are to be found among all the others = all those representations and concepts that play a *co*-determining role in every relation. For example: each object is *an* object, but each on the other hand is *another* (each is different from the other). This results in the following: unity, otherness, difference, multiplicity. This third type of dove is found everywhere.

Whoever possesses such an aviary possesses the doves in this cage, in this container, but does so in different ways. First, by sitting in a house, in a room, and having the doves under a roof. In this way, he can possess them and add to his possession. But he can also grasp a dove inside the container. There is the fundamental possibility of taking something out of this domain and *having* it in a *stronger* sense, taking on a *relationship of Being* with it. This is *the* difference, that something can be *absent* and *present*.

---

2. {Gap in Hallwachs's transcript. Editor's conjecture based on the lecture course of the same name from Winter Semester 1931–1932 (GA 34), p. 305.}

§38. Clarification of the double sense of δόξα. Mistakes are made possible by the bifurcation of δόξα into presencing and making-present

What does this clarification show us? We see the possibility of δόξα as a correct view. To return to our example: we take the man we meet, who looks like Theaetetus and also is Theaetetus, as Theaetetus. What is going on here?

First of all: what is given to us is what confronts us, the particular appearance of a particular person. At the same time, we look *at* what we encounter, we look at it as Theaetetus. Here we are moving within a remarkable mode of grasping things.

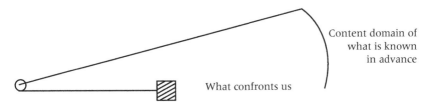

Content domain of what is known in advance

What confronts us

We can picture it this way: the person confronts us; we take him as Theaetetus. We grasp him on the basis of a particular way of representing him, on the basis of our knowledge of Theaetetus. In experiencing what confronts me as Theaetetus I do not simply take in what I perceive, but I take in what I perceive *as* Theaetetus in a *re-grasping* = in such a way that I have a definite view of him. I already know in advance who and what Theaetetus is, regardless of whether he is confronting me or not. I grasp what confronts me on the basis of a knowledge by virtue of which I can make Theaetetus present to myself at any time.

Human beings move in the direction of what immediately confronts them, but *at the same time* they move within the grasping of the *content domain,* that is, what they have experienced earlier. All cognition has this remarkable *double character.* δόξα is *both.* When I have a view of something, I see what I encounter from a particular perspective. This double meaning is not accidental; *every view is intrinsically bifurcated in accordance with its essence.* With this, the solution to the question has in principle been found.

If we now move on to *false belief,* if we take what confronts us as Socrates instead of Theaetetus, what we took to be impossible in the preliminary investigation is now the case.

I have a particular view of the one confronting me, a particular familiarity with him (snub-nosed, popeyed), the appearance of a particular person, but in actuality I have *no* acquaintance with the one confronting me, inasmuch as I take him for Socrates. Here we have a simultaneous familiarity and unfamiliarity that concern two different objects.

The second difficulty lies in the fact that what confronts me in δόξα (as a false view) is not null, but is such that what is actually confronting me is taken as something else. What we have here is a certain exchange, in that I take him for Socrates instead of Theaetetus. This switch is a *confusion*.

When I *exchange* an object, I give away one object in return for the other; but when I *confuse* them, this means that I hold onto the object and grasp the other together with it. Both are held together in this distinctive grasp. This *bifurcation is a fundamental structure of* δόξα; it *makes it intrinsically possible* that I can either *grasp* what is present at hand confronting me, or *mistake* it.

The *domain* of *making-present* is always *broader* than what is present at hand. So I can always either grasp or mistake the object on the basis of the domain. With this it is given that *untruth, falsehood, is built into this fundamental constitution of human Dasein*, that it always moves in the *present* and at the same time in *making-present*.

This *bifurcation* makes possible both truth and the false. These, truth and falsehood, stand under the same conditions, namely, that the domain is broader than the object. Whether truth or untruth is attained is always a question of *decision*, a question of *struggle*.

---

§39. The essence of truth as historical man's struggle with untruth. Untruth is posited with the enabling of the essence of truth

The *essence of truth* is the *struggle* with *untruth*, where *untruth* is *posited with the enabling of the essence of truth*. This struggle, as struggle, is always a specific struggle. Truth is always truth *for us*.

For us today, the true is not so much some particular truth as it is knowing about the essence of truth itself. We grasp this more deeply if we grasp what the *bifurcation* means.

What this says is that man, insofar as he exists, must always stand fast by that to which he is immediately bound, and that he *exists* only in what he projects himself into and what he gives form to in the sense of *binding* to the given and *projecting* upon what is freely created.

What is conceived formally here as the inner constitution of man is nothing other than the distinguishing fact that man—man as *historical*—exists in the togetherness of a historical people, with a specific, *historical mission*, and exists in the preservation of the forces that carry him forward and to which he is bound. δόξα is just the offshoot, formally conceived, of this distinguishing feature. This fundamental constitution is the *domain* within which the *struggle for the truth* must play itself out.

If we today stand before the question of whether a people just this once grasps its full essence, then this means that we are asking whether the people is strong enough—whether it, in itself, has the will to itself, to stand up to the will to its own essence. It means asking whether we will grapple with this, whether we will take on as our task this knowing and will to know in their full intensity and hardness, or whether we are of the opinion that culture and spiritual life are a supplement that produces itself by itself, while we look on as if it were a game.

So we stand or fall by the will to *knowledge and spirit.* Today, there is much talk of *blood and soil* as forces that are frequently invoked. The literati, who are still around even today, have seized upon these forces. Blood and soil are indeed powerful and necessary, but they are *not sufficient* conditions for the Dasein of a people.

Other conditions are *knowledge and spirit,* but not as an addendum to a list. Knowledge first brings a direction and path to the blood's flow, first brings to the soil the fecundity of what it can bring to term. Knowledge lets the nobility of the soil yield what the soil can bring to term.

The decision lies in whether we are capable of taking on all this with adequate originality and strength—whether we are capable of giving our Dasein a real weight and a real gravity; only if we succeed in this shall we create the possibility of *greatness* for ourselves.

Great things are revealed only to great men and to a great people. Small men take small things as huge.

The *true* is something for us to *achieve,* the decision about our mission. Only through the decision of this struggle will we create the possibility of a *fate.* There is fate only where a human being exposes himself, *in a free decision,* to the *danger of his Dasein.*

APPENDIX I

Notes and drafts for the lecture course of Summer Semester 1933

1. The fundamental question of philosophy

We do not know, without further inquiry, *whether* there is such a question for philosophy at all and what it is; whether philosophy still can be and is allowed to be at all; whether we should even *preserve* philosophy out of respect for the tradition. Or what a fundamental question is at all!

These questions may all be very important and profoundly critical—and yet they may be posed in the wrong place and at the wrong time and, if only for this reason, *erroneously.*

So, then—technically—only *after* the introduction, if at all.

2. {The fundamental question of philosophy}

Historically spiritual action only on the basis of a *knowing* about the future of the people. Never to substitute policies and institutions for this action—on the contrary.

But *this knowing is a knowing that makes demands.* Questioning, philosophizing—from the ground up, by asking the fundamental question.

On what basis? Neither by decree, nor by whim, nor by compact, nor by arbitrary preference. From the real urgency of our Dasein in the necessity of questioning. This questioning *on the basis of its inception* and origin.

3. {The fundamental question of philosophy}

We are asking the fundamental question of philosophy. What question is that, how to find it? Not to be launched by decree; instead, it {would have to} assail us as the innermost and most extreme urgency and necessity.

The fundamental question by way of *philosophy;* it demands {?} reflection: what is philosophy? But what philosophy is can be demonstrated only if its task is known, and so through *the fundamental question that philosophy poses. Circle?* Both are the same question. The question about the essence of philosophy is the question about its fundamental question, and vice versa.

Who and what decides about this? Arbitrariness, naiveté, the accidental needs of an era? It is already decided. What does that mean? Only whether we can rediscover this decision, that is, whether we are equal to it, whether, for us, *necessity and what is unavoidable* . . .

When did the decision about philosophy happen? When a *people*— its Greek *human beings*—set out . . . (Berve I!).[1] This *decision* is not past; not settled, just *unredeemed* and unfulfilled—because the age is no longer equal to it.

This *decision*—how it *endures and how it grows* as a *distant en-joining.* Whether we will to expose ourselves to it, will to join in with it (it is not gone, the question is *when* we will catch up!), that is, whether we will greatness and the long will to the fulfillment of our spiritual mission among peoples. For what is philosophy? Once again: the very same *Greeks* coined the word!

φιλοσοφία [philosophy] → ← the secret mission——wanderer {?}
Division:
1. The end and those who awaken the inception. Question of Being! How, here?
   Kierkegaard: Christian, "existence" of the individual before God. Time—eternity.
   Nietzsche: antiquity. Being—becoming, time—eternity
2. *Taking up the inception.*
   a) Unfolding the distant enjoining; inception and the principal steps. *Überlegungen II.*[2]
   b) Confrontation with Nietzsche's *doctrine of Being.*
3. The *rift.*
4. Exposure. *The German casts itself loose into* . . .

---

1. {Helmut Berve, *Griechische Geschichte,* vol. 2 (Freiburg im Breisgau: Herder, 1931/1933). (*Geschichte der führenden Völker,* ed. Heinrich Finke, Hermann Junker, and Gustav Schnürer, vols. 4/5.) First half: *Von den Anfängen bis Pericles* (1931).}

2. {*Überlegungen II* is scheduled to be published in volume 94 of the *Gesamtausgabe, Überlegungen A.*}

4. The fundamental question of philosophy

So: what is philosophy? What fundamental question results from the concept of philosophy? This way cannot be traveled. At most, the reverse: the essence of philosophy from the fundamental question.

But *which* is the fundamental, grounding question? What kind of question is it in the first place? *A question that grounds!* That questioning which grounds, which leads *to the ground and away beyond it;* the originary, the first and last, the deepest and most far-reaching questioning; that questioning in which questioning as questioning happens as what it is and how it is: questioning as questioning. The essence of questioning. *Questioning as effective formation.*

The *what* and *whether* questions (modalities!). Not a "theoretical" preparation for some activity, much less for mere research!

The questioner. To *stand* in the rift; to be *exposed* to it. Existence and the *understanding of Being.*

Foundation for the possibility of all this? What are we getting into here? Where are we taking ourselves? *Questioning and attuning!* The fundamental attunement that now most assails us.

5. The fundamental question of philosophy

The fundamental question of philosophy is the question of Being. (A powerful pronouncement! Empowered by what?) But this fundamental, grounding question is not to be taken here as the chief question among a set of related questions; instead, it is to be taken in the essential sense of *the* question that *grounds* all philosophical questions and thereby any actual question at all—and this in a multiple sense.

This *grounding* is itself ground-less, abyssal, and in *this* sense, ungrounded. But it can happen only if present-at-hand philosophy is compelled to end; this means, if experience tells us that this philosophy, *as* present-at-hand, is precisely at an end.

To bring about this end is the *preliminary labor* of every authentic philosophy. But this preliminary labor is already the unfolding forward reach into that within which what is coming must move and take shape. In preliminary labor, the distant enjoining is already at work, and at the same time it is the grounding confrontation with the first inception.

Note: this has nothing to do with a theory of knowledge that limps along after some present-at-hand philosophy. It has nothing to do with attaining a useful and universally recognized "definition" of philosophy. Above all, it never has anything to do with empty "groundwork" for what will never be actual.

6. The fundamental question of philosophy

The fundamental question is the questioning that evokes the essence, the empowerment that opens up, through which philosophy sets itself back on its mission—not fantastically climbing up to an in-itself that there must be at any price. Philosophy belongs to the history of what *is*—and within this, philosophy has its portion. (To hold open the questionworthiness of Being and to preserve the hardness of the clarity of the concept and the depth and breadth of great moods amid beings.)

The necessary impetus of the fundamental question is the question of Being as the disempowerment of Being (cf. *Überlegungen II*, pp. 127-28).[3] *The first impediment to the disempowerment through the empowerment of the rift.* A preparatory step for this is the destruction, properly understood (*Überlegungen II*, p. 124),[4] of the modalities in their inceptive roots (Aristotle).

To follow the question of the modalities back to the essence. But in this, there is *no* inner opposition to Being and the question of Being (cf. *Überlegungen II*, pp. 90ff.).[5]

But certainly *prepare for this question*, among other things, and that means according to the maxims in the notes: the fundamental question (see the following pages).

7. The fundamental question of philosophy

Introduction. Note: no more reacting to misguided demands for an illusory rigor; so-called introductory questions and questions of relevance—definitions of philosophy; and *how* we should define and are unable to define. All this discussion ends fruitlessly; it enervates and disappoints; along such mistaken pathways—which lead only into the trap of the traditional, baseless business of philosophy—it really becomes very difficult to engage in this essential questioning.

But neither is it the phony liveliness of idle talk about the situation; nor is it programs and promises.

The world is being reconstructed. Man stands at the awakening of a renewed grounding of his essence.

3. {Cf. above, [German] p. 268, note.}
4. {Ibid.}
5. {Ibid.}

How do we recognize this? Not in the situation. Erroneous perspective. Whether *we* are able to determine this at all, like some "fact"? If not, on what basis then do we speak? Assertions, assurances? No! Instead, a hint that we give to "ourselves"—based on an understanding that is *not wizardry* but derives just as little from the self-satisfaction of mere observation. An understanding that places what is obviously accessible in another light and thereby simplifies it according to what is essential. On this basis, only an opportunity for an initial understanding of *the political excitement of the youth.* (Cf. *Überlegungen II*, pp. 81ff.).[6]

This not as a "symptom" of the "situation"—not in order to remain attached to this, much less to build upon it; instead, simply to indicate with this onto which path it must be brought, a path that must be opened up. This pathfinding is itself what comes first and what alone is essential.

Labor camps, militias, settlers, leagues, landscape—seizing beings oneself, taking hold of the soil.

At the same time: the boundlessness of the sciences, the unrestrainedness of technology, the limitlessness of the free economy. How the sciences, technology, the economy have, in their own dispersal, worn themselves down. They all lose their basis and perspective—wearing out and breaking down.

This means, at bottom, *staying back—the understanding of Being;* and this—not joining in or following, much less moving ahead, but simply hanging back—creates a hanging, a curtain; this curtain veils what *is* and reinforces a great untruth—error.

But at the same time: evasion—even, and especially, among those who see this analytically in *Christianity* and in *faith.* No questioning and no concept of its *activity.*

*   *   *

Most immediate goal: to open up the full questionableness of Being, by establishing ourselves in its essence (its falling to us and its inevitability). This questionableness preserves the assignation of beings and brings forth and creates receptivity.

The questionableness of Being as the blaze of the flame in the hearth of what *is.* The paths into questionableness—there are many of these and they cannot be evaluated in advance. Instead, go down *one.*

For this, first the pathway to Being; and where and how to find it? "In" what *is,* in beings; and here again, not what is contrived, unusual, and complicated-confusing; instead, what is close by, simple, and nevertheless somehow inevitable.

6. {Ibid.}

The real—the first indication of what falls to us, the ac-cidental [*des Zu-fälligen*]. In the accidental, the undefined glimmerings of the rift.

All this has its entire basis exclusively in what is at issue. Nothing about the illusory critique of "theory of knowledge," nothing about the "modalities" and the like; instead, to let the pathway run into the rift. Nothing about the "subject" and so on, but instead *the world on fire*, exposure to the mood.—Alone-ness.

Not just talk of questionableness, because, on the one hand, there is enough that is questionable, and, on the other, no real questioning—instead, simply *move forward with questioning*.

---

8. {The fundamental question of philosophy}

A. Preparation.—B. Asking the fundamental question.

On A.

1. The simple reflection: the fundamental question based on philosophy. What is philosophy?
2. *Destruction.* Out from the captivity of the term and its line of thought. To be struck by the fact that another Dasein has cast itself free into another Being.
   a) Is philosophy required? Only a *semblance* remains? Possibility and necessity of *cessation*, end. Merely a semblance and *superfluous besides* (command, decree, calling upon tradition), because until now intuition {?}, perhaps a fundamental trait {?}, *precisely the opposite*. Genuine *urgent need*.
   b) But only decidable when we know *what* philosophy is. Where do we get this? A concept handed down.—Not just from today, but also not an arbitrary, handed-down has-been. Or from the *condition of urgent need?* The ancients.— The name and concept, passion, questioning. What is it "not," then? *But what remains?* The second *urgent need*.
   c) *Distant* enjoining? *Not redeemed*.
3. *The engagement in our actuality. What is Being?* (Cf. 2b.)
   a) Unprepared for history; *and nevertheless* to will it, *our* history—positively and the *questionworthy*.
   b) For this: calling—call—*university*. On this path and passageway ("philosophy"), *leadership* in *science*. The *questionworthy*. Wrestling over the clarity of our own essence as a people. *Questioning*. (Cf. under B, mission.)
   c) We *ask both*, even if only falteringly, etc. *Questioning, and no "problems"—our mission;* and perhaps on the way to 2c {distant enjoining}.

Our mission, redeeming and catching up with the distant enjoining?? We take up the mission by *questioning. What, and how?* History, πόλις, meta-political, "ground." Not fostering culture and the like; instead: *world, Dasein.*

A. (Preparation) in the inception: not from philosophy to the fundamental question; instead, from questioning into the ground; a fundamental, grounding questioning in philosophy.

On B.

To attune oneself through questioning to the mission; *thinking of the uncustomary! Withstanding,* not *evading,* not to *thrust aside* as mere "thoughts."

1. The rift. (Law—rank; leadership—following; the *whole* of the *people;* greatness—hardness—urgent need; possibility—actuality—necessity; history {?}.)
2. Exposure to *Being* ("distinction").

The end—inception! — enjoining.

---

9. Cessation

How often, how fruitlessly—and how far from inceptively—"philosophy" toils at the "question of the inception." The comical fretting that there must be no circle, that there must be an orderly sequence and construction.—Whom is all this for?

Neither an unrestrained self-formation of philosophy in some direction of its own progress, nor the overzealous, cheap mania for being effective according to the illusory reality of the present day. All of this breaks against the urgent need of the inevitable {?} *cessation.*

What does this mean, then? Do not the paradoxes of the inception announce themselves here in reverse order? Cessation only as not ceasing and going forward. But not this, not forward, but going back and through to the inception. Really to grasp and now to carry the end into the *inception!* In this way to attain the inception.

These are all attempts at cessation—this will to originality, to originary groundwork, to *simplification,* to de-construction.

To cease [*Auf-hören*] : to listen [*Hören*] instead of talking; by no means ending what is essential. Instead, *turning around and turning toward.*

To cease with philosophy—to make it hearken to its essence. *De-construction and cessation.*

10. Our historical meditation

We receive pushes and impulses from history only in the essential confrontation with history.

The implementation of such an attack should aim at *Hegel*. This has nothing to do with a refutation in the usual style. Moreover, there is all too much that is correct in philosophy; what is rare is the true.

The *biographical* in bare outlines—*on the basis of the whole German movement*. Until now, the term has been seen mostly as humanism or as *patriotic*, but really neither philosophical nor political.

Hegel in his *main position*, that means the fundamental discipline, "metaphysics." *History of "metaphysics" as a word and a concept.*

This might create the impression that we are trotting out historians' curiosities here and burdening our memory with them. But right away something else shows itself—a *fundamental piece* of the *spiritual fate* of the West, in which we are *implicated*. And this applies, once and for all, to all considerations of historical facts in this lecture course: not an empty and baseless outline and enumeration of names, titles, and numbers; instead, *history,* as it *comes up behind us* and gathers itself in *essential steps*. History, as it *enters our future, moving out beyond us,* and assails us from there.

Our historical meditation does not work with the wide-ranging depiction of cultures, ages, and "personalities" and with the "literature" on these, but dares to enter the hard and naked simplicity of the essential in our spiritual fate—*solely* in order to face the equally hard and naked, simple task that is our *own*. Note: it does not need to be extensively confirmed that this involves the most fundamental labor and that general overviews are of no help.

11. Kant's authentic work
{re: [German] p. 26}

The *Critique of Pure Reason* (1781): *how things stand with metaphysics:* (a) what it wills, (b) what it is capable of doing;— (a) what it is entitled to, (b) what is denied it. To distinguish, to separate (κρίνειν) according to its inner possibility and its procedure—*ratio*—free of experience, *pure reason*.

But to do so in a really thorough examination and investigation (not a program). The *guideline* for this—which *question?* [Metaphysical] cognition as synthetic, extending [our knowledge], supersensory, free of experience, a priori. The Kantian *question* that *leads* his entire critique: how is synthetic cognition possible a priori?

The solution (division of the work): 1. in what sense possible, in what sense not. 2. On what grounds—man. 3. In *what scope:* regulative: practical reason.

Metaphysics of metaphysics—not "theory of knowledge," but *the position in the world of man as such; hence Kant's concept of "natural metaphysics."*

- (a)   Man—an impulse to the supersensible, *anima naturaliter christiana* [the soul is Christian by nature].
- (b)   At the same time, constant error; natural illusion, taking what is thought for what *is.*

Kant and Luther!—Yes and no!—*In any case the Christian world.*
    Cf. above. Even if today's "natural worldview" has been de-Christianized in its particular content in many ways and has no basis, its *fundamental form* has nevertheless *remained* and in one way or another has *then been filled out with substitute forms.*

----

12. {Remembering our intention}

Remembering our intention.—*Questioning:* a knowing that demands, that quarrels, that honors.—Fundamental question of philosophy.—Historical confrontation.—Hegel.—"Metaphysics," *word and concept.*—The issue.—Preeminent stage: Kant.
    What are the determining forces at which the confrontation aims? (religious-Christian way of thinking)
    We seek the fundamental question—not there—hidden, held down. To draw it out from darkness.
    Our Dasein—attacking *what!*

----

13. The confrontation with Hegel's metaphysics

What philosophical con-frontation is (on the basis of the essence of philosophical truth).
    Not formal refutation and polemic, the demonstration of mere incorrect points, but *con-frontation—scission;* for us this is a decision *for and against.*
    Not with particular scholarly opinions or systems, nor with an indefinite, general, comprehensive notion of everything and nothing, but with the whole of history in its innermost happening—hinting beyond us *within history.*
    Against what? Against the two determining powers.

1. The world-concept of Christian faith—
2. the mathematical as ideal of knowledge.

Not against these as such, but *against the fact that* they are the *determining* powers in metaphysics.

Why against them? Why *shouldn't they be?* Because they have *not arisen originally* from the fundamental question of philosophy and are not *rooted in it;* but to the contrary

(a) the Christian world-concept had to lose and deny the fundamental question,
(b) the mathematical was not equal to it—concealed, given up, forgotten.

----

14. The confrontation with Hegel
(Kierkegaard and Nietzsche)

As con-frontation: to separate, to reject, and to decide anew—with respect to the determining powers: Christianity and the *mathematical-logical* (not *against* logos!).

Against what? The fact that these two powers are in general determinative for "metaphysics"? Why *should this not* be? Because *neither* is rooted in the philosophical fundamental question.

I. Instead:
    (a) {Christianity} denied this question and *had to do so,*
    (b) {the mathematical} was not equal to the question, but externalized, deformed, and diverted it—and thus at bottom abandoned it.
II. Because through these, philosophy in general *no longer arrives at a ground and basis,* does not resist either of the world powers that determine it: instead (to the contrary—it is held fast in *semblance*) it clings to "worldview" or "scientificity."

But *neither has binding force* in the seriousness and extremity of Dasein; *neither is pregnant with an origin.*

All this—because the fundamental question is no longer a question anymore, and in the end is no longer even recognized as such.

What the fundamental question is not, what it is and the only way it can happen. First lecture.[7]

----

7. {Cf. the main text of the lecture course, §§1–2, esp. [German] pp. 5–6.}

15. {The Christian and the mathematical in Hegel}

The Christian concept of the world—*beings as a whole* (↔Being) *determined.*

The mathematical—certainty in the face of truth / Being.

How are both determinative? How the mathematical alters the concept of Being: *bonum* as *perfectum* [the good as the perfect]—"Logos."

How now—having gone through Kant—the whole outline. *Metaphysics in Hegel, metaphysics as logic: everything*—and yet it leaves out the fundamental question. Expropriation of philosophy, for this fundamental question is not some arbitrary pursuit of an obsolete question, a compensatory solution to some theoretical obscurity, but the ground and basis of Dasein is different. Cf. principle of contradiction and its foundation. Cf. first lecture.[8]

Confrontation—to begin with, neither the Christian nor the mathematical, but the *ground* for why both of these can have such influence in philosophy; (a) because for its part, philosophy has never been rooted, (b) and because philosophy no longer adequately has a basis and necessity, but is delivered over to the observation {?} of private worldviews or of "science."

Neither has binding force and neither *achieves an origin.* But this is the case because they are not based on the fundamental question, and because this question itself is no longer a question and is no longer questionable. What con-frontation [means] here now—essential, decisive.

16. Kierkegaard and Hegel—Nietzsche and Hegel

Kierkegaard wills precisely *Christianity*—originally *New Testament and Protestant Christianity* (the opposite of cultural Christendom)—in such a way that he leaves the Hegelian system untouched and works entirely with its means.

Nietzsche does {seek} the fundamental confrontation with Christianity, but he gets stuck in the *biological way of thinking* and in a simple acceptance of the usual "logic" and its necessity; he does not arrive at the question of Being as such.

At the same time, a radical con-frontation—separation—with Kierkegaard and Nietzsche.

* * *

1. Uncertainty as questionworthiness (against the mathematical).
2. The announcement that "God is dead" (against the theological).

8. {Cf. the main text of the lecture course, "Introduction," §§1-4.}

1. and 2. together.
Exposure to fate—the rift and what is German.

---

17. {Inception and semblance}

The greater the inception, the more insistent the semblance. *The semblance of Being* and the *guiding question* of ancient philosophy. Cf. *Überlegungen* II, p. 95.[9]
Semblance of Being and the Christian attitude toward the world.
The way back from the guiding question to the fundamental question with the help of the principle of possibility. (*Überlegungen* II, pp. 107, 113, 133)
Thrown off the track! *"Onto-logy." Originary {?} inception and the track!*

*   *   *

Hegel

Completion of the inception that was relegated to semblance!
In general—*which Dasein, history?*
The guiding problem according to the lecture;[10] *"logic"—onto-theo-logy.* (Winter Semester 1930–1931)[11]
"Differenz{schrift}"[12] (Summer Semester 1929)[13]—"phenomenology"—"logic"—"encyclopedia."

9. {*Überlegungen II* is scheduled to be published in volume 94 of the *Gesamtausgabe, Überlegungen A.*}

10. {Martin Heidegger, "Hegel und das Problem der Metaphysik." Lecture at the scientific congress in Amsterdam, 22 March 1930. Scheduled for publication in GA 80, *Vorträge (1915-1967)*.}

11. {Martin Heidegger, *Hegels Phänomenologie des Geistes,* Freiburg lecture course, Winter Semester 1930-1931 (GA 32), ed. Ingtraud Görland (Frankfurt am Main: Klostermann, 1980; 3rd edition, 1997).} [English translation: *Hegel's Phenomenology of Spirit,* trans. Parvis Emad and Kenneth Maly (Bloomington: Indiana University Press, 1994).]

12. {G. W. F. Hegel, *Differenz des Fichte'schen und Schelling'schen Systems der Philosophie, in Beziehung auf Reinhold's Beyträge zur leichtern Übersicht des Zustands der Philosophie bey dem Anfange des neunzehnten Jahrhunderts.* Erstes Heft (Jena, 1801). In *Sämtliche Werke, Jubiläumsausgabe in 20 Bänden,* ed. Hermann Glockner (1927 sqq.), vol. I, pp. 33-168.} [English translation: *The Difference Between Fichte's and Schelling's System of Philosophy,* trans. H. S. Harris and Walter Cerf (Albany: State University of New York Press, 1977).]

13. {Martin Heidegger, *Der deutsche Idealismus (Fichte, Schelling, Hegel) und die philosophische Problemlage der Gegenwart,* Freiburg lecture course, Summer Semester 1929 (GA 28), ed. Claudius Strube (Frankfurt am Main: Klostermann, 1997), cf. pp. 195ff., esp. 196-97.}

APPENDIX II

Notes and drafts for the lecture course of
Winter Semester 1933–1934

1. Thomas: *veritas; intellectus*
(Quaestiones de veritate, quaest. I, art. 1-12)[1]

... ubi invenitur *perfecta ratio* veritatis [where we find the *complete account* of truth] (cf. quaest. I, art. 2). . . . per posterius invenitur verum in rebus, per prius autem in intellectu [the true is found secondarily in things, but primarily in the intellect] (cf. ibid.). Relation to Aristotle, *Metaphysics* E 4! And: in intellectu divino (creans) *mensurante, non mensurato* [in the divine (creating) intellect that is *measuring, not measured*]. *Pre*-formation; intellectus humanus speculativus [the human theoretical intellect] is imitative; intellectus humanus practicus [the human practical intellect] is preformative or constructive in a certain way.

Why {primarily in the intellect}? Because veritas = adaequatio [truth = conformity] and *Veri enim ratio consistit in adaequatione rei et intellectus* [*for the definition of the true consists in the conformity of thing and intellect*] (art. 3); {*verum*} *aequalitas diversorum est* [(*the true*) *is an equality of diverse things*] (ibid.), "equality" (as-similation).

So there is veritas where *intellectus* (vel enuntiatio, quae intellectum significat [or articulation, which indicates intellect], art. 5c) begins to

---

1. {*Sancti Thomae Aquinatis doctoris angelici ordinis praedicatorum Opera Omnia: Tomus IX: Quaestiones disputatae, Volumen secundum, completens De veritate et Quaestiones quodlibeticas* (Parmae: Typis Petri Fiaccadori, 1859).} [Modern edition: *Sancti Thomae de Aquino Opera omnia iussu Leonis XIII P. M. edita* (Rome: Commissio Leonina, 1970–1976), vol. 22, pp. 1-3. English translation: Thomas Aquinas, *Truth*, vol. I, trans. Robert W. Mulligan, S. J. (Chicago: Regnery, 1952; repr. Indianapolis: Hackett, 1994). The translation here is ours. In this section of Heidegger's text, which uses Latin extensively, italics are used only for emphasis and not to indicate foreign words.]

have *something of its own* that the res [thing] does *not* have—but this content proper to the intellect is correspondens [corresponding]! Intellectus
dividens et componens [the intellect separates and combines], so necessarily [it involves] *reflectio* supra se (reditus) [*reflection* on itself (return)]
(art. 9). Intellectus . . . adaequatur rebus, quarum cognitionem habet
[the intellect is conformed to the things of which it has knowledge] (art.
8c). What does this mean? Here deduced formally from the idea of *adaequatio* [*conformity*] (cf. art. 5c: commensuratio, verum = commensura-
tum; "aequalitas," convenientia [having a common measure, the true =
the commensurate; "equality," agreement]), without a phenomenal look
at the inner presuppositions that lie in ἀ-λήθεια; cf. *Being and Time.*
    Intellectus . . . formans quidditates, non habet nisi similitudinem
rei existentis extra animam, sicut et sensus inquantum accipit spe-
ciem rei sensibilis [the intellect forming essences has only a likeness of
the thing existing outside the soul, like a sense inasmuch as a sense
grasps the form of a sensible thing] (art. 3).

                              *   *   *

Whatness has only selfsameness, thus no diversitas [diversity]—here
no possibility of *adaequatio,* veritas [*conformity,* truth].
    Everything based on "difference," "equality," "similarity," as though
it were a matter of a relationship between things.
    But why is the intellectus formans quidditates [intellect forming
essences, or whatnesses] nevertheless posterius—verum [secondarily
true]? (definitio, i. e. per ordinem ad compositionem [definition, i.e.,
from order to composition]). Cf. art. 3c, end: everything based on
adaequari [to be conformed]!
    Intellectus (intus legere) proprie = apprehensio quidditatem—and
thus non est *falsitas in intellectu.* [Intellect ([etymologically] to collect
within) properly = apprehension of whatness—and thus there is no
falsehood in the intellect.] Quidditas: proprie objectum intellectus.
[Whatness: properly the object of intellect.] (Cf. art. 2.) Intellectus "in
cognoscendo quod quid est"—semper verum? [Intellect "in knowing
that which is"—always true?] What does this mean? Cf. above, art. 3.
How do the two go together? Adaequatio simply taken as present at
hand: it is given, i.e., it is an ens creatum [created being]. With this, a
seeming objectivity of all beings in which I was merely operating. In
this, man only a *functionary,* a *hireling.*

-----

2. {The dominant conception of truth as correctness}

The dominant conception of the essence of truth: *correctness*—fact of
measurement.

Agreement between proposition and thing. From early on *and in different worlds:* Kant, Thomas, Aristotle. Despite his {Kant's} definition of cognition, that cognition does not direct itself to objects, but objects to cognition. A proposition that has nothing to do with subjectivism. The common interpretation of Kant. This conception {agreement of proposition and thing} has a peculiar *prominence* and *obstinacy.* To *decide* about it—hopeless!

To look *at* it more closely:

1. so *obviously intelligible*—so unintelligible and questionable; example.
2. *place of truth:* propositions; *validity; reason.* Being-true of propositions—Being! *Turned on its head! the essential relation of truth and Being!*

Very old—the Greeks; and yet *different in early times. Which conception* is originary and tenable?

---

3. Context

Question of the essence of truth—first about the essence of essence. Heraclitus's saying—*truth* of this saying? *Preliminary concept* of truth: ἀλήθεια—"correctness." Preliminary understanding of the words and language and "existence" of man.

---

4. {The question of truth as question of a historical decision}

Our answer to the question of the essence of truth must pass through a *decision;* it is not thought up in some free-floating way. *This decision in a confrontation* with the *tradition in which we have been standing for a long time: the history of our Dasein.*

Two fundamental conceptions of the essence of truth: unconcealment—correctness. Overpowering power of the latter in itself—or powerlessness of the former? *Why?*

The struggle between them—not brought to a resolution! Where? *Plato's philosophy.* Story of the *cave.* μῦθος—λόγος. *This treatment* of the *story* already leads into the center of the question of the essence of *truth.* A decisive *step* in its interpretation.

---

5. Recapitulation of the lecture, 9 January 1934

The question of the *essence* of truth: not about an abstract and separated concept in itself—the more universal the emptier, the less binding.

Essence—what *is essencing*—our Dasein—as this historical Dasein of ours—must thoroughly rule and determine. But *not* to contrive something arbitrarily *today,* but in the *confrontation* with the *tradition* that sustains and conditions us.

Two fundamental lines in conceiving of essence: (1) truth as unconcealment, (2) truth as correctness. *Both* in the first creative initiation among the Greeks. The first became powerless—forgotten—while the second became self-evident in its spreading dominance.

Both are there, where a *final resolution* and *definite spiritual forms of the world* [are established] for the next two millennia.

Plato's doctrine of ideas. Idea: 1. Representation in itself, ideal, *rule* and *value,* norm.

2. Representing—pure consciousness, consciousness in general, reason of *humanity,* of *Man* in himself.

Everything that *we* must struggle against and overcome—has its *roots* here. *Essence of Being—essence of man.* We—fundamental experience and fundamental attitude: finitude, temporality, historicity, thrownness, mission, individuation.

Philosophy different from the *ground up.*

For this, to *begin* with the *inception!* To be a match for the *fundamental powers.*

Plato: not a new *interpretive grasp* of Plato—*makes no difference;* decisive is the *grasping of our future Dasein* itself.

---

6. {Plato's allegory of the cave}

Plato—allegory of the cave. This *mythos*—no efforts to *define.* History of man—different stages and ἀλήθεια *different at each stage.*

Stage III: factual situation clarified

1. Idea and light
2. Light and freedom
3. Freedom and beings.

Connection of these four factual situations—the essence of ἀλήθεια.

---

7. {On the inner order of our questioning}

We must once again secure the simple trajectory of the inner order of our questioning as a whole. We are asking the question: what is truth?

Two answers: (1) unconcealment, ἀλήθεια; (2) correctness, *adaequatio.* (1) the inceptive, (2) the later and now dominant answer.

Connection of the two: Whether the first one is inceptive only in the temporal historical {sense}, or on the basis of its essence *according to the origin. And if according to the origin* and *therefore paramount* and determinative—*why* has it become *powerless?*

The answers: not simply *different* definitions with different content, but *interpretations* of different orientations of experience; these are based on *fundamental positions* of Dasein. *Difference* between such fundamental positions. *Change in the history of man,* and in fact in the essential ground, not just different *cultural periods!*

Their *juxtaposition* and *opposition* already early on, most clearly in *Platonic philosophy. Plato's answer: in* and *through* the *history of the release* of the human being from the cave. The four stages; in [stage] 3 the *high point,* but only in 4 the fulfillment. In 3 the *decisive point passed over,* deferred to the end of the interpretation, in order, as it were, to *survey the whole* from the *highest peak.*

The *highest idea: the good;* its clarification by answering *two main questions:*

  I. What does Plato understand by the highest idea of the good?
  II. What does this highest idea tell us about the *totality* we are asking about: about the *essence* of truth?

On I.

1. The highest idea as intensification of the essence of idea in general: *what originally makes possible,* ὄντως ὄν, ὄν ἀληθινόν [what genuinely is, true being]; and the Greek word for good: ἀγαθός. Only the originary word that grows from immediate Dasein—no *content,* no value and realm of values somehow in addition to other realms!
2. How Plato himself exhibits this highest idea.
    (1) In a sensory image—by the sun and sensory perception with the eyes. *The relationship of corresponding.* The fundamental factual situation—the yoke. The function and essence of the ἀγαθόν.
    (2) The explicit features:
        (a) ἐπέκεινα τῆς οὐσίας, ὑπερέχων πρεσβείᾳ καὶ δυνάμει, over and above, paramount, towering over [Being] in age, source, supremacy and power.
        (b) κυρία—παρασχομένη ἀλήθειαν καὶ νοῦν. Mastery— *granting-binding* [truth and intellect].

The paramount, masterful, granting-binding: *the empowering (what originally makes possible); cf.* (1) → covering!

On II.

What we should gather from the insight into the *essence of the highest idea—the good—*for the *essence of truth.*

1. That "truth," ἀλήθεια, is *itself not ultimate,* but stands *beneath a higher empowerment;* the "that" and "how."
2. That this is so *not only* for "truth," but also for *"Being."*
3. That not only are both thus in general under something higher, but both are under something higher as the *yoke;* what *yokes* them is precisely what empowers *both* to their essential connection.
4. That what empowers ἀλήθεια to its essence stands in an originary relation to the existence of man—as what *binds him in liberation.*
5. That this liberation is a *history* of man in which his essence is transformed from the ground up. Therefore 521c5: so this *is not,* as it seems, a *mere turning of a potsherd in the hand, but instead* leading the essence of man forth and out from a certain night-like day;[2] it is the ascent to beings (as such), and we say of this happening that it is *philosophizing.*
6. In brief and condensed: *the question of the essence of truth is the question of the essential history of man.* To pursue {?} in meditation—*through and into philosophizing. Phaedrus 243b5. Republic* 514a—the introductory words to the whole story at the start of book VII deliberately set aside. Now to be understood: "After this, make yourself an image of our essence and understand this {our essence} then according to its binding-fast and also its lack of binding discipline" (514a1-2).
   (1) ἡ ἡμετέρα φύσις [our nature or Being]
   (2) παιδεία τε καὶ ἀπαιδευσία
   (3) παιδεία neither "cultivation" nor "education" nor "formation," but the *binding-fast of Dasein based on the holding-fast that holds firm* in the face of the *empowerment* to history and fate. Note: and yet right in a certain way, *because with Plato* something else begins.
7. The fundamental happening of this history: *philosophy. But* keep the misconceptions and nonconceptions distant—and at the same time: elaborate the originary concept.

* * *

What philosophy is *not,* cf. above §28c, [German] pp. 206ff., esp. 208.

What it is? The fundamental happening in human Dasein, insofar as this Dasein is seen as spiritual-historical. In what does this fundamental happening consist? → *What is man?* Whence the answer to this question? *Biology, psychology, anthropology, typology.* These sciences give *a variety of information—and yet no answer?* No *answer,* because they *do not question*

2. [Reading *nächtlichen Tag* for *nächsten Trug* ("close-lying deception"). Cf. above, German pp. 206, 217.]

at all; they do not question, because they already start out with an answer. *Man as something that is also given, that is present at hand, that consists of body, soul, and spirit.* These sciences are only the *separate development and presentation of these components.*

What the sciences say is *correct—and yet deeply untrue.* Presentations of facts on the basis of an answer that has already been presupposed, that is not put into question at all. But the *answer* is already the *prejudice* and *advance decision about the essence of humanity.*

But at the foundation of this prejudice lies *a quite definite way* of *experiencing* the something that we call the human being: the sort of thing that consists of different pieces, facts, which pieces belong to it, *all of which* is at hand in it. The {. . .}.[3] In every question a decision already *before* the answer and thus the circle of *possible* answers already *staked out.* And this fundamental decision comes from the fundamental experience, and accordingly so does the form of the question.

On the grounds of the experience we mentioned there grows the question: *what is man?* But there is nothing objectionable in this question; how else should we ask *if we are asking about man at all? However—* there is *still another* possibility and *necessity* of asking about man; not "What is man?" but *"Who is man?"*

But according to what we just presented, is there a fundamental decision *here as well?* By all means! And which one? That man is a *self.*[4]

But this characterization is *not the determination of something present at hand,* but *addresses us as our vocation. Self: being that is delivered over to itself in its Being; "consciousness" only a consequence.* For a being that *is a self does not only know something about itself,* but it itself is *properly left to its own discretion and decision,* namely, in *how* it is—i.e., *how* it takes its *own Being, how its own Being is an issue for it.*

This—that there is a being for whom its own Being is an issue—itself belongs *to the originary constitution of its Being.* Hence I call the Being of the self *care.* Nothing to do with meddlesome fussing and the anxiousness of neurotics.

Care is the *condition of possibility for resoluteness,* readiness, engagement, labor, mastery, heroism; *and where there are such, there are necessarily* innocuousness, busy-ness, cowardice, money-grubbing, slavery and cowardice; and not just as a regrettable addition, but as *essential necessity.*

Care and historicity. Care as the condition of possibility of the political essence of man.

---

3. {One word illegible (margin cut off).}
4. {Cf. above, §§22, 24, 25, 28.}

Care as existence: what and *who—categories* and *existentialia*. Cf. *Being and Time* / "On the Essence of Ground."[5]

Care *as self: "I" and "we"*; and *struggle* and *predominance* and in each case mastery *of both.*

Who is man? This question decides and determines the question, *"What is philosophy?"*—decides in general about philosophy as such, whether it can and must be, or not.

But this question has still *quite different questions* behind and before it! Can man know and find his *essence* in the first place *beginning with himself?* To go *to the limits! How do we know that we know,* and can know, *who we are? Whence the truth about man? Of what sort* is this truth? *What is truth?* This question: the question *of the essential history of man*—and that is philosophizing: *standing fast in the questioning about Being and truth.*

Bending back! Circle! Certainly—but work through it.

We must stand fast in the face of the *question, precisely in the context* from which we have now spoken *in summary: the highest peak,* ἀγαθόν. Here not the simplistic solution, but precisely the *beginning of true questionworthiness.*

I. *Questionworthiness.* Which question endures and *intensifies?*
   ἀγαθόν: *what persists, stands fast!* But: *how* and *where?* ζυγόν for ὁρᾶν [yoke for seeing] (understanding of Being) and ὁρώμενον [the visible] (openness, unconcealment). Where does this happen? "In" the human being—"in"?? But the other (ἀλήθεια) with things, with beings, and yet precisely un-derangeable {?}. *In the human being—with things; relation of the two,* in each case from one side.
   Furthermore: *what, who is man?* The question about the yoke (ἀγαθόν) still *not decided* at all, perhaps *not even adequately asked.*
   Ego, res cogitans—res extensa [I, thinking thing—extended thing]; subject—object; "relation"! Why is the question inadequate? Because οὐσία = *something present at hand! Greek concept of Being!* What and how constituted, *subjectum, substantia, accidens.*
   The question of the yoke as such is precisely suppressed, instead of this *and together with it the elements made independent and thus the approach to the question.*

II. *What is the ground for this disregard for the question of the yoke?* "Doctrine of ideas," because οὐσία as ἰδέα! thereby entrenched. *Idea as interpretation of Being.* Ambiguity: (1) granting passage, (2) itself a being, object, present at hand, *higher—lower—domains, strata;* χωρισμός, gap!

---

5. ["On the Essence of Ground," trans. William McNeill, in Martin Heidegger, *Pathmarks*, ed. William McNeill (Cambridge: Cambridge University Press, 1998).]

III. *But* doctrine of ideas *at the same time basis for the suppression of* ἀλήθεια.
  1. What is seen—but itself the *being itself,* the what. But not Being-seen in seeing. The *what* itself *as a being in itself;* relation accidental. Correspondingly ἀλήθεια—not qua unconcealment.
  2. The seen as *prototype,* derivative, imitation, representation; *agreement,* ὁμοίωσις. *Stratification of domains!*
  3. *Suppression* of ἀλήθεια *as predominance* of *adaequatio.*
IV. *Remarkable:* Plato makes one more approach and yet precisely ἀλήθεια is *suppressed. Ineffectual,* ἀλήθεια no longer determines questioning. *Nevertheless looking out* into the inception. *The struggle for a defeat of* ἀλήθεια *as opposed to* ὁμοίωσις. The dominance of *adaequatio* since then.
V. But why not leave it at that?
  1. The aporia of *"agreement in itself." Impossibility.*
    (1) *What* agrees, *completely different in kind.*
    (2) *With what,* how to measure? But a standard already revealed in advance.
  2. Does not reach *the essential truths* at all, cf.
    (1) truth of the essential determination of man,
    (2) truth of a mission and vocation,
    (3) *truth* of taking a position and deciding,
    (4) *truth* of a work of art.
In short: wherever essential, it is inadequate, if not completely superfluous.

So: to lead the question back to *inception—hopeless and senseless* at once, yet not cut off. *To make a new inception* on the ground of the *fundamental experiences* of our historical Dasein. *To question again!* By all means.

The insight attained: (1) that the question is inadequate, (2) that the main difficulty lies precisely in this: in attaining the sufficiently originary and broad approach to the question.

Where the failure? Un-concealment not interrogated as such, Being not interrogated as such, especially and *originally.*

Un-concealment—to ask about it: what this means. Cf. above, §§29 and 30.

8. {Truth—untruth; transition to *Theaetetus*}

1. *Word-concept and essence of ἀλήθεια,* cf. Winter Semester 1931–1932;[6] also word-concept and essence of ψεῦδος.
2. How at the basis of assertions that are common among us—*true propositions*—there lies ἀλήθεια. (The first step in the truth lecture.)[7] Yet *veritas* as *principaliter in intellectu* [*truth* as *principally in the intellect*].—Middle Ages (*Deus*)—Descartes, modernity—*certum,* certainty, taking-as-true (Nietzsche, cf. *Beyond Good and Evil*).

9. Translation and elucidation of Plato, *Theaetetus* 184-87

This is the essential passage that sustains everything. Here the turning point is also especially clear, the turning point that Greek thought carries out in contrast to its inception, in order to make the transition into "metaphysics," i.e., to ground metaphysics on the doctrine of Being as ἰδέα and truth as ὁμοίωσις. Now ψυχή and ἔρως—ἰδέα—ἀγαθόν. Only now does "philosophy" begin.

10. *Theaetetus* 184b ff.

In this reflection it comes to light that *the relation* does not consist of or in the organs of the body.

The relation (συντείνειν) is ἰδέα—seeing of what is seen,
having sight of what can be seen
sightfulness.

νοεῖν   appearance
presencing

The relation is the "soul" itself—it is not at first a soul on its own and then further, hooked on and into it, as it were, a cord that connects it to things.

6. {Martin Heidegger, *Vom Wesen der Wahrheit: Zu Platons Höhlengleichnis und Theätet* (GA 34), ed. Hermann Mörchen (Freiburg: Vittorio Klostermann, 1988; 2nd rev. edition, 1997).} [English translation: *The Essence of Truth: On Plato's Cave Allegory and "Theaetetus,"* trans. Ted Sadler (London and New York: Continuum, 2005).]

7. {Martin Heidegger, "On the Essence of Truth," a lecture delivered, among other places, in fall and winter 1930 in Bremen, Marburg, Karlsruhe, and Freiburg, and in summer 1932 in Dresden. The much-revised text of this lecture was first published in 1943 by Vittorio Klostermann, Frankfurt am Main (8th exp. edition, 1997; with marginal notes by Heidegger from his personal copy). The lecture was also included in the anthology *Wegmarken* [*Pathmarks,* ed. William McNeill].}

What is the soul? and how this implies that what shows itself is beings in their Being; therefore this—and indeed οὐσία (πρῶτον—
μάλιστα) [beingness (first—most)] *before all* ("a priori").

To what extent the "soul" now shows itself and the intention of the
dialogue first reveals and fulfills itself requires no further explanation.

---

11. *Theaetetus* 184d {re: §33c}

"Soul" as name for the relation to Being (presencing of appearance)
and thus to unconcealment.

ψυχή—as ἰδέα τις μία εἰς ἣν πάντα τὰ ὄντα ἢ ὄντα συντείνει [soul
as some single *idea* to which all beings as beings converge] (cf. 184d3-
4).[8] All that *is* gathers itself—stretching out to this single sight (*ambiguous*), i.e., this sight first catches sight in apprehension of something
like what appears, something presencing in such and such a way.

Soul: name *for the relation to Being.*

(Body and living thing are let into this relation—if the Greek human
being is. *Not* soul *inspired into the body,* but *bodying let into the soul.* But
ψυχή [soul] does anticipate the later *animus* and *anima* (ζωή [life]).)

Being—beingness: πρῶτον—τοῦτο γὰρ μάλιστα ἐπὶ πάντων
παρέπεται (186a2-3); what already inserts itself in advance the earliest,
what shows itself, turns itself *toward* us, the pre-ceding. μάλιστα
πρῶτον, therefore πρότερον, *prius, a priori* [first of all, therefore prior, in
advance].

---

8. {Quoted freely from 184d3-4: εἰς μίαν ἰδέαν, εἴτε ψυχὴν . . . πάντα ταῦτα
συντείνει [to a single *idea*, be it the soul . . . to which all these things converge].}

Editor's Afterword

The two lecture courses collected in the present double volume under the bibliographical title *Being and Truth* stem from Martin Heidegger's year as rector. The lecture course *The Fundamental Question of Philosophy* was held in Summer Semester 1933 for two hours per week, as was the lecture course *On the Essence of Truth* in Winter Semester 1933-1934. The latter began, according to extant transcripts by attendees, on 7 November 1933, and ended 27 February 1934. The transcripts do not provide any such dates for the lecture course of Summer Semester 1933. However, the brevity of the text of the course allows us to surmise that because of the extraordinary and unaccustomed duties of the office of rector, Heidegger canceled some sessions of the course in Summer Semester 1933.

As bases for the edition of the lecture course of Summer Semester 1933, the editor had available:

1. The photocopy of the manuscript made available by the Deutscher Literaturarchiv, which comprises 22 consecutively numbered pages written in oblong format, as well as numerous inserted and appended additions in various formats, but for the most part in DIN A5 format.
2. The transcript of the manuscript typed by the editor in 1978 (about 100 pages in DIN A4 format, including additions).
3. A handwritten student transcript by Wilhelm Hallwachs, of 117 DIN A5 pages, written for the most part on both sides of the page in a large hand; this transcript presumably represents a tran scription of an originally stenographic record.
4. A typewritten student transcript by Adolph Kolping, of 35 DIN A4 pages, as a transcription of a heavily abbreviated handwritten transcript.

For the edition of the lecture course of Winter Semester 1933–1934, the editor had available:

1. The photocopy of the manuscript of the newly composed introduction to the repetition of this lecture course, which was held for the first time in Winter Semester 1931–1932; this introduction comprises 24 pages written in oblong format, as well as 14 inserted notes, predominantly in DIN A5 format and in part numbered consecutively.
2. A typewritten transcript of the manuscript of the introduction prepared by the editor in spring 1980.
3. The original of the handwritten transcript of the lecture course by Wilhelm Hallwachs, comprising 199 DIN A5 pages, predominantly written on both sides in broad handwriting, again presumably a transcript of an originally stenographic record.
4. A typewritten transcript of Hallwachs's transcript (no. 3) prepared by the editor in 1985, comprising 199 pages in DIN A4 format.
5. A typewritten student transcript of 44 closely written DIN A4 pages by Arnold Bergsträsser; this is a transcript of a handwritten record that reproduces the text of the lecture course only in abbreviated form.
6. The photocopy of the manuscript of the lecture course of the same name from Winter Semester 1931–1932.

As regards the bases of the edition, the lecture course *On the Essence of Truth* (Winter Semester 1933–1934) represents a special case. It does repeat the lecture course of the same name from Winter Semester 1931–1932 (GA 34),[1] but in a form that is altered in several ways. A newly composed introduction that deals with Heraclitus's πόλεμος fragment, the interpretation of the Platonic allegory of the cave that has been expanded with more extensive recapitulations, the abbreviated interpretation of the dialogue *Theaetetus,* and the multitude of allusions that are "political" in the broader sense give the lecture course as a whole a changed form. Since Heidegger did not elaborate a new manuscript for the main part of the course, the obligation of historical veracity was enough to demand that the altered form of the main part and the numerous "political" interpolations be reproduced by printing the thorough transcript of the lecture course by Wilhelm Hallwachs.

1. [See *Vom Wesen der Wahrheit. Zu Platons Höhlengleichnis und Theätet (WS 1931–32),* ed. Hermann Mörchen (Frankfurt am Main: Vittorio Klostermann, 1988; rev. edition, 1997); and *The Essence of Truth: On Plato's Cave Allegory and "Theaetetus,"* trans. Ted Sadler (London and New York: Continuum, 2005).]

Our reproduction of the Hallwachs transcript is interrupted in the session of 30 January 1934 by a handwritten textual passage by Heidegger presenting a talk on the first anniversary of the National Socialist seizure of power; in this talk, Heidegger deals in an extremely critical way with a speech given on the previous day by the author Kolbenheyer and with the (National Socialist) picture of humanity and the world presented in this lecture. This original text passage (pp. 209ff.)[2] is printed in italics in order to distinguish it from the text that stems from the Hallwachs transcript; accordingly, emphasized words are set in roman type.[3]

*   *   *

For the editions of these lecture courses, the typescripts that had already been prepared by the editor at the end of the seventies and in the eighties were carefully collated with the handwritten originals and photocopies; errors in the transcripts were corrected, and numerous remaining flaws and questionable readings were resolved. Orthography and punctuation were revised in accordance with modern German rules (though not the newest ones), as long as they were not (recurrent) peculiarities of Heidegger's writing style.

The section headings and subheadings derive primarily from the editor. They were chosen in close reliance on formulations in the text. An exception in the Summer Semester 1933 course is the confrontation with Descartes, for which Heidegger provided short, title-like notes in the margin of the main text; these have been adopted as headings. The higher-level headings of parts and chapters are predominantly by Heidegger, or are taken from the corresponding divisions in the text. They were supplemented in a few cases with formulations from the text.

The italicized words in the text generally follow Heidegger's underlining in the manuscripts, but underlinings that are purely for the purpose of oral delivery or intonation have not been retained. In some cases, crucial sentences and formulations have been emphasized in italics by the editor.[4] Braces in quotations indicate additions and explanations by Heidegger; outside quotations they indicate the editor's conjectures, and editor's notes are identified in the same way. Undecipherable words [and gaps in the manuscript] are indicated in footnotes; questionable readings are signaled by a question mark in braces. [Translators' additions and notes are enclosed in square brackets

2. [All page numbers here refer to the German pagination.]

3. [In the judgment of the translators, these alterations of the type are not necessary for the English reader.]

4. [The remainder of this paragraph has been slightly modified to reflect the typography of the translation.]

throughout. All footnotes are Heidegger's unless they are marked as stemming from the editor or translators.]

*   *   *

The lecture course *The Fundamental Question of Philosophy,* from Summer Semester 1933, takes a first step in developing the question of Being by distinguishing it from Christian assumptions and the mathematical-logical concepts of foundation in the metaphysical systems of the eighteenth century (Wolff, Baumgarten). This development reaches its "completion" in Hegel's metaphysics as theo-logic, in which the logic of the pure essentialities grasps the truth (the self-knowledge) of reason as absolute spirit. Authentic metaphysics as higher logic appears as the system of the absolute self-consciousness of God.

The questionworthiness of this completion of metaphysics as theo-logic is shown in the fact that the deepest urgency of questionworthiness that held sway in the inception of Western philosophy gives way in the struggle with the unmastered powers of truth and with the errancy of the highest beatitude of the supersession of all opposites. In the powerlessness of mere conceptual oppositions, all genuine questioning fails and dies out in the empty eternity of what lacks all decision.

The lecture course *On the Essence of Truth,* from Winter Semester 1933–1934, repeats the lecture course of the same name from Winter Semester 1931–1932 (GA 34) in a form that is altered in several ways. The lecture course asks about the early and deeper ground for the historical transformation of the essence of truth from unconcealment (ἀ-λήθεια) to correctness (of the assertion). It is true that in Plato the highest idea, the idea of the good, is presented as the yoke uniting sight and what can be seen, and thus as the empowerment of Being and unconcealment; however, as the higher empowering factor, it remains essentially unquestioned regarding its own Being. The omission of the question of the essence of unconcealment, from which the unconcealed can be wrested, finally leads into the historical transformation of the essence of truth and untruth as the history of man.

*   *   *

Both lecture courses do show Heidegger drawing closer to contemporary political diction, but the gap between his fundamental position as a thinker and National Socialist ideology remains unbridgeable. As regards their purely philosophical fundamental claims, both courses could also have been held in another situation. Heidegger's sympathy for the pathos of the uprising and revolution is unmistakably countered by the emphatic warning that the revolution is taking place on the basis of a distorted picture of humanity and the world that corresponds to the realm of shadows of the cave dwellers in Plato's allegory. The worldview of National Socialism, as Heidegger's criticism of Kolbenheyer's speech makes clear (pp. 209ff.), is for Heidegger a derivative amalgam of modern metaphysics and of the sciences that arise in its wake. The dilemma for Heidegger lay in the fact that one had to preserve, extend, and deepen the mood of the uprising and revolution for the sake of the spiritual-political upheaval that he held to be necessary at the end (i.e., in the questionworthy "completion") of metaphysics, an upheaval that would overcome it in "another inception"— but the criticism of the unspeakable picture of humanity and the world in National Socialism could no longer be expressed openly, at least as long as one did not want to rob oneself completely of the possibility of being effective (through academic instruction). However, the freeing of the revolutionary mood from the political worldview of National Socialist ideology was made more difficult not only by the necessity of a disguised way of speaking, but also by the fact that Heidegger's thinking was itself in the midst of a revolution. The simple answers of National Socialist ideology, disseminated and supported by an immense propagandistic expenditure, could no longer be dislodged by emphasizing the indispensability and necessity of a more original and foundational questioning (about Being and its truth).

The repetition of the lecture course of the same name from Winter Semester 1931–1932 in the second half of the rectoral year gives the central interpretation of Plato's myth of the cave an orientation toward matters of worldview and politics. The philosopher knows of the attraction of the shadow-pictures in the cave and the resistance of the cave dwellers to releasing themselves from these pictures. The philosopher who returns into the cave as liberator knows in addition about his endangerment: namely, the danger of being mocked, misunderstood, ignored, or even made into an enemy and threatened with death "at the hands of the powerful cave dwellers who set the standards in the cave" (p. 182), on account of his strange view of things. "Speaking out from solitude, he speaks at the decisive moment. He speaks with the danger that what he says may suddenly turn into its opposite" [p. 183].

But the philosopher does not give up. If he cannot lead all the prisoners out of the cave, he will attempt "to seize this or that person whom he thinks he has recognized {as one who can be addressed and is open}[5] and lead him up the steep path, not through a one-time act but through the happening of history itself" (ibid.).

Thus, Heidegger's interpretation of the philosopher who turns back into the cave as liberator, and of his intention and endangerment, mirrors his self-understanding in his "political" engagement during his year

5. Here the braces mark the editor's conjecture.

as rector and his subsequent academic activity during the period of National Socialism. In his Nietzsche interpretations of the second half of the 1930s, Heidegger succeeds in essentially unmasking Nazi ideology as a mere means of seizing, retaining, and increasing power.

* * *

I owe great thanks above all to Jutta Heidegger, as well as to Dr. Hermann Heidegger and Dr. Peter von Ruckteschell, for their conscientious collation of the final typescript with the manuscript. For help with deciphering gaps and questionable readings, I thank Prof. Friedrich-Wilhelm von Herrmann and Dr. Hermann Heidegger. I owe thanks to Dr. Robin Rollinger and Dr. Thomas Vongehr of the Husserl Archives of the University of Freiburg for deciphering three stenographic insertions. For the careful correction of the proofs I am grateful to Dr. Peter von Ruckteschell and Dr. Ino Augsberg, as well as to Dr. Hermann Heidegger in particular, once again.

Freiburg im Breisgau, September 2001   Hartmut Tietjen

German-English Glossary

Page numbers refer to the pagination of the German edition.

Abbau	deconstruction
Abbild	copy. *See also* Bild
Anblick	look; image (p. 170)
Anfang	inception
Angst	angst (p. 95)
Anschein	illusion, semblance
Ansehen	respect
Ansicht	view; vista. *See also* Blick
anwesen	to presence
Anwesenheit	presentness (p. 152)
Aufbruch	awakening (p. 14). A reference to the National Socialist revolution.
Aufgeschlossenheit	disclosedness (pp. 111, 113, 114)
aufheben	supersede (pp. 74–75, 77)
Auftrag	mission, vocation
Auseinandersetzung	confrontation
Aussehen	appearance, look; what a thing looks like (p. 152). This is not necessarily a *deceptive* appearance, which Heidegger usually calls *Schein*. The appearance of a thing may be a genuine self-display.
begegnen	confront, encounter, come upon
Beginn	beginning. See p. 11 for the contrast with *Anfang*, inception.
Behalt	the preserve (p. 259)
beherrschen	rule, dominate

Bereich	domain
Beruf	vocation
Berufung	calling
besinnen	reflect, contemplate, meditate
Bestimmung	vocation; determination, definition, feature, characterization, characteristic, type
Bild	image
Bindung	binding, obligation (p. 213)
Blick	view, gaze
blicken	to view, to look
Boden	basis; soil (pp. 263, 271). A charged term in political contexts, evoking the nationalist slogan *Blut und Boden*, "blood and soil."
Dasein	Dasein; existence (p. 51), determinate Being (p. 73). See the translators' foreword for the meaning of this term in Heidegger. We use "existence" and "determinate Being" in the context of other philosophers' thought.
eigentlich	authentic, genuine, real, true, proper. When this term arguably has some of the force of the concept of *Eigentlichkeit* in *Being and Time,* we use "authentic"; elsewhere it is simply an intensifier.
Einsatz	engagement
entbergen	unconceal
Entschlossenheit	resoluteness
Erkenntnis	cognition, knowledge, realization
ermächtigen	empower
Erscheinung	phenomenon
Existenz	existence. See pp. 177, 218–19 for Heidegger's explanations of the term.
existenziell	existentiell (pp. 24, 211). The "existentiell" is defined in *Being and Time* as that which concerns a particular way of existing.

Führer	Führer (pp. 211, 225)
Führerschaft, Führung	leadership (pp. 3, 4, 273, 274)
Gefüge	structure, organization, (power) relations, interrelation, conjunction (p. 4)
Gegenwart	presence
Gegenwärtigung	presencing
Geist, geistig	spirit, spiritual. See the translators' foreword for a discussion of these terms.
Geltung	validity
Gerede	idle talk
Geschichte	history, story. See translators' note, p. 136.
Geschichtlichkeit	historicity
Geschick	destiny
Geschlecht	generation (p. 4), lineage (pp. 90 n., 178)
Gleichheit	equivalence, equality
Grund	ground, foundation
Grund-	fundamental, ground-
Halt	standpoint, steadfastness (p. 207)
Haltung	attitude, deportment, how we hold ourselves (p. 200)
Haltungslosigkeit	lack of binding discipline (p. 291)
das Helle	the clear (p. 155). *See also* Lichtung
Herkunft	provenance, heritage (pp. 12, 86)
Herrschaft	mastery, rule
herrschen	rule, dominate, reign
Her-stellen, Herausstellen	setting-forth (pp. 93, 116)
Irre	errancy (pp. 77, 237, 302)
irren	err
Irrtum	error
Kampf	struggle. See the translators' foreword for a discussion of this term.
Kraft	strength
Leiblichkeit	bodily Being (p. 211)
lichten; Lichtung	to clear (pp. 160, 177); clearing (p. 160)

Mensch; Menschen	human being, humanity, man; human beings, people. The term is gender-neutral. In Heidegger's discussions of the allegory of the cave, *der Mensch* is sometimes ambiguous between "humanity" and "the [particular] human being."
Menschenstamm	ethnicity (p. 89). *See also* Stammesart
Mitanwesenheit	co-presence (pp. 114–15)
Miteinandersein	being-with-one-another (pp. 57, 158, 194)
Mitsein	being-with (p. 14)
Nation	nation
nichtig	null
das Nichts	the nothing
Not	urgency, urgent need, needs
nötigen	compel by need (p. 100)
offenbaren	reveal
Offenbarkeit	openness; revelation (p. 168). The condition in which beings are revealed to us. Heidegger uses this term as a near synonym for *Unverborgenheit*, unconcealment.
Offenbarung, Offenbarwerden	revelation
Offenheit	openedness (p. 110). A silent, receptive attention to beings in their Being.
Phänomen	phenomenon
präsentieren	to present
Präsenz	Presence (p. 152)
Rede	discourse
reden	speak; talk; discourse
Sache	matter, thing
Satz	proposition, statement
Schein	semblance, seeming, illusion
scheinbar	illusory, apparent
Schicksal	fate
schweigen	keep silent